Jane Addams

A CENTENNIAL READER

New York
The Macmillan Company
1960

Preface

Jane Addams regarded as the two major undertakings of her life Hull-House, the social settlement that she founded, and the organization to promote peace efforts of which she was international president for twenty years, the Women's International League for Peace and Freedom. When, therefore, the centennial of her birth approached, it was natural for the peace workers to enlist the cooperation of the social and settlement workers for a united celebration in honor of this great American woman.

Among the many forms which the commemoration has taken is this volume—an anthology of selections from Miss Addams' writings. The able initiative for setting into motion the early plans was supplied by Carmelita Chase Hinton, chairman of the WILPF Centennial Committee. The extracts were chosen by several members of the WILPF with the objective of showing to new readers the sweep of the author's penetrating mind, the richness of her human sympathies, and the felicity of her English style. Some of the social problems to which Miss Addams addressed herself are now largely solved; the integrity, intelligence, and indomitability which she applied to her own world are undated principles of public service.

To point out the validity of Jane Addams' philosophy for today's problems the WILPF asked several persons distinguished in their fields to supply introductions to the book and its various parts. It is a warm satisfaction to see thus set forth fresh responses to Miss Addams' thought and personality.

The Women's International League for Peace and Freedom wishes to express particular appreciation to Professor William L. Neumann of Goucher College for his generosity as consulting editor, his valuable suggestions and criticisms. The professional editorial experience offered by Lois Leighton Comings has also been gratefully accepted.

Collection of the extracts has been greatly assisted by the cooperation of the staff of the Swarthmore College Peace Collection, which has an unrivaled library of Jane Addams' books and papers, by the Free Library of Philadelphia, and by the Friends Free Library of Germantown. Indebtedness is acknowledged for the help given throughout the preparation of the book by Claire Holcomb Walsh of the Centennial Committee staff; special mention must also be made of the long hours contributed by members of the WILPF as volunteer typists of the material and the extra work carried at the Philadelphia office of the WILPF.

Certain practices adopted in dealing with the reprinting of the extracts should be explained. Many, but not all, of the chapter and section headings have been taken from Jane Addams' writings. The boldface figures in brackets at the beginning of each series of quotations indicate the year of publication of the paragraphs that follow. The sources of the excerpts are given in the section of References at the end of the book.

The original texts have been reprinted exactly with the following exceptions: (1) the single ellipsis indication (. . .) has been used for all omissions, regardless of length; (2) when a quotation begins in the middle of its sentence without immediate reference to what precedes, a capital letter has been used for the first word; (3) obvious typographical errors and misspellings have been corrected, including the titles of a few organizations; and (4) a minimum of changes have been made in punctuation to facilitate understanding.

The Women's International League for Peace and Freedom acknowledges with thanks the courteous permission of the heirs of Jane Addams and the following publishers to use excerpts from Jane Addams' writings in the books listed:

Thomas Y. Crowell: "Subjective Necessity for Social Settlements" and "Objective Necessity of a Social Settlement" in Jane Addams and others, *Philanthropy and Social Progress* (1893); "The Settlement as a Factor in the Labor Movement" in Residents of Hull House, *Hull House Maps and Papers* (1895).

Dodd, Mead & Company: "Introduction" in Graham Taylor, *Religion in Social Action* (1913).

The Macmillan Company: *Democracy and Social Ethics* (1902); *Newer Ideals of Peace* (1907); *The Spirit of Youth and the City Streets* (1909); *Twenty Years at Hull-House* (1910); *A New Conscience and an Ancient Evil* (1912); *The Long Road of Woman's Memory* (1916); *Peace and Bread in Time of War* (1922); *The Second Twenty Years at Hull-House* (1930); *The Excellent Becomes the Permanent* (1932)—all by Jane Addams; and *Women at The Hague* (1915) by Jane Addams and others.

Acknowledgment of similar courtesy is also gratefully made for material by Jane Addams in the following periodicals and reports: *Rockford* (Ill.) *Daily Register*, April 21, 1880; *International Journal of Ethics*, April, 1898; *American Journal of Sociology* (University of Chicago Press), January, 1899; *Annals of the American Academy of Political and Social Science*, May, 1899; *Atlantic Monthly*, March, 1899; *Thirteenth Annual Report, Universal Peace Congress*, 1904; *Ladies' Home Journal*, January, 1910, and June, 1913 (copyright by the Curtis Publishing Company 1909 and 1913); *Proceedings, Conference on Charities and Corrections*, 1910 and 1911; *Survey*, November, 1912, and August, 1930; *Journal of Home Economics*, September, 1918; *Proceedings, National Conference of Social Welfare*, 1930; *Liberty*, March 12, 1932.

For the Women's International League for Peace and Freedom,
EMILY COOPER JOHNSON, *Editor*

Prefatory Note on Jane Addams' Life

The eighth child in the family of a prosperous miller, Jane Addams was born in the prairie town of Cedarville in northern Illinois on September 6, 1860. Her mother died before she reached the age of three, and it was her father who played the major role in her early training. He was by conviction but not by affiliation a Quaker, an active citizen who served eight terms in the Illinois Senate and a man widely known in his state for his devotion to fine principles.

At the age of seventeen Jane Addams entered nearby Rockford Seminary, where she received a classical education and developed an interest in the biological sciences. After graduation in 1881 she went to Philadelphia to prepare herself for admission to the Woman's Medical College. Illness, complicated by a spinal defect and the shock of her father's death, forced her to break off her studies and to spend many months in bed. On the advice of doctors, in the fall of 1883 she went to Europe, where she spent two restless years in travel, expanding her interest in art, architecture, and languages.

During a second trip to Europe in 1887–1888 Jane Addams

reached a decision to work amidst the poor and to establish a center where educated young women could live and put their social principles into action. She visited Toynbee Hall in the slums of London's East End and found there one prototype of the settlement she envisioned. Returning to the United States she rented an old mansion on South Halsted Street in Chicago, the former residence of a real estate millionaire, Charles Hull. In September of 1889 she and Ellen Gates Starr, a college classmate and kindred spirit, moved into Hull-House with the hope of providing a center for the social life of the impoverished working people, many of them immigrants, in the surrounding city area.

In a few years the Halsted Street residence became a major center of community life and a wide variety of civic improvement and cultural enrichment projects originated within its walls. It soon attracted the services of many outstanding individuals and by gifts of land and money was able greatly to enlarge its program. A working girls' home, a day nursery, a Labor Museum, a Boys' Club, a Little Theater, and many other activities were initiated by the Hull-House director and her capable aides.

Jane Addams' name became well known throughout Chicago and Illinois as she fought for legislation and action to improve the working and living conditions of the laboring people. Her influence extended in widening circles as she and her co-workers attacked the evils of urban life and the political corruption and lethargy which supported them. She began speaking to many civic groups and reaching out to a larger audience by rewriting these talks and publishing them in the popular magazines of her time. The vigor and literary quality of her appeal for better human relationships brought her work to the attention of millions.

In 1895 the Halsted center made its first contribution to sociological knowledge with the publication of *Hull House Maps and Papers,* describing the living conditions of the nineteen different nationalities packed into the Nineteenth Ward of Chicago. In 1902 *Democracy and Social Ethics* appeared, bringing together a series of Jane Addams' articles on the major human problems she saw around her. In 1909 she published *The Spirit of Youth and the City Streets,* calling attention to the serious conditions of juvenile delinquency in urban living. *A New Conscience and an Ancient Evil* appeared in

1912, urging a new approach to the problem of prostitution through woman suffrage. In 1916 an interesting analysis of feminine psychology appeared with the title *The Long Road of Woman's Memory*. But the book which became a classic, reaching an international group of readers, was the autobiographical *Twenty Years at Hull-House*, published in 1910 and reprinted several times.

With the outbreak of the first World War in 1914 Jane Addams spent a larger segment of her time in behalf of world peace. In 1906 she had written *Newer Ideals of Peace*, attacking the problem of militarism in civic life. In 1915 she took part in the organization of the Woman's Peace Party and was elected national chairman. In devoting herself to the objectives of this organization she attended the International Women's Conference at The Hague in 1915 and headed the commission selected by that conference to seek an end to the war. She visited heads of government in the capitals of ten neutral and warring nations, arguing for a program of mediation and negotiation to stop hostilities. An account of this first major international effort by women against war was published in 1915, *Women at The Hague*, written with her co-workers Emily Balch and Alice Hamilton.

In 1916 Jane Addams supported the reelection of Woodrow Wilson, a man who she hoped would play the role of mediator. When the President took the United States into war she held to her pacifist position and became the object of severe criticism. Her concern for a lasting peace took her to Zurich in 1919 as head of the American delegation to the Second Women's Peace Conference. It was at this meeting that the Women's International League for Peace and Freedom was formed. Jane Addams was elected the first president, a post which she held for the rest of her life.

During the decade of the twenties she continued her travels and work for the Women's International League while at the same time maintaining her home at Hull-House. She continued her writing as well and in 1922 published *Peace and Bread in Time of War*, an account of women's work for peace. *The Second Twenty Years at Hull-House* appeared in 1930, covering the period of her life from 1909 to 1929. In 1931 she and Dr. Nicholas Murray Butler were co-recipients of the Nobel Peace Prize. This award was a great tribute to Miss Addams' international endeavors.

Writing and speaking engagements continued to occupy her last years. *The Excellent Becomes the Permanent,* a series of memorial addresses given for outstanding American men and women, was published in 1932. In 1935 she completed *My Friend Julia Lathrop,* a biography of a Hull-House co-worker who was named by President Taft in 1912 as head of the newly formed Children's Bureau.

After a life never long free from illness, Jane Addams died on May 21, 1935, at the age of seventy-four. She was buried in the family plot in the town of her birth, Cedarville, Illinois.

WILLIAM L. NEUMANN, *Consulting Editor*

Contents

Introduction

by WILLIAM O. DOUGLAS

Associate Justice of the Supreme Court of the United States

Jane Addams (1860–1935) was long a champion of the democratic ideal in the daily affairs of people. She wrote and spoke about it; and she represented that philosophy in many conferences at home and abroad. Yet she was not content to be merely an advocate who could live in ease and comfort on the dividends which that advocacy would return. Like St. Francis she did something about it. Hull-House in Chicago became her base of operations. She lived and worked among the underprivileged of her day. The newly arrived immigrants of the eighties and nineties had her as friend and counsellor. She tried to translate to them the American conception of freedom and equal justice under law. She helped greatly in welding racial groups—that carried with them from Europe ancient antagonisms—into a viable American community. And when the police descended on these people, as police in Europe had done from time immemorial, Jane Addams was their protector and defender.

She lived in a time when fear of subversives charged American minds with intolerance and suspicion. In the early days it was the "anarchists" who generated the fear. They were the refugees from Russia who had shaken their fists at Czars; and we were easily convinced that they came here to undermine and destroy the American system. Jane Addams was not their exponent; she only insisted that they be treated according to the command of our Bill of Rights. The result was that she too was denounced. Her name was on lists of subversives. Yet she was an honor to those lists. For she exemplified the best in our tradition—tolerance for the expression of ideas we hate; punishment of people only for their deeds, never for their beliefs; outlawry of police brutality and the practice of holding prisoners incommunicado; equal justice under law.

Jane Addams walked a lonely road during and for some years following World War I, for she was deeply committed to the cause of world peace, disarmament, and the conscientious objector. But she was wise enough to avoid the pitfalls of self-pity or the heroics of martyrdom. She walked proudly and with dignity; and she remained true to her ideals. In time she was awarded the Nobel Peace Prize.

Thanks to her, Hull-House generated potent forces in our local and national affairs. It was a musical and literary center and the home of the little theater. It was a haven for the oppressed in troubled times. It was a rallying ground for those with lost causes. At Hull-House victims of sweatshops got guidance and renewed courage. At Hull-House the proponents of trade unionism found encouragement and inspiration. At Hull-House children who worked long hours in miserable factories at last found a powerful advocate. Hull-House served as an investigating agency and as legislative counsel, so to speak. For it was through the efforts of Hull-House that some of our basic factory legislation was passed.

Jane Addams had interests that covered every subject where flesh and blood and the human spirit were in jeopardy. She was straight in the Lincoln tradition; and it was to the famous Lincoln statue in Chicago she often, in her loneliness, went for succor. There have been few like her in the long centuries of history who have combined the capacity to speak the teachings of Christ and at the same time to apply them in the mundane affairs of life. Some of her precepts sound strange to the ears that Madison Avenue has reconditioned. She speaks of the glory, the dignity, the therapy of manual labor—not of labor-saving devices. She saw promise in the youth who was different; and she stoutly rebelled at any trend to orthodoxy and conformity. So it is that in many ways the words of Jane Addams are today a real tonic, even though they were written about conditions that we like to think have passed away.

WILLIAM O. DOUGLAS

Social Work

Introduction by **HELEN HALL**

Director of the Henry Street Settlement, New York City

Extracts selected and arranged by

Lydia Lewis Rickman

Jane Addams' character and achievements are a very proud part of the history of social work. The reach of her mind and the breadth of her courage brought new dimensions to the profession. Her superb powers of interpretation played a large part in public understanding of social work when it was feeling its way to greater competence, evolving new disciplines, and taking on new responsibilities. In spite of her far-reaching concern for the social maladjustments of her day, or rather because of it, she used every opportunity to strengthen social work itself. She was the first woman president of the National Conference of Social Work, elected in 1909. She was a founder and the first president of the National Federation of Settlements and served on its Board until her death in 1935. I remember how impressed I was with her interest in every single thing that was discussed even though our meetings ran from early morning until late at night. She never dominated the discussion but had a keen bit of wisdom for each problem as it came up. The give and take was very lively as John Elliott, Lillian Wald, Mary Simkovitch, Paul Kellogg, Albert Kennedy, and many others pooled their neighborhood experience with passion and humor.

While Jane Addams' feeling of responsibility, made potent by her many gifts, took her well beyond any one profession, and many movements look to her as their initiating force, settlements can in justice claim her particularly as their own—not only because she founded Hull-House in 1889 but because she so completely exemplifies the settlement method at its best. In everything she did she made it clear that her concern sprang from her firsthand contacts. In settling on Halsted Street she deliberately put herself in a position to know intimately the people who were having the hardest time to survive in the city of Chicago. It was a neighborhood where the obstacles to living were greatest, and where democracy stumbled and halted in its upward struggle. Her work at Hull-House from the beginning was an effort, as she says, to add social democracy to its political expression. The services at Hull-House grew in answer to this need. The neighbors and residents learned from each other. The desire for dignity, beauty, self-expression, found answers in the shops, the clubs, a labor museum, an art gallery, a theater, music, pottery, discussion groups, and all the continually changing projects springing from the creative atmosphere fostered there.

But even as Jane Addams experimented with immediate answers to her neighbors' needs she faced the necessity for the fundamental changes which took her far afield. She never dodged an issue no matter where it led her. Laws affecting immigrants, child labor, prostitution, labor's right to organize, the status of women, political reform at its roots, and social justice through the Progressive Party—and her passion for peace —all these and many more she saw as urgent demands upon her creative efforts and interpretative skills. Perhaps this does not sound so difficult as we look back upon it, but most of these were sharply controversial issues in Miss Addams' day, and she was vilified as few other people, particularly in her efforts to bring management and labor together and, even more cruelly, for her stand on peace when our country was at war. It is hard to imagine what her fellow citizens' bitterness toward her must have meant to anyone so sensitive and highly organized. It has always seemed to me that she was perhaps better able to withstand the pressures of adverse criticism because her convictions were so firmly rooted in her neighborhood experience and she could always go back to the source of her strength. In the Second World War a new member of the Board of the National Federation of Settlements once asked, when a resolution involving international relations was discussed, why settlements should go so far afield as war to express themselves. I could not but think of the prayers for peace at the end of every mothers' club meeting and the "Welcome Home" signs over tenement doors when a soldier came back from the army.

While Jane Addams was obviously moved by the emotional impact of her personal experiences at Hull-House and strengthened by the moral indignation she felt toward suffering and injustice of any kind, she did not stop at interpretation. A large part of her genius lay in getting things done. Jane Addams had a very practical bent and a tremendous capacity for hard work. When I sent, for her comment, some stories of unemployed families as part of a study the National Federation of Settlements was making in 1928, her reply, written by hand, came almost by return mail.

Jane Addams' championship of women seemed to spring more from compassion than feminism. Their helplessness ranked next to children's as she saw them struggling so barehanded to hold their own in a city slum. However, as for women's lack of the right to vote, she never failed to express a healthy scorn for this blind hangover from the past which kept women from sharing fully as citizens in a democracy.

Aside from her own devotion and capacity, part of her success must have come from her ability to pick gifted people and to strengthen their hands as they worked. She recognized the capacities of those around her, no matter who they were, rich or poor, and drew them into her orbit of accomplishment. Hull-House grew, as did her most far-reaching endeavors, as a result of her understanding of people and her ability to attract the most adventurous people of her day. That Jane Addams could work with people of equal strength and genius is proved by the names of her many associates who, with her, shared in turning philanthropy into social work. At the same time they were making possible much of the protective legislation of that day. She worked with two of her most distinguished contemporaries, Lillian Wald and Florence Kelley, in establishing the first White House Conference for Children, out of which the Children's Bureau grew. Their determination that the federal government should be interested in the welfare of American children proved impossible to withstand.

As Jane Addam writes, her neighbors seem to jog her elbow, illuminating her concern with the stories of their individual lives. So her whole life's work was also illuminated by her genius. To all she did she brought the clarity and self-discipline of the artist. In commenting on a fellow worker she once said, "It is good for a social worker to be an artist too." It is surely good for all of us that this social worker was an artist, for these gifts of hers have brought enrichment to all of us who are privileged to practice the art of healing through the profession of social work.

And we are indebted to her deeply philosophical mind as she took the tragedies and joys of those around her and fitted them into their place in history—making what had gone before, what was, and what should be into an understandable pattern of life, invested always with her own warmth and insight.

HELEN HALL

FIRST DAYS AT HULL-HOUSE

[1910]   It is hard to tell just when the very simple plan which afterward developed into the Settlement began to form itself in my mind. . . . But I gradually became convinced that it would be a good thing to rent a house in a part of the city where many primitive and actual needs are found, in which young women who had been given over too exclusively to study, might restore a balance of activity along traditional lines and learn of life from life itself; where they might try out some of the things they had been taught and put truth to "the ultimate test of the conduct it dictates or inspires." I do not remember to have mentioned this plan to any one until . . . April, 1888. . . .

. . . I can well recall the stumbling and uncertainty with which I finally set it forth to Miss Starr, my old-time school friend. . . . I even dared to hope that she might join in carrying out the plan, but nevertheless I told it in the fear of that disheartening experience which is so apt to afflict our most cherished plans when they are at last divulged, when we suddenly feel that there is nothing there to talk about, and as the golden dream slips through our fingers we are left to wonder at our own fatuous belief. But gradually the comfort of Miss Starr's companionship, the vigor and enthusiasm which she brought to bear upon it, told both in the growth of the plan and upon the sense of its validity, so that . . . the scheme had become convincing and tangible although still most hazy in detail.

A month later we parted in Paris, Miss Starr to go back to Italy, and I to journey on to London to secure as many suggestions as possible from those wonderful places of which we had heard, Toynbee Hall and the People's Palace. So that it finally came about that in June, 1888, . . . I found myself at Toynbee Hall . . . with high expectations and a certain belief that whatever perplexities and discouragement concerning the life of the poor were in store for me, I should at least know something at first hand and have the solace of daily activity. . . .

The next January found Miss Starr and myself in Chicago searching for a neighborhood in which we might put our plans into execution. . . . From the very first the plan received courteous attention, and discussion while often skeptical, was always friendly. . . .

. . . With the advice of several of the oldest residents of Chicago . . . we decided upon a location somewhere near the junction of Blue Island Avenue, Halsted Street, and Harrison Street. I was surprised and overjoyed on the very first day of our search for quarters to come upon the hospitable old house . . . which had passed through many changes since it had been built in 1856 for the homestead of one of Chicago's pioneer citizens, Mr. Charles J. Hull, and although battered by its vicissitudes, was essentially sound. . . . [It] responded kindly to repairs, its wide hall and open fireplaces always insuring it a gracious aspect. . . .

We furnished the house as we would have furnished it were it in another part of the city, with the photographs and other impedimenta we had collected in Europe, and with a few bits of family mahogany. While all the new furniture which was bought was enduring in quality, we were careful to keep it in character with the fine old residence. Probably no young matron ever placed her own things in her own house with more pleasure than that with which we first furnished Hull-House. We believed that the Settlement may logically bring to its aid all those adjuncts which the cultivated man regards as good and suggestive of the best life of the past.

On the 18th of September, 1889, Miss Starr and I moved into it. . . . In our enthusiasm over "settling," the first night we forgot not only to lock but to close a side door opening on Polk Street, and were much pleased in the morning to find that we possessed a fine illustration of the honesty and kindliness of our new neighbors.

Our first guest was an interesting young woman who lived in a neighboring tenement, whose widowed mother aided her in the support of the family by scrubbing a downtown theater every night.

The mother, of English birth, was well bred and carefully educated, but was in the midst of that bitter struggle which awaits so many strangers in American cities who find that their social position tends to be measured solely by the standards of living they are able to maintain. Our guest has long since married the struggling young lawyer to whom she was then engaged, and he is now leading his profession in an eastern city. She recalls that month's experience always with a sense of amusement over the fact that the succession of visitors who came to see the new Settlement invariably questioned her most minutely concerning "these people" without once suspecting that they were talking to one who had been identified with the neighborhood from childhood. I at least was able to draw a lesson from the incident, and I never addressed a Chicago audience on the subject of the Settlement and its vicinity without inviting a neighbor to go with me, that I might curb any hasty generalization by the consciousness that I had an auditor who knew the conditions more intimately than I could hope to do. . . .

In the very first weeks of our residence Miss Starr started a reading party in George Eliot's "Romola," which was attended by a group of young women who followed the wonderful tale with unflagging interest. The weekly reading was held in our little upstairs dining room, and two members of the club came to dinner each week, not only that they might be received as guests, but that they might help us wash the dishes afterwards and so make the table ready for the stacks of Florentine photographs.

Our "first resident," as she gayly designated herself, was a charming old lady who gave five consecutive readings from Hawthorne to a most appreciative audience, interspersing the magic tales most delightfully with recollections of the elusive and fascinating author. . . . We thus early found the type of class which through all the years has remained most popular—a combination of a social atmosphere with serious study. . . .

In those early days we were often asked why we had come to live on Halsted Street when we could afford to live somewhere else. . . . In time it came to seem natural to all of us that the Settlement should be there. If it is natural to feed the hungry and care for the sick, it is certainly natural to give pleasure to the young, comfort to the aged, and to minister to the deep-seated craving for social intercourse that all men feel. Whoever does it is rewarded by something which, if not gratitude, is at least spontaneous and vital and lacks that irksome sense of obligation with which a substantial benefit is too often acknowledged. . . .

. . . I think that time has also justified our early contention that the mere foothold of a house, easily accessible, ample in space, hospitable and tolerant in spirit, situated in the midst of the large foreign colonies which so easily isolate themselves in American cities, would be in itself a serviceable thing for Chicago. I am not so sure that we succeeded in our endeavors "to make social intercourse express the growing sense of the economic unity of society and to add the social function to democracy." But Hull-House was soberly opened on the theory that the dependence of classes on each other is reciprocal; and that as the social relation is essentially a reciprocal relation, it gives a form of expression that has peculiar value. . . .

We early found ourselves spending many hours in efforts to secure support for deserted women, insurance for bewildered widows, damages for injured operators, furniture from the clutches of the installment store. The Settlement is valuable as an information and interpretation bureau. It constantly acts between the various institutions of the city and the people for whose benefit these institutions were erected. The hospitals, the county agencies, and State asylums are often but vague rumors to the people who need them most. Another function of the Settlement to its neighborhood resembles that of the big brother whose mere presence on the playground protects the little one from bullies. . . .

. . . In spite of some untoward experiences, we were constantly impressed with the uniform kindness and courtesy we received. Perhaps these first days laid the simple human foundations which are certainly essential for continuous living among the poor: first, genuine preference for residence in an industrial quarter to any other part of the city, because it is interesting and makes the human appeal; and second, the conviction, in the words of Canon Barnett, that the things which make men alike are finer and better than the things that keep them apart, and that these basic likenesses, if they are properly accentuated, easily transcend the less essential differences of race, language, creed and tradition.

Perhaps even in those first days we made a beginning toward that object which was afterwards stated in our charter: "To provide a center for a higher civic and social life; to institute and maintain educational and philanthropic enterprises, and to investigate and improve the conditions in the industrial districts of Chicago."

SOCIAL SETTLEMENTS

[1910]   The Subjective Necessity for Social Settlements

The Ethical Culture Societies held a summer school at Plymouth, Massachusetts, in 1892, to which they invited several people representing the then new Settlement movement, that they might discuss with others the general theme of Philanthropy and Social Progress.

I venture to produce here parts of a lecture I delivered in Plymouth, both because I have found it impossible to formulate with the same freshness those early motives and strivings, and because, when published with other papers given that summer, it was received by the Settlement people themselves as a satisfactory statement.

I remember one golden summer afternoon during the sessions of the summer school that several of us met on the shores of a pond in a pine wood a few miles from Plymouth, to discuss our new movement. . . .

. . . Some of us had numbered our years as far as thirty, and we all carefully avoided the extravagance of statement which characterizes youth, and yet I doubt if anywhere on the continent that summer could have been found a group of people more genuinely interested in social development or more sincerely convinced that they had found a clew by which the conditions in crowded cities might be understood and the agencies for social betterment developed.

We were all careful to avoid saying that we had found a "life work," perhaps with an instinctive dread of expending all our energy in vows of constancy, as so often happens; and yet it is interesting to note that all of the people whom I have recalled as the enthusiasts at that little conference, have remained attached to Settlements in actual residence for longer or shorter periods each year during the eighteen years which have elapsed since then, although they have also been closely identified as publicists or governmental officials with movements outside. It is as if they had discovered that the Settlement was too valuable as a method, as a way of approach, to the social question to be abandoned, although they had long since discovered that it was not a "social movement" in itself. This, however, is anticipating the future, whereas the following paper on "The Subjective Necessity for Social Settlements" should have a chance to speak for itself. It is perhaps too late in the day to express regret for its stilted title.

[1893]   Hull-House, which was Chicago's first Settlement, was established in September, 1889. It represented no association, but was opened by two women, backed by many friends, in the belief that the mere foothold of a house, easily accessible, ample in space, hospitable and tolerant in spirit, situated in the midst of the large foreign colonies which so easily isolate themselves in American cities, would be in itself a serviceable thing for Chicago. Hull-House endeavors to make social intercourse express the growing sense of the economic unity of society. It is an effort to add the social function to democracy. It was opened on the theory that the dependence of classes on each other is reciprocal; and that as "the social relation is essentially a reciprocal relation, it gave a form of expression that has peculiar value."

This paper is an attempt to treat of the subjective necessity for Social Settlements, to analyze the motives which underlie a movement based not only upon conviction, but genuine emotion. Hull-House of Chicago is used as an illustration, but so far as the analysis is faithful, it obtains wherever educated young people are seeking an outlet for that sentiment of universal brotherhood which the best spirit of our times is forcing from an emotion into a motive. . . .

. . . The social organism has broken down through large districts of our great cities. Many of the people living there are very poor, the majority of them without leisure or energy for anything but the gain of subsistence. They move often from one wretched lodging to another. They live for the moment side by side, many of them without knowledge of each other, without fellowship, without local tradition or public spirit, without social organization of any kind. Practically nothing is done to remedy this. The people who might do it, who have the social tact and training, the large houses, and the traditions and custom of hospitality, live in other parts of the city. The club-houses, libraries, galleries, and semi-public conveniences for social life are also blocks away. We find working-men organized into armies of producers because men of executive ability and business sagacity have found it to their interests thus to organize them. But these working-men are not organized socially; although living in crowded tenement-houses, they are living without a corresponding social contact. The chaos is as great as it would be were they working in huge factories without foreman or superintendent. Their ideas and resources are cramped. The desire for higher social pleasure is extinct. They have no share in the traditions and social energy which make for progress. Too often their only place of meeting is a saloon, their only host a bartender; a local demagogue forms their public opinion. Men of ability and refinement, of social power and university cultivation, stay away from them. Personally, I believe the men who lose most are those who thus stay away. But the paradox is here: when cultivated people do stay away from a certain portion of the population, when all social advantages are persistently withheld, it may be for years, the result itself is pointed at as a reason, is used as an argument, for the continued withholding.

It is constantly said that because the masses have never had social advantages they do not want them, that they are heavy and dull, and that it will take political or philanthropic machinery to change them. This divides a city into rich and poor; into the favored, who express their sense of the social obligation by gifts of money, and into the unfavored, who express it by clamoring for a "share"— both of them actuated by a vague sense of justice. This division of the city would be more justifiable, however, if the people who thus isolate themselves on certain streets and use their social ability for each other gained enough thereby and added sufficient to the sum total of social progress to justify the withholding of the pleasures and results of that progress from so many people who ought to have them. But they cannot accomplish this. "The social spirit discharges itself in many forms, and no one form is adequate to its total expression." We are all uncomfortable in regard to the sincerity of our best phrases, because we hesitate to translate our philosophy into the deed.

It is inevitable that those who feel most keenly this insincerity and partial living should be our young people, our so-called educated young people who accomplish little toward the solution of this social problem, and who bear the brunt of being cultivated into unnourished, over-sensitive lives. They have been shut off from the common labor by which they live and which is a great source of moral and physical health. They feel a fatal want of harmony between their theory and their lives, a lack of coordination between thought and action. I think it is hard for us to realize how seriously many of them are taking to the notion of human brotherhood, how eagerly they long to give tangible expression to the democratic ideal. . . .

"There is nothing after disease, indigence, and a sense of guilt so fatal to health and to life itself as the want of a proper outlet for active faculties." I have seen young girls suffer and grow sensibly lowered in vitality in the first years after they leave school. In our attempt then to give a girl pleasure and freedom from care we succeed, for the most part, in making her pitifully miserable. She finds "life" so different from what she expected it to be. She is besotted with innocent little ambitions, and does not understand this apparent waste of herself, this elaborate preparation, if no work is provided for her. There is a heritage of noble obligation which young people accept and long to perpetuate. The desire for action, the wish to right wrong and alleviate suffering, haunts them daily. Society smiles at it indulgently instead of making it of value to itself. . . .

We have in America a fast-growing number of cultivated young people who have no recognized outlet for their active faculties. They hear constantly of the great social maladjustment, but no way is provided for them to change it, and their uselessness hangs about them heavily. Huxley declares that the sense of uselessness is the severest shock which the human system can sustain, and that, if persistently sustained, it results in atrophy of function. These young people have had advantages of college, of European travel and economic study, but they are sustaining this shock of inaction. . . .

We are fast feeling the pressure of the need and meeting the necessity for Settlements in America. Our young people feel nervously the need of putting theory into action, and respond quickly to the Settlement form of activity. . . .

I believe that there is a distinct turning among many young men and women toward the simple acceptance of Christ's message. They resent the assumption that Christianity is a set of ideas which belong to the religious consciousness, whatever that may be, that it is a thing to be proclaimed and instituted apart from the social life of the community. They insist that it shall seek a simple and natural expression in the social organism itself. . . .

I cannot, of course, speak for other Settlements, but it would, I think, be unfair to Hull-House not to emphasize the conviction with which the first residents went there, that it would simply be a foolish and an unwarrantable expenditure of force to oppose or to antagonize any individual or set of people in the neighborhood; that whatever of good the House had to offer should be put into positive terms; that its residents should live with opposition to no man, with recognition of the good in every man, even the meanest. . . . Certain it is that spiritual force is found in the Settlement movement, and it is also true that this force must be evoked and must be called into play before the success of any Settlement is assured. There must be the over-mastering belief that all that is noblest in life is common to men as men, in order to accentuate the likenesses and ignore the differences which are found among the people whom the Settlement constantly brings into juxtaposition. . . .

The Settlement, then, is an experimental effort to aid in the solution of the social and industrial problems which are engendered by the modern conditions of life in a great city. It insists that these problems are not confined to any one portion of a city. It is an attempt to relieve, at the same time, the over-accumulation at one end of society and the destitution at the other; but it assumes that this over-accumulation and destitution is most sorely felt in the things that pertain to social and educational advantage. From its very nature it can stand for no political or social propaganda. It must, in a sense, give the warm welcome of an inn to all such propagandas, if perchance one of them be found an angel. The one thing to be dreaded in the Settlement is that it lose its flexibility, its power of quick adaptation, its readiness to change its methods as its environment may demand. It must be open to conviction and must have a deep and abiding sense of tolerance. It must be hospitable and ready for experiment. It should demand from its residents a scientific patience in the accumulation of facts and the steady holding of their sympathies as one of the best instruments for that accumulation. It must be grounded in a philosophy whose foundation is on the solidarity of the human race, a philosophy which will not waver when the race happens to be represented by a drunken woman or an idiot boy. Its residents must be emptied of all conceit of opinion and all self-assertion, and ready to arouse and interpret the public opinion of their neighborhood. They must be content to live quietly side by side with their neighbors until they grow into a sense of relationship and mutual interests. Their neighbors are held apart by differences of race and language which the residents can more easily overcome. They are bound to see the needs of their neighborhood as a whole, to furnish data for legislation, and use their influence to secure it. In short, residents are pledged to devote themselves to the duties of good citizenship and to the arousing of the social energies which too largely lie dormant in every neighborhood given over to industrialism. They are bound to regard the entire life of their city as organic, to make an effort to unify it, and to protest against its over-differentiation. . . .

. . . It is easy in writing a paper to make all philosophy point one particular moral and all history adorn one particular tale; but I hope you forgive me for reminding you that the best speculative philosophy sets forth the solidarity of the human race; that the highest moralists have taught that without the advance and improvement of the whole no man can hope for any lasting improvement in his own moral or material individual condition. The subjective necessity for Social Settlements is identical with that necessity which urges us on toward social and individual salvation.

[1893]   The Objective Necessity for Social Settlements

Hull-House . . . once stood in the suburbs, but the city has steadily grown up around it and its site now has corners on three or four more or less distinct foreign colonies. . . . This ward has a population

of about fifty thousand, and at the last presidential election registered 7072 voters. It has had no unusual political scandal connected
with it, but its aldermen are generally saloon-keepers and its political manipulations are those to be found in the crowded wards
where the activities of the petty politician are unchecked.

The policy of the public authorities of never taking an initiative,
and always waiting to be urged to do their duty, is fatal in a ward
where there is no initiative among the citizens. The idea underlying
our self-government breaks down in such a ward. The streets are
inexpressibly dirty, the number of schools inadequate, factory legislation unenforced, the street-lighting bad, the paving miserable and
altogether lacking in the alleys and smaller streets, and the stables
defy all laws of sanitation. Hundreds of houses are unconnected
with the street sewer. The older and richer inhabitants seem anxious
to move away as rapidly as they can afford it. They make room for
newly arrived immigrants who are densely ignorant of civic duties.
This substitution of the older inhabitants is accomplished industrially also in the south and east quarters of the ward. The Hebrews
and Italians do the finishing for the great clothing-manufacturers
formerly done by Americans, Irish, and Germans, who refused to
submit to the extremely low prices to which the sweating system
has reduced their successors. As the design of the sweating system
is the elimination of rent from the manufacture of clothing, the
"outside work" is begun after the clothing leaves the cutter. An
unscrupulous contractor regards no basement as too dark, no stable
loft too foul, no rear shanty too provisional, no tenement room too
small for his workroom, as these conditions imply low rental. Hence
these shops abound in the worst of the foreign districts, where the
sweater easily finds his cheap basement and his home finishers.
There is a constant tendency to employ school-children, as much
of the home and shop work can easily be done by children. . . .

Our ward contains two hundred and fifty-five saloons; our own
precinct boasts of eight, and the one directly north of us twenty.
This allows one saloon to every twenty-eight voters, and there is no
doubt that the saloon is the centre of the liveliest political and social
life of the ward. . . .

This site for a Settlement was selected in the first instance because
of its diversity and the variety of activity for which it presented an

opportunity. It has been the aim of the residents to respond to all sides of the neighborhood life: not to the poor people alone, nor to the well-to-do, nor to the young in contradistinction to the old, but to the neighborhood as a whole, "men, women, and children taken in families as the Lord mixes them." . . .

A Settlement which regards social intercourse as the terms of its expression logically brings to its aid all those adjuncts which have been found by experience to free social life. . . . It ignores none of the surroundings which one associates with a life of simple refinement. The amount of luxury which an individual indulges in is a thing which has to be determined by each for himself. It must always be a relative thing. The one test which the Settlement is bound to respect is that its particular amount of luxury shall tend to "free" the social expression of its neighbors, and not cumber that expression. The residents at Hull-House find that the better in quality and taste their surroundings are, the more they contribute to the general enjoyment. . . .

It is much easier to deal with the first generation of crowded city life than with the second or third, because it is more natural and cast in a simpler mould. The Italian and Bohemian peasants who live in Chicago still put on their bright holiday clothes on a Sunday and go to visit their cousins. They tramp along with at least a suggestion of having once walked over ploughed fields and breathed country air. The second generation of city poor have no holiday clothes and consider their cousins "a bad lot." I have heard a drunken man, in a maudlin stage, babble of his good country mother and imagine he was driving the cows home, and I knew that his little son, who laughed loud at him, would be drunk earlier in life, and would have no such pastoral interlude to his ravings. Hospitality still survives among foreigners, although it is buried under false pride among the poorest Americans. One thing seemed clear in regard to entertaining these foreigners: to preserve and keep for them whatever of value their past life contained and to bring them in contact with a better type of Americans. For two years, every Saturday evening, our Italian neighbors were our guests; entire families came. These evenings were very popular during our first winter at Hull-House. Many educated Italians helped us, and the house became known as a place where Italians were welcome and where national holidays were observed. They come to us with their petty lawsuits, sad relics of the *vendetta,* with their incorrigible boys, with their hospital cases, with their aspirations for American clothes, and with their needs for an interpreter.

Friday evening is devoted to Germans and is similar in purpose; but owing to the superior education of our Teutonic guests and the clever leading of a cultivated German woman, we can bring out the best of that cozy social intercourse which is found in its perfection in the "Fatherland." They sing a great deal in the tender minor of the German folksong or in the rousing spirit of the Rhine, and they are slowly but persistently pursuing a course in German history and literature. The relationship by no means ends with social civilities, and the acquaintance made there has brought about radical changes in the lives of many friendless families. I recall one peasant woman, straight from the fields of Germany. Her two years in America had been spent in patiently carrying water up and down two flights of stairs, and in washing the heavy flannel suits of iron-foundry workers. For this her pay had averaged thirty-five cents a day. Three of her daughters had fallen victims to the vice of the city. The mother was bewildered and distressed, but understood nothing. We were able to induce the betrayer of one daughter to marry her; the second, after a tedious lawsuit, supported his child; with the third we were able to do nothing. This woman is now living with her family in a little house seventeen miles from the city. She has made two payments on her land and is a lesson to all beholders as she pastures her cow up and down the railroad tracks and makes money from her ten acres. She did not need charity. She had an immense capacity for hard work, but she sadly needed "heading." She is our most shining example, but I think of many forlorn cases of German and Bohemian peasants in need of neighborly help.

Perhaps of more value than to the newly arrived peasant is the service of the Settlement to those foreigners who speak English fairly well, and who have been so successful in material affairs that they are totally absorbed by them. Their social life is too often reduced to a sense of comradeship. The lives of many Germans, for instance, are law-abiding, but inexpressibly dull. They have resigned poetry and romance with the other good things of the Fatherland. There is a strong family affection between them and their English-speaking children, but their pleasures are not in common and they seldom go out together. Perhaps the greatest value of the Settlement to them is in simply placing large and pleasant rooms with musical facilities at their disposal, and in reviving their almost forgotten enthusiasm for Körner and Schiller. I have seen sons and daughters stand in complete surprise as their mother's knitting-needles softly beat time to the song she was singing, or her worn face turned rosy under the hand-clapping as she made an old-fashioned curtsy at the end of a German poem. It was easy to fancy a growing touch of respect in her children's manner to her, and a rising enthusiasm for German literature and reminiscence on the part of all the family, an effort to bring together the old life and the new, a respect for the older cultivation, and not quite so much assurance that the new was the best. . . .

. . . In every neighborhood where poorer people live, because rents are supposed to be cheaper there, is an element which, although uncertain in the individual, in the aggregate can be counted upon. It is composed of people of former education and opportunity who have cherished ambitions and prospects, but who are caricatures of what they meant to be—"hollow ghosts which blame the living men." There are times in many lives when there is a cessation of energy and loss of power. Men and women of education and refinement come to live in a cheaper neighborhood because they lack the power of making money, because of ill health, because of an unfortunate marriage, or for various other reasons which do not imply criminality or stupidity. Among them are those who, in spite of untoward circumstances, keep up some sort of an intellectual life, those who are "great for books" as their neighbors say. To such the Settlement is a genuine refuge. In addition to these there are many young women who teach in the public schools, young men who work at various occupations, but who are bent upon self-improvement and are preparing for professions. It is of these that the College Extension classes are composed. The majority of the two hundred students live within the radius of six blocks from the house, although a few of them come from other parts of the city. The educational effort of Hull-House always has been held by the residents to be subordinate to its social life, and, as it were, a part of it. What is now known as the College Extension course, a series of lectures and classes held in the evening on the general plan of University Extension, had its origin in an informal club which, during the first winter, read "Romola" with the original residents. . . .

The relation of students and faculty to each other and to the residents is that of guest and hostess, and those students who have been longest in relation to the Settlement feel the responsibility of old friends of the house to new guests. A good deal of tutoring is constantly going on among the students themselves in the rooms of Hull-House. At the close of each term the residents give a reception to students and faculty, which is one of the chief social events of the season. Upon this comfortable social basis very good work has been done in the College Extension courses. Literature classes until recently have been the most popular. The last winter's Shakespeare class had a regular attendance of forty. The mathematical classes have always been large and flourishing. The faculty, consisting of college men and women, numbers thirty-five. Many of them have taught constantly at the house for two years, but their numbers are often re-enforced. During the last term a class in physics, preparatory for a class in electricity, was composed largely of workmen in the Western Electric Works, which are within a few blocks of Hull-House. . . .

The industrial education of Hull-House has always been somewhat limited. From the beginning we have had large and enthusiastic cooking classes, first in the Hull-House kitchen, and later in a tiny cottage across the yard which has been fitted up for the purpose. We have also always had sewing, mending, and embroidery classes. This leads me to speak of the children who meet weekly at Hull-House, whose organization is between classes and clubs. There are three hundred of them who come on three days, not counting, of course, the children who come to the house merely as depositors in the Penny Provident Fund Savings Bank. A hundred Italian girls come on Monday. They sew and carry home a new garment, which becomes a pattern for the entire family. Tuesday afternoon has always been devoted to school-boys' clubs: they are practically storytelling clubs. The most popular stories are legends and tales of chivalry. The one hundred and fifty little girls on Friday afternoon are not very unlike the boys, although they want to sew while they are hearing their stories. The value of these clubs, I believe, lies almost entirely in their success in arousing the higher imagination. We have had a kindergarten at Hull-House ever since we have lived there. Every morning miniature Italians, Hebrews, French, Irish, and Germans assemble in our drawing-room, and nothing seems to excite admiration in the neighborhood so much as the fact that we "put up with them." . . .

Helpful resources from the neighborhood itself constantly develop, physicians, benefit societies, ministers and priests are always ready to co-operate in any given case. Young girls from the neighborhood assist in the children's classes, mothers help in the nursery, young men teach in the gymnasium, or secure students for an experimental course of lectures. We constantly rely more and more on neighborhood assistance. . . .

It is difficult to classify the Working People's Social Science Club which meets weekly at Hull-House. It is social, educational and civic in character, the latter chiefly because it strongly connects the House with the labor problems in their political and social aspects. . . . There is still need . . . for many of these clubs where men who differ widely in their social theories can meet for discussion, where representatives of the various economic schools can modify each other, and at least learn tolerance and the futility of endeavoring to convince the world of the truth of one position. To meet in a social-science club is more educational than to meet in a single-tax club, or a socialistic chapter, or a personal-rights league, although the millennium may seem farther off after such a meeting. In addition to this modification of view there is doubtless a distinct modification of attitude. Last spring the Hull-House Social Science Club heard a series of talks on municipal and county affairs by the heads of the various departments. During the discussion following the address on "The Chicago Police," a working-man had the pleasure of telling the chief of police that he had been arrested, obliged to pay two dollars and a half, and had lost three days' work, because he had come out of the wrong gate when he was working on the World's Fair grounds. The chief sighed, expressed his regret, and made no defence. The speaker sat down bewildered; evidently for the first time in his life he realized that blunders cut the heart of more than the victim.

Is it possible for men, however far apart in outward circumstances, for the capitalist and the working-man, to use the common phrase, to meet as individuals beneath a friendly roof, open their minds each to each, and not have their "class theories" insensibly modified by the kindly attrition of a personal acquaintance? In the light of our experience I should say not. . . .

I am always sorry to have Hull-House regarded as philanthropy, although it doubtless has strong philanthropic tendencies, and has several distinct charitable departments which are conscientiously carried on. It is unfair, however, to apply the word philanthropic to the activities of the House as a whole. Charles Booth, in his brilliant chapter on "The Unemployed," expresses regret that the problems of the working class are so often confounded with the problems of the inefficient, the idle, and distressed. To confound thus two problems is to render the solution of both impossible. Hull-House, while endeavoring to fulfil its obligations to neighbors of varying needs, will do great harm if it confounds distinct problems. Working people live in the same streets with those in need of charity, but they themselves, so long as they have health and good wages, require and want none of it. As one of their number has said, they require only that their aspirations be recognized and stimulated, and the means of attaining them put at their disposal. Hull-House makes a constant effort to secure these means for its neighbors, but to call that effort philanthropy is to use the word unfairly and to underestimate the duties of good citizenship.

[1902]   Charitable Relationships

. . . Probably there is no relation in life which our democracy is changing more rapidly than the charitable relation—that relation which obtains between benefactor and beneficiary; at the same time there is no point of contact in our modern experience which reveals so clearly the lack of that equality which democracy implies. We have reached the moment when democracy has made such inroads upon this relationship, that the complacency of the old-fashioned charitable man is gone forever; while, at the same time, the very need and existence of charity denies us the consolation and freedom which democracy will at last give.

. . . The daintily clad charitable visitor who steps into the little house made untidy by the vigorous efforts of her hostess, the washer-woman, is no longer sure of her superiority to the latter; she recognizes that her hostess after all represents social value and industrial use, as over against her own parasitic cleanliness and a social standing attained only through status.

The only families who apply for aid to the charitable agencies are those who have come to grief on the industrial side; it may be through sickness, through loss of work, or for other guiltless and inevitable reasons; but the fact remains that they are industrially ailing, and must be bolstered and helped into industrial health. The charity visitor, let us assume, is a young college woman, well-bred and open-minded; when she visits the family assigned to her, she is often embarrassed to find herself obliged to lay all the stress of her teaching and advice upon the industrial virtues, and to treat the members of the family almost exclusively as factors in the industrial system. She insists that they must work and be self-supporting, that the most dangerous of all situations is idleness, that seeking one's own pleasure, while ignoring claims and responsibilities, is the most ignoble of actions. The members of her assigned family may have other charms and virtues—they may possibly be kind and considerate of each other, generous to their friends, but it is her business to stick to the industrial side. As she daily holds up these standards, it often occurs to the mind of the sensitive visitor, whose conscience has been made tender by much talk of brotherhood and equality, that she has no right to say these things; that her untrained hands are no more fitted to cope with actual conditions than those of her broken-down family.

The grandmother of the charity visitor could have done the industrial preaching very well, because she did have the industrial virtues and housewifely training. In a generation our experiences have changed, and our views with them; but we still keep on in the old methods, which could be applied when our consciences were in line with them, but which are daily becoming more difficult as we divide up into people who work with their hands and those who do not. The charity visitor belonging to the latter class is perplexed by recognitions and suggestions which the situation forces upon her. Our democracy has taught us to apply our moral teaching all around, and the moralist is rapidly becoming so sensitive that when his life does not exemplify his ethical convictions, he finds it difficult to preach.

Added to this is a consciousness, in the mind of the visitor, of a genuine misunderstanding of her motives by the recipients of her charity, and by their neighbors. Let us take a neighborhood of poor people, and test their ethical standards by those of the charity visitor, who comes with the best desire in the world to help them out of their distress. A most striking incongruity, at once apparent, is the difference between the emotional kindness with which relief is given by one poor neighbor to another poor neighbor, and the guarded care with which relief is given by a charity visitor to a charity recipient. The neighborhood mind is at once confronted not only by the difference of method, but by an absolute clashing of two ethical standards.

A very little familiarity with the poor districts of any city is sufficient to show how primitive and genuine are the neighborly relations. There is the greatest willingness to lend or borrow anything, and all the residents of the given tenement know the most intimate family affairs of all the others. The fact that the economic condition of all alike is on a most precarious level makes the ready outflow of sympathy and material assistance the most natural thing in the world. There are numberless instances of self-sacrifice quite unknown in the circles where greater economic advantages make that kind of intimate knowledge of one's neighbors impossible.

. . . The subject of clothes indeed perplexes the visitor constantly, and the result of her reflections may be summed up somewhat in this wise: The girl who has a definite social standing, who has been to a fashionable school or to a college, whose family live in a house seen and known by all her friends and associates, may afford to be very simple, or even shabby as to her clothes, if she likes. But the working girl, whose family lives in a tenement, or moves from one small apartment to another, who has little social standing and has to make her own place, knows full well how much habit and style of dress has to do with her position. Her income goes into her clothing, out of all proportion to the amount which she spends upon other things. But, if social advancement is her aim, it is the most sensible thing she can do. She is judged largely by her clothes. Her house furnishing, with its pitiful little decorations, her scanty supply of books, are never seen by the people whose social opinions she most values. Her clothes are her background, and from them she is largely judged. It is due to this fact that girls' clubs succeed best in the business part of town, where "working girls" and "young ladies" meet upon an equal footing, and where the clothes superficially look very much alike. Bright and ambitious girls will come to these down-town clubs to eat lunch and rest at noon, to study all sorts of subjects and listen to lectures, when they might hesitate a long time before joining a club identified with their own neighborhood, where they would be judged not solely on their own merits and the unconscious social standing afforded by good clothes, but by other surroundings which are not nearly up to these.

. . . In some very successful down-town clubs the home address is not given at all, and only the "business address" is required. Have we worked out our democracy further in regard to clothes than anything else?

[1899]   A Function of the Social Settlement

The word "settlement," which we have borrowed from London, is apt to grate a little upon American ears. It is not, after all, so long ago that Americans who settled were those who had adventured into a new country, where they were pioneers in the midst of difficult surroundings. The word still implies migrating from one condition of life to another totally unlike it, and against this implication the resident of an American settlement takes alarm.

We do not like to acknowledge that Americans are divided into "two nations," as her prime minister once admitted of England. We are not willing, openly and profoundly, to assume that American citizens are broken up into classes, even if we make that assumption the preface to a plea that the superior class has duties to the inferior. Our democracy is still our most precious possession, and we do well to resent any inroads upon it, even although they may be made in the name of philanthropy. . . .

The dominating interest in knowledge has become its use, the conditions under which, and ways in which, it may be most effectively employed in human conduct; . . . certain people have consciously formed themselves into groups for the express purpose of

effective application. These groups which are called settlements
have naturally sought the spots where the dearth of this applied
knowledge was most obvious, the depressed quarters of great cities.
They gravitate to these spots, not with the object of finding clinical
material, not to found "sociological laboratories," not, indeed, with
the analytical motive at all, but rather in a reaction from that motive, with a desire to use synthetically and directly whatever knowledge they, as a group, may possess, to test its validity and to discover
the conditions under which this knowledge may be employed. . . .

My definition of a settlement is that it is an attempt to express
the meaning of life in terms of life itself, in forms of activity. There
is no doubt that the deed often reveals when the idea does not, just
as art makes us understand and feel what might be incomprehensible and inexpressible in the form of an argument. . . .

[The settlement's] social relations are successful as it touches to
life the dreary and isolated, and brings them into a fuller participation of the common inheritance. Its teaching is successful as it
makes easy and available that which was difficult and remote. Its
most valuable function, as yet, lies along the line of interpretation
and synthesis.

ACTIVITIES AND EXPERIENCES
AT HULL-HOUSE

[1910]   Problems of Poverty

. . . There was in the earliest undertakings at Hull-House a touch
of the artist's enthusiasm when he translates his inner vision through
his chosen material into outward form. Keenly conscious of the
social confusion all about us and the hard economic struggle, we
at times believed that the very struggle itself might become a
source of strength. The devotion of the mothers to their children,
the dread of the men lest they fail to provide for the family dependent upon their daily exertions, at moments seemed to us the
secret stores of strength from which society is fed, the invisible
array of passion and feeling which are the surest protectors of the
world. We fatuously hoped that we might pluck from the human

tragedy itself a consciousness of a common destiny which should bring its own healing, that we might extract from life's very misfortunes a power of coöperation which should be effective against them.

Of course there was always present the harrowing consciousness of the difference in economic condition between ourselves and our neighbors. Even if we had gone to live in the most wretched tenement, there would have always been an essential difference between them and ourselves, for we should have had a sense of security in regard to illness and old age and the lack of these two securities are the specters which most persistently haunt the poor. Could we, in spite of this, make their individual efforts more effective through organization and possibly complement them by small efforts of our own? . . .

That neglected and forlorn old age is daily brought to the attention of a Settlement which undertakes to bear its share of the neighborhood burden imposed by poverty, was pathetically clear to us during our first months of residence at Hull-House. One day a boy of ten led a tottering old lady into the House, saying that she had slept for six weeks in their kitchen on a bed made up next to the stove; that she had come when her son died, although none of them had ever seen her before; but because her son had "once worked in the same shop with Pa, she thought of him when she had nowhere to go." The little fellow concluded by saying that our house was so much bigger than theirs that he thought we would have more room for beds. The old woman herself said absolutely nothing, but looking on with that gripping fear of the poorhouse in her eyes, she was a living embodiment of that dread which is so heart-breaking that the occupants of the County Infirmary themselves seem scarcely less wretched than those who are making their last stand against it. . . .

. . . For several years . . . I invited five or six old women to take a two weeks' vacation from the poorhouse which they eagerly and even gayly accepted. Almost all the old men in the County Infirmary wander away each summer taking their chances of finding food or shelter and return much refreshed by the little "tramp," but the old women cannot do this unless they have some help from the outside, and yet the expenditure of a very little money secures for them the coveted vacation. I found that a few pennies paid their car fare into town, a dollar a week procured lodging with an old acquaintance; assured of two meals a day in the Hull-House coffee-house they could count upon numerous cups of tea among old friends to whom they would airily state that they had "come out for a little change" and hadn't yet made up their minds about "going in again for the winter." They thus enjoyed a two weeks' vacation to the top of their bent and returned with wondrous tales of their adventures, with which they regaled the other paupers during the long winter. . . .

The lack of municipal regulation already referred to was, in the early days of Hull-House, paralleled by the inadequacy of the charitable efforts of the city and an unfounded optimism that there was no real poverty among us. Twenty years ago there was no Charity Organization Society in Chicago and the Visiting Nurse Association had not yet begun its beneficent work, while the relief societies, although conscientiously administered, were inadequate in extent and antiquated in method.

As social reformers gave themselves over to discussion of general principles, so the poor invariably accused poverty itself of their destruction. . . .

This spirit of generalization and lack of organization among the charitable forces of the city was painfully revealed in that terrible winter after the World's Fair, when the general financial depression throughout the country was much intensified in Chicago by the numbers of unemployed stranded at the close of the exposition. When the first cold weather came the police stations and the very corridors of the city hall were crowded by men who could afford no other lodging. . . .

. . . A huge mass meeting . . . resulted in a temporary organization, later [developed] into the Civic Federation. I was a member of the committee of five appointed to carry out the suggestions made in this remarkable meeting, and our first concern was to appoint a committee to deal with the unemployed. But when has a committee ever dealt satisfactorily with the unemployed? Relief stations were opened in the various parts of the city, temporary lodging houses were established, Hull-House undertaking to lodge the homeless women who could be received nowhere else; employment stations were opened giving sewing to the women, and street sweeping for the men was organized. It was in connection with the latter that the perplexing question of the danger of permanently lowering wages at such a crisis, in the praiseworthy effort to bring speedy relief, was brought home to me. I insisted that it was better to have the men work half a day for seventy-five cents, than a whole day for a dollar, better that they should earn three dollars in two days than in three days. I resigned from the street cleaning committee in despair of making the rest of the committee understand that, as our real object was not street cleaning but the help of the unemployed, we must treat the situation in such wise that the men would not be worse off when they returned to their normal occupations. The discussion opened up situations new to me and carried me far afield in perhaps the most serious economic reading I have ever done.

A beginning also was then made toward a Bureau of Organized Charities, the main office being put in charge of a young man recently come from Boston, who lived at Hull-House. But to employ scientific methods for the first time at such a moment involved difficulties, and the most painful episode of the winter for me came from an attempt on my part to conform to carefully received instructions. A shipping clerk whom I had known for a long time had lost his place, as so many people had that year, and came to the relief station established at Hull-House four or five times to secure help for his family. I told him one day of the opportunity for work on the drainage canal and intimated that if any employment were obtainable, he ought to exhaust that possibility before asking for help. The man replied that he had always worked indoors and that he could not endure outside work in winter. I am grateful to remember that I was too uncertain to be severe, although I held to my instructions. He did not come again for relief, but worked for two days digging on the canal, where he contracted pneumonia and died a week later. I have never lost trace of the two little children he left behind him, although I cannot see them without a bitter consciousness that it was at their expense I learned that life cannot be administered by definite rules and regulations; that wisdom to deal with a man's difficulties comes only through some knowledge of his life and habits as a whole. . . .

. . . There are also the families who, during times of business depression, are obliged to seek help from the county or some benevolent society, but who are themselves most anxious not to be confounded with the pauper class, with whom indeed they do not in the least belong. . . .

I remember one family in which the father had been out of work for this same winter, most of the furniture had been pawned, and as the worn-out shoes could not be replaced the children could not go to school. The mother was ill and barely able to come for the supplies and medicines. Two years later she invited me to supper one Sunday evening in the little home which had been completely restored, and she gave as the reason for the invitation that she couldn't bear to have me remember them as they had been during that one winter, which she insisted had been unique in her twelve years of married life. She said that it was as if she had met me, not as I am ordinarily, but as I should appear misshapen with rheumatism or with a face distorted by neuralgic pain; that it was not fair to judge poor people that way.

[1910]   The Jane Club

At a meeting of working girls held at Hull-House during a strike in a large shoe factory, the discussions made it clear that the strikers who had been most easily frightened, and therefore first to capitulate, were naturally those girls who were paying board and were afraid of being put out if they fell too far behind. After a recital of a case of peculiar hardship one of them exclaimed: "Wouldn't it be fine if we had a boarding club of our own, and then we could stand by each other in a time like this?" After that events moved quickly. We read aloud together Beatrice Potter's [later Beatrice Webb] little book on "Coöperation," and discussed all the difficulties and fascinations of such an undertaking, and on the first of May, 1891, two comfortable apartments near Hull-House were rented and furnished. The Settlement was responsible for the furniture and paid the first month's rent, but beyond that the members managed the club themselves. The undertaking "marched," as the French say, from the very first, and always on its own feet. Although there were difficulties, none of them proved insurmountable, which was a matter for great satisfaction in the face of a statement made by the head of the United States Department of Labor, who, on a visit to the club when it was but two years old, said that his department had investigated many coöperative undertakings, and that none founded and managed by women had ever succeeded. At the end of the third year the club occupied all of the six apartments which the original building contained, and numbered fifty members.

It was in connection with our efforts to secure a building for the Jane Club, that we first found ourselves in the dilemma between the needs of our neighbors and the kind-hearted response upon which we had come to rely for their relief. The adapted apartments in which the Jane Club was housed were inevitably more or less uncomfortable, and we felt that the success of the club justified the erection of a building for its sole use.

Up to that time, our history had been as the minor peace of the early Church. We had had the most generous interpretation of our efforts. Of course, many people were indifferent to the idea of the Settlement; others looked on with tolerant and sometimes cynical amusement which we would often encounter in a good story related at our expense; but all this was remote and unreal to us and we were sure that if the critics could but touch "the life of the people," they would understand.

The situation changed markedly after the Pullman strike, and our efforts to secure factory legislation later brought upon us a certain amount of distrust and suspicion; until then we had been considered merely a kindly philanthropic undertaking whose new form gave us a certain idealistic glamour. But sterner tests were coming and one of the first was in connection with the new building for the Jane Club. A trustee of Hull-House came to see us one day with the good news that a friend of his was ready to give twenty thousand dollars with which to build the desired new clubhouse. When, however, he divulged the name of his generous friend, it proved to be that of a man who was notorious for underpaying the girls in his establishment and concerning whom there were even darker stories. It seemed clearly impossible to erect a clubhouse for working girls with such money and we at once said that we must decline the offer. The trustee of Hull-House was put in the most embarrassing situation; he had, of course, induced the man to give the money and had had no thought but that it would be eagerly received; he would now be obliged to return with the astonishing, not to say insulting, news that the money was considered unfit. . . .

In the course of time a new club house was built by an old friend of Hull-House much interested in working girls, and this has been occupied for twelve years by the very successful coöperating Jane Club. . . .

A little incident of this time illustrated to me the confusion in the minds of at least many older men between religious teaching and advancing morality. One morning I received a letter from the head of a Settlement in New York expressing his perplexity over the fact that his board of trustees had asked money from a man notorious for his unscrupulous business methods. . . . The very morning when my mind was full of the questions raised by this letter, I received a call from the daughter of the same business man whom my friend considered so unscrupulous. She was passing through Chicago and came to ask me to give her some arguments which she might later use with her father to confute the charge that Settlements were irreligious. She said, "You see, he has been asked to give money to our Settlement and would like to do it, if his conscience was only clear; he disapproves of Settlements because they give no religious instruction; he has always been a very devout man."

[1910]   A Modern Lear

After the Pullman strike I made an attempt to analyze in a paper which I called *The Modern King Lear,* the inevitable revolt of human nature against the plans Mr. Pullman had made for his employees, the miscarriage of which appeared to him such black ingratitude. It seemed to me unendurable not to make some effort to gather together the social implications of the failure of this benevolent employer and its relation to the demand for a more democratic administration of industry.

[1912*]   . . . During the discussions which followed the Pullman strike, the defenders of the situation were broadly divided between

* The following was written and read to the Chicago Woman's Club shortly after the Pullman strike of 1894, but owing to the controversial nature of the issue was not accepted for publication until 1912.

the people pleading for individual benevolence and those insisting upon social righteousness; between those who held that the philanthropy of the president of the Pullman company had been most ungratefully received and those who maintained that the situation was the inevitable outcome of the social consciousness developing among working people.

In the midst of these discussions the writer found her mind dwelling upon a comparison which modified and softened all her judgments. Her attention was caught by the similarity of ingratitude suffered by an indulgent employer and an indulgent parent. King Lear often came to her mind. We have all shared the family relationship and our code of ethics concerning it is somewhat settled. We also bear a part in the industrial relationship, but our ethics concerning that are still uncertain. . . .

This older tragedy implied maladjustment; the forces of the tragedy were personal and passionate. This modern tragedy in its inception is a maladjustment between two large bodies of men, an employing company and a mass of employees. It deals not with personal relationships, but with industrial relationships. . . .

In shops such as those at Pullman, indeed, in all manufacturing affairs since the industrial revolution, industry is organized into a vast social operation. The shops are managed, however, not for the development of the workman thus socialized, but for the interests of the company owning the capital. The divergence between the social form and the individual aim becomes greater as the employees are more highly socialized and dependent, just as the clash in a family is more vital in proportion to the development and closeness of the family tie. The president of the Pullman company went further than the usual employer does. He socialized not only the factory but the form in which his workmen were living. He built and, in a great measure, regulated an entire town. This again might have worked out into a successful associated effort, if he had had in view the sole good of the inhabitants thus socialized, if he had called upon them for self-expression and had made the town a growth and manifestation of their wants and needs. But, unfortunately, the end to be obtained became ultimately commercial and not social, having in view the payment to the company of at least 4 per cent on the money invested, so that with this rigid requirement there could be no adaptation of rent to wages, much less to needs. The rents became statical and the wages competitive, shifting inevitably with the demands of trade. . . .

The theater was complete in equipment and beautiful in design, but too costly for a troupe who depended upon the patronage of mechanics, as the church was too expensive to be rented continuously. . . .

He fostered his employees for many years, gave them sanitary houses and beautiful parks, but in their extreme need, when they were struggling with the most difficult question which the times could present to them, when, if ever, they required the assistance of a trained mind and a comprehensive outlook, he lost his touch and had nothing wherewith to help them. He did not see the situation. He had been ignorant of their gropings toward justice. His conception of goodness for them had been cleanliness, decency of living, and above all, thrift and temperance. He had provided them means for all this; had gone further, and given them opportunities for enjoyment and comradeship. But he suddenly found his town in the sweep of world-wide moral impulse. A movement had been going on about him and through the souls of his workingmen of which he had been unconscious. He had only heard of this movement by rumor. The men who consorted with him at his club and in his business had spoken but little of it, and when they had discussed it had contemptuously called it the "Labor Movement," headed by deadbeats and agitators. Of the force and power of this movement, of all the vitality within it, of that conception of duty which induces men to go without food and to see their wives and children suffer for the sake of securing better wages for fellow-workmen whom they have never seen, this president had dreamed absolutely nothing. But his town had at last become swept into this larger movement, so that the giving up of comfortable homes, of beautiful surroundings, seemed as naught to the men within its grasp. . . .

The president of this company desired that his employees should possess the individual and family virtues, but did nothing to cherish in them those social virtues which his own age demanded. He rather substituted for that sense of responsibility to the community, a feeling of gratitude to himself, who had provided them with public buildings, and had laid out for them a simulacrum of public life.

Is it strange that when the genuine feeling of the age struck his town this belated and almost feudal virtue of personal gratitude fell before it? . . .

He felt himself right from the *commercial* standpoint, and could not see the situation from the *social* standpoint . . . Mazzini once preached, "the consent of men and your own conscience are two wings given you whereby you may rise to God." It is so easy for the good and powerful to think that they can rise by following the dictates of conscience, by pursuing their own ideals, leaving those ideals unconnected with the consent of their fellow-men. . . .

The man who insists upon consent, who moves with the people, is bound to consult the feasible right as well as the absolute right. He is often obliged to attain only Mr. Lincoln's "best possible," and often to have the sickening sense of compromising with his best convictions. He has to move along with those whom he rules toward a goal that neither he nor they see very clearly till they come to it. He has to discover what people really want, and then "provide the channels in which the growing moral force of their lives shall flow." What he does attain, however, is not the result of his individual striving, as a solitary mountain climber beyond the sight of the valley multitude, but it is underpinned and upheld by the sentiments and aspirations of many others. Progress has been slower perpendicularly, but incomparably greater because lateral. . . .

Is it too much to hope that some of us will carefully consider this modern tragedy, if perchance it may contain a warning for the troublous times in which we live? By considering the dramatic failure of the liberal employer's plans for his employees we may possibly be spared useless industrial tragedies in the uncertain future which lies ahead of us. . . .

[1910]   . . . The last picture of the Pullman strike which I distinctly recall was three years later when one of the strike leaders came to see me. Although out of work for most of the time since the strike, he had been undisturbed for six months in the repair shops of a street car company, under an assumed name, but he had at that moment been discovered and dismissed. He was a superior type of English workingman, but as he stood there, broken and discouraged, believing himself so black-listed that his skill could never be used again, filled with sorrow over the loss of his wife who had recently died after an illness with distressing mental symptoms, realizing keenly the lack of the respectable way of living he had always until now been able to maintain, he seemed to me an epitome of the wretched human waste such a strike implies.

I recall a time of great perplexity in the summer of 1894, when Chicago was filled with federal troops sent there by the President of the United States, and their presence was resented by the governor of the state, that I walked the wearisome way from Hull-House to Lincoln Park—for no cars were running regularly at that moment of sympathetic strikes—in order to look at and gain magnanimous counsel, if I might, from the marvelous St. Gaudens statue which had been but recently placed at the entrance of the park. Some of Lincoln's immortal words were cut into the stone at his feet, and never did a distracted town more sorely need the healing of "with charity towards all" than did Chicago at that moment, and the tolerance of the man who had won charity for those on both sides of "an irrepressible conflict."

[1898]   Ethical Survivals in Municipal Corruption

In . . . this paper . . . the writer is giving her own experiences from an eight years' residence in a ward of Chicago which has, during all that time, returned to the city council a notoriously corrupt politician. To say that all the men who vote for him are also corrupt, or that they approve of his dealings, is manifestly unfair; but to find the motives from which the votes are cast is not an easy matter.

The status of ethics attained in a given community is difficult to determine, and a newly-arrived resident is almost sure to make mistakes. He often fatuously attempts to correct public morals and change civic ideals without knowing the processes by which the present corrupt standards were obtained, and [is] sometimes quite ignorant of the motives and temptations of those who naively hold those standards.

Living together as we do, within the narrow boundary of a Chicago ward, fifty thousand people of a score of different tongues and nationalities, the writer is much impressed with the fact that all that holds us together—Latin, Celt, Teuton, Jew, and Slav, as we are—is our intrinsic human nature,—the few basic experiences which we hold in common. Our social ethics have been determined much more by example than by precept. . . .

Granting, then, that morality develops far earlier in the form of moral fact than in the higher form of moral ideas, it becomes obvious that ideas only operate upon the popular mind through will and character, and that goodness has to be dramatized before it reaches the mass of men. Ethics as well as political opinions may be discussed and disseminated among the sophisticated by lectures and printed pages, but to the common people they can only come through example,—through a personality which seizes the popular imagination. . . .

Nothing is more certain than that the quality which a heterogeneous population, living in one of the less sophisticated wards, most admires is the quality of simple goodness; that the man who attracts them is the one whom they believe to be a good man. . . . Abstract virtues are too difficult for their untrained minds to apprehend, and many of them are still simple enough to believe that power and wealth come only to good people.

The successful candidate, then, must be a good man according to the standards of his constituents. He must not attempt to hold up a morality beyond them, nor must he attempt to reform or change the standard. His safety lies in doing on a large scale the good deeds which his constituents are able to do only on a small scale. If he believes what they believe, and does what they are all cherishing a secret ambition to do, he will dazzle them by his success and win their confidence. . . . It seems to such a man entirely fitting that he should help a constituent out of trouble just because he is in trouble, irrespective of the justice involved.

The alderman, therefore, bails out his constituents when they are arrested, or says a good word to the police justice when they appear before him for trial; uses his "pull" with the magistrate when they are likely to be fined for a civil misdemeanor, or sees what he can do to "fix up matters" with the State's attorney, when the charge is really a serious one.

A gray-faced woman visited Hull-House one morning and asked
that her son be helped out of the city prison, because he was her
last support. The alderman had always done it for her, but the boy
had been arrested so often that even his patience, the most colossal
she had ever known, had given way. One of her boys was in the
penitentiary, and one of them in the reform school for a term of
years, and if this one, her Benjamin, were sent up she would have
no wages forthcoming. The alderman had bailed them out and
spoken to the judges many times since they were little fellows. He
had begun when her husband was still living, but he had kept on
long after she was a widow, and when the boys were still too young
to vote, which the neighbors all said was "mighty good of him."
The mother had no notion of the indifference for law which this
course had fostered in her sons; she was only in despair that her
long-suffering and powerful friend had at last come to the position
when he could no longer serve her and could only give his sympathy.
It did not occur to any of those concerned that the sense of justice
was thus slowly undermined and law-breaking encouraged. . . .

The alderman may himself be quite sincere in his acts of kindness.
In certain stages of moral evolution, a man is incapable of unsel-
fish action, the results of which will not benefit some one of his
acquaintances; still more, of conduct that does not aim to assist any
individual whatsoever; and it is a long step in moral progress to
appreciate the work done by the individual for the community. . . .
The alderman gives presents at weddings and christenings. He
seizes these days of family festivities for making friends. It is
easiest to reach people in the holiday mood of expansive good-will,
but on their side it seems natural and kindly that he should do it.
. . . If . . . [he] seizes upon festivities for expressions of his good-
will, much more does he seize upon periods of sorrow. At a funeral
he has the double advantage of ministering to a genuine craving
for comfort and solace, and at the same time of assisting at an
important social function. . . .

. . . The tendency to speak lightly of the faults of the dead and to
judge them gently is transferred to the living, and many a man at
such a time has formulated a lenient judgment of political corruption and has heard kindly speeches which he has remembered on
election day. "Ah, well, he has a big Irish heart. He is good to the
widow and the fatherless." "He knows the poor better than the big

guns who are always talking about civil service and reform." . . .
Such a man understands what the people want, and ministers
just as truly to a great human need as the musician or the artist
does. . . .

The question does, of course, occur to many minds, Where does the
money come from with which to dramatize so successfully? The
more primitive people accept the truthful statement of its sources
without any shock to their moral sense. To their simple minds he
gets it "from the rich," and so long as he again gives it out to the
poor, as a true Robin Hood, with open hand, they have no objections to offer. Their ethics are quite honestly those of the merry-
making foresters. The next less primitive people of the vicinage
are quite willing to admit that he leads "the gang" in the city council, and sells out the city franchises; that he makes deals with the
franchise-seeking companies; that he guarantees to steer dubious
measures through the council, for which he demands liberal pay;
that he is, in short, a successful boodler. But when there is intellect
enough to get this point of view, there is also enough to make the
contention that this is universally done; that all the aldermen do it
more or less successfully, but that the alderman of the Nineteenth
Ward is unique in being so generous; that such a state of affairs is
to be deplored, of course, but that that is the way business is run,
and we are fortunate when a kind-hearted man who is close to the
people gets a large share of the boodle. . . . The sense of just dealing comes apparently much later than the desire for protection and
kindness. On the whole, the gifts and favors are taken quite simply,
as an evidence of good and loving kindness, or are accepted as
inevitable political measures. . . .

[A] curious experience during . . . [a] campaign against our
corrupt alderman was the difference of standards between the imported speakers and the audience. One man high in the council
of the "better element," one evening, used as an example of the
philanthropic politician an alderman of the vicinity recently dead,
who was devotedly loved and mourned by his constituents. When
the audience caught the familiar name in the midst of platitudes,
they brightened up wonderfully. But, as the speaker went on, they
first looked puzzled, then astounded, and gradually their astonishment turned to indignation. The speaker, all unconscious of the

situation, went on, imagining, perhaps, that he was addressing his usual audience, and totally unaware that he was perpetrating an outrage upon the finest feelings of the people who were sitting before him. He certainly succeeded in irrevocably injuring the chances of the candidate for whom he was speaking. The speaker's standard of ethics was upright dealing in positions of public trust. The standard of ethics held by his audience was, being good to the poor and speaking gently of the dead. If he considered them corrupt and illiterate voters, they quite honestly held him a blackguard. . . .

Kinship of a common moral nature is the last and most comprehensive of all bases of union. The meaning of life is, after all, to search out and then to conform our activities to our new knowledge. And if we discover that men of low ideals and corrupt practice are forming popular political standards simply because such men stand by and for and with the people, then nothing remains but to obtain a like sense of identification before we can hope to modify ethical standards.

[1902]   During the campaign [against the alderman], when it was found hard to secure enough local speakers of the moral tone which was desired, orators were imported from other parts of the town, from the so-called "better element." Suddenly it was rumored on all sides that, while the money and speakers for the reform candidate were coming from the swells, the money which was backing the corrupt alderman also came from a swell source; that the president of a street-car combination, for whom he performed constant offices in the city council, was ready to back him to the extent of fifty thousand dollars; that this president, too, was a good man, and sat in high places; that he had recently given a large sum of money to an educational institution and was therefore as philanthropic, not to say good and upright, as any man in town; that the corrupt alderman had the sanction of the highest authorities, and that the lecturers who were talking against corruption, and the buying and selling of franchises, were only the cranks, and not the solid business men who had developed and built up Chicago.

All parts of the community are bound together in ethical development. If the so-called more enlightened members accept corporate gifts from the man who buys up the council, and the so-called less enlightened members accept individual gifts from the man who sells out the council, we surely must take our punishment together. There is the difference, of course, that in the first case we act collectively, and in the second case individually; but is the punishment which follows the first any lighter or less far-reaching in its consequences than the more obvious one which follows the second? . . .

After all, what the corrupt alderman demands from his followers and largely depends upon is a sense of loyalty, a standing-by the man who is good to you, who understands you, and who gets you out of trouble. All the social life of the voter from the time he was a little boy and played "craps" with his "own push," and not with some other "push," has been founded on this sense of loyalty and of standing in with his friends. Now that he is a man, he likes the sense of being inside a political organization, of being trusted with political gossip, of belonging to a set of fellows who understand things, and whose interests are being cared for by a strong friend in the city council itself. All this is perfectly legitimate, and all in the line of the development of a strong civic loyalty, if it were merely socialized and enlarged. . . .

In order, however, to give him a sense of conviction that his individual needs must be merged into the needs of the many, and are only important as they are thus merged, the appeal cannot be made along the line of self-interest. The demand should be universalized; in this process it would also become clarified, and the basis of our political organization become perforce social and ethical. . . .

As the acceptance of democracy brings a certain life-giving power, so it has its own sanctions and comforts. Perhaps the most obvious one is the curious sense which comes to us from time to time, that we belong to the whole, that a certain basic well-being can never be taken away from us whatever the turn of fortune. Tolstoy has portrayed the experience in "Master and Man." The former saves his servant from freezing, by protecting him with the heat of his body, and his dying hours are filled with an ineffable sense of healing and well-being. Such experiences, of which we have all had glimpses, anticipate in our relation to the living that peace of mind which envelops us when we meditate upon the great multitude of the dead. It is akin to the assurance that the dead understand, because they have entered into the Great Experience, and therefore must comprehend all lesser ones; that all the misunderstandings we have in life are due to partial experience, and all life's fretting comes of our limited intelligence; when the last and Great Experience comes, it is, perforce, attended by mercy and forgiveness. Consciously to accept Democracy and its manifold experiences is to anticipate that peace and freedom.

[1910]   Public Activities and Investigations

One of the striking features of our neighborhood twenty years ago, and one to which we never became reconciled, was the presence of huge wooden garbage boxes fastened to the street pavement in which the undisturbed refuse accumulated day by day. The system of garbage collecting was inadequate throughout the city but it became the greatest menace in a ward such as ours, where the normal amount of waste was much increased by the decayed fruit and vegetables discarded by the Italian and Greek fruit peddlers, and by the residuum left over from the piles of filthy rags which were fished out of the city dumps and brought to the homes of the rag pickers for further sorting and washing.

The children of our neighborhood twenty years ago played their games in and around these huge garbage boxes. They were the first objects that the toddling child learned to climb; their bulk afforded a barricade and their contents provided missiles in all the battles of the older boys; and finally they became the seats upon which absorbed lovers held enchanted converse. . . .

It is easy for even the most conscientious citizen of Chicago to forget the foul smells of the stockyards and the garbage dumps, when he is living so far from them that he is only occasionally made conscious of their existence, but the residents of a Settlement are perforce constantly surrounded by them. During our first three years on Halsted Street, we had established a small incinerator at Hull-House and we had many times reported the untoward conditions of the ward to the city hall. We had also arranged many talks for the immigrants, pointing out that although a woman may sweep her own doorway in her native village and allow the refuse to innocently decay in the open air and sunshine, in a crowded city quarter, if the garbage is not properly collected and destroyed, a tenement-house mother may see her children sicken and die, and that the immigrants must therefore, not only keep their own houses clean, but must also help the authorities to keep the city clean. . . .

The Hull-House Woman's Club had been organized the year before. . . . The members came together, however, in quite a new way that summer when we discussed with them the high death rate so persistent in our ward. After several club meetings devoted to the subject, despite the fact that the death rate rose highest in the congested foreign colonies and not in the streets in which most of the Irish American club women lived, twelve of their number undertook in connection with the residents, to carefully investigate the condition of the alleys. . . . It required both civic enterprise and moral conviction to be willing to do this three evenings a week during the hottest and most uncomfortable months of the year. Nevertheless, a certain number of women persisted, as did the residents, and three city inspectors in succession were transferred from the ward because of unsatisfactory services. Still the death rate remained high and the condition seemed little improved throughout the next winter. In sheer desperation, the following spring when the city contracts were awarded for the removal of garbage, with the backing of two well-known business men, I put in a bid for the garbage removal of the nineteenth ward. My paper was thrown out on a technicality but the incident induced the mayor to appoint me the garbage inspector of the ward.

The salary was a thousand dollars a year, and the loss of that political "plum" made a great stir among the politicians. The position was no sinecure whether regarded from the point of view of getting up at six in the morning to see that the men were early at work; or of following the loaded wagons, uneasily dropping their contents at intervals, to their dreary destination at the dump; or of insisting that the contractor must increase the number of his wagons from nine to thirteen and from thirteen to seventeen, although he assured me that he lost money on every one and that the former inspector had let him off with seven; or of taking careless landlords into court because they would not provide the proper garbage receptacles; or of arresting the tenant who tried to make the garbage wagons carry away the contents of his stable.

With the two or three residents who nobly stood by, we set up six of those doleful incinerators which are supposed to burn garbage with the fuel collected in the alley itself. The one factory in town which could utilize old tin cans was a window weight factory, and we deluged that with ten times as many tin cans as it could use— much less would pay for. We made desperate attempts to have the dead animals removed by the contractor who was paid most liberally by the city for that purpose but who, we slowly discovered, always made the police ambulances do the work, delivering the carcasses upon freight cars for shipment to a soap factory in Indiana where they were sold for a good price although the contractor himself was the largest stockholder in the concern. Perhaps our greatest achievement was the discovery of a pavement eighteen inches under the surface in a narrow street, although after it was found we triumphantly discovered a record of its existence in the city archives. The Italians living on the street were much interested but displayed little astonishment, perhaps because they were accustomed to see buried cities exhumed. This pavement became the *casus belli* between myself and the street commissioner when I insisted that its restoration belonged to him, after I had removed the first eight inches of garbage. The matter was finally settled by the mayor himself, who permitted me to drive him to the entrance of the street in what the children called my "garbage phaëton" and who took my side of the controversy. . . .

. . . The spectacle of eight hours' work for eight hours' pay, the even-handed justice to all citizens irrespective of "pull," the dividing of responsibility between landlord and tenant, and the readiness to enforce obedience to law from both, was, perhaps, one of the most valuable demonstrations which could have been made. Such daily living on the part of the office holder is of infinitely more value than many talks on civics for, after all, we credit most easily that which we see. The careful inspection combined with other causes brought about a great improvement in the cleanliness and comfort of the neighborhood and one happy day, when the death rate of our ward was found to have dropped from third to seventh in the list of city wards and was so reported to our Woman's Club, the applause which followed recorded the genuine sense of participation in the result, and a public spirit which had "made good." . . .

Of course our experience in inspecting only made us more conscious of the wretched housing conditions over which we had been distressed from the first. It was during the World's Fair summer that one of the Hull-House residents in a public address upon housing reform used as an example of indifferent landlordism a large block in the neighborhood occupied by small tenements and stables unconnected with a street sewer, as was much similar property in the vicinity. In the lecture the resident spared neither a description of the property nor the name of the owner. The young man who owned the property was justly indignant at this public method of attack and promptly came to investigate the condition of the property. Together we made a careful tour of the houses and stables and in the face of the conditions that we found there, I could not but agree with him that supplying South Italian peasants with sanitary appliances seemed a difficult undertaking. Nevertheless, he was unwilling that the block should remain in its deplorable state, and he finally cut through the dilemma with the rash proposition that he would give a free lease of the entire tract to Hull-House, accompanying the offer, however, with the warning remark, that if we should choose to use the income from the rents in sanitary improvements we should be throwing our money away.

Even when we decided that the houses were so bad that we could not undertake the task of improving them, he was game and stuck to his proposition that we should have a free lease. We finally submitted a plan that the houses should be torn down and the entire tract turned into a playground, although cautious advisers intimated that it would be very inconsistent to ask for subscriptions for the support of Hull-House when we were known to have thrown away an income of two thousand dollars a year. We, however, felt that a spectacle of inconsistency was better than one of bad landlordism and so the worst of the houses were demolished, the best three were sold and moved across the street under careful provision that they might never be used for junk-shops or saloons, and a public playground was finally established. . . .

During fifteen years this public-spirited owner of the property paid all the taxes, and when the block was finally sold he made possible the playground equipment of a near-by school yard. On the other hand, the dispossessed tenants, a group of whom had to be evicted by legal process before their houses could be torn down, have never ceased to mourn their former estates. Only the other day I met upon the street an old Italian harness maker, who said that he had never succeeded so well anywhere else nor found a place that "seemed so much like Italy." . . .

One of the first lessons we learned at Hull-House was that private beneficence is totally inadequate to deal with the vast numbers of the city's disinherited. We also quickly came to realize that there are certain types of wretchedness from which every private philanthropy shrinks and which are cared for only in those wards of the county hospital provided for the wrecks of vicious living or in the city's isolation hospital for smallpox patients. . . .

. . . This aspect of governmental responsibility was unforgettably borne in upon me during the smallpox epidemic following the World's Fair, when one of the residents, Mrs. Kelley, as State Factory Inspector was much concerned in discovering and destroying clothing which was being finished in houses containing unreported cases of smallpox. The deputy most successful in locating such cases lived at Hull-House during the epidemic because he did not wish to expose his own family. Another resident, Miss Lathrop, as a member of the State Board of Charities, went back and forth to the crowded pest house which had been hastily constructed on a stretch of prairie west of the city. As Hull-House was already so exposed, it seemed best for the special smallpox inspectors from the Board of Health to take their meals and change their clothing there before they went to their respective homes. All of these officials had accepted without question and as implicit in public office, the obligation to carry on the dangerous and difficult undertakings for which private philanthropy is unfitted, as if the commonality of compassion represented by the state was more comprehending than that of any individual group.

It was as early as our second winter on Halsted Street that one of the Hull-House residents received an appointment from the Cook County agent as a county visitor. She reported at the agency each morning, and all the cases within a radius of ten blocks from Hull-House were given to her for investigation. This gave her a legitimate opportunity for knowing the poorest people in the neighborhood and also for understanding the county method of outdoor relief. The commissioners were at first dubious of the value of such a visitor and predicted that a woman would be a perfect "coal chute" for giving away county supplies, but they gradually came to depend upon her suggestion and advice. . . .

In our first two summers we had maintained three baths in the basement of our own house for the use of the neighborhood and they afforded some experience and argument for the erection of the first public bathhouse in Chicago, which was built on a neighboring street and opened under the city Board of Health. The lot upon which it was erected belonged to a friend of Hull-House who offered it to the city without rent, and this enabled the city to erect the first public bath from the small appropriation of ten thousand dollars. Great fear was expressed by the public authorities that the baths would not be used and the old story of the bathtubs in model tenements which had been turned into coal bins was often quoted to us. We were supplied, however, with the incontrovertible argument that in our adjacent third square mile there were in 1892 but three bathtubs and that this fact was much complained of by many of the tenement-house dwellers. Our contention was justified by the immediate and overflowing use of the public baths, as we had before been sustained in the contention that an immigrant population would respond to opportunities for reading when the Public Library Board had established a branch reading room at Hull-House.

[1912]   Prostitution

In every large city throughout the world thousands of women are so set aside as outcasts from decent society that it is considered an impropriety to speak the very word which designates them. Lecky calls this type of woman "the most mournful and the most awful figure in history": he says that "she remains, while creeds and civilizations rise and fall, the eternal sacrifice of humanity, blasted for the sins of the people." But evils so old that they are imbedded in man's earliest history have been known to sway before an enlightened public opinion and in the end to give way to a growing conscience, which regards them first as a moral affront and at length as an utter impossibility. Thus the generation just before us, our own fathers, uprooted the enormous upas of slavery, "the tree that was literally as old as the race of man," although slavery doubtless had its beginnings in the captives of man's earliest warfare, even as this existing evil thus originated. . . .

Throughout this volume the phrase "social evil" is used to designate the sexual commerce permitted to exist in every large city, usually in a segregated district, wherein the chastity of women is bought and sold. Modifications of legal codes regarding marriage and divorce, moral judgments concerning the entire group of questions centering about illicit affection between men and women, are quite other questions which are not considered here. Such problems must always remain distinct from those of commercialized vice, as must the treatment of an irreducible minimum of prostitution, which will doubtless long exist, quite as society still retains an irreducible minimum of murders. . . .

Nothing is gained by making the situation better or worse than it is, nor in anywise different from what it is. This ancient evil is indeed social in the sense of community responsibility and can only be understood and at length remedied when we face the fact and measure the resources which may at length be massed against it. . . .

. . . Although economic pressure as a reason for entering an illicit life has thus been brought out in court by the evidence in a surprising number of cases, there is no doubt that it is often exaggerated; a girl always prefers to think that economic pressure is the reason for her downfall, even when the immediate causes have been her love of pleasure, her desire for finery, or the influence of evil companions. It is easy for her, as for all of us, to be deceived as to real motives. . . .

. . . Devotion and self-sacrifice [are often] poured out upon the miserable man who in the beginning was responsible for the girl's entrance into the life and who constantly receives her earnings. She supports him in the luxurious life he may be living in another part of the town, takes an almost maternal pride in his good clothes and general prosperity, and regards him as the one person in all the world who understands her plight. . . .

Most of the cases of economic responsibility, however, . . . arise from a desire to fulfill family obligations such as would be accepted by any conscientious girl. . . .

... The following story ... is of a girl who had come to Chicago at the age of fifteen from a small town in Indiana. Her father was too old to work and her mother was a dependent invalid. The brother who cared for the parents, with the help of the girl's own slender wages earned in the country store of the little town, became ill with rheumatism. In her desire to earn more money the country girl came to the nearest large city, Chicago, to work in a department store. The highest wage she could earn ... was ... inadequate even for her own needs and she was constantly filled with a corroding worry for "the folks at home." In a moment of panic, a fellow clerk who was "wise" showed her that it was possible to add to her wages by making appointments for money in the noon hour at down-town hotels. Having earned money in this way for a few months, the young girl made an arrangement with an older woman to be on call in the evenings whenever she was summoned by telephone, thus joining that large clandestine group of apparently respectable girls, most of whom yield to temptation only when hard pressed by debt incurred during illness or non-employment, or when they are facing some immediate necessity. This practice has become so general in the larger American cities as to be systematically conducted. . . . For a long time the young saleswoman kept her position in the department store, retaining her honest wages for herself, but sending everything else to her family. At length, however, she changed from her clandestine life to an openly professional one when she needed enough money to send her brother to Hot Springs, Arkansas, where she maintained him for a year. She explained that because he was now restored to health and able to support the family once more, she had left the life "forever and ever," expecting to return to her home in Indiana. She suspected that her brother knew of her experience, although she was sure that her parents did not, and she hoped that as she was not yet seventeen, she might be able to make a fresh start. Fortunately the poor child did not know how difficult that would be. . . .

[Another girl] has since married a man who wishes to protect her from the influence of her old life, but although not yet twenty years old and making an honest effort, what she has undergone has apparently so far warped and weakened her will that she is only partially successful in keeping her resolutions, and she sends each month to her parents in France . . . [money], which she confesses to have earned illicitly. It is as if the shameful experiences to which this little convent-bred Breton girl was forcibly subjected, had finally become registered in every fibre of her being until the forced demoralization has became genuine. She is . . . powerless . . . to save herself from her subjective temptations. . . .

Such demoralization is, of course, most valuable to the white slave trader, for when a girl has become thoroughly accustomed to the life and testifies that she is in it of her own free will, she puts herself beyond the protection of the law. She belongs to a legally degraded class, without redress in courts of justice for personal outrages. . . .

. . . It is easy to see why it thus becomes part of the business to break down a girl's moral nature by all those horrible devices which are constantly used by the owner of the white slave. . . . Our civilization becomes permanently tainted with the vicious practices designed to accelerate the demoralization of unwilling victims in order to make them commercially valuable. . . .

The suggestive presence of such women on the streets is perhaps one of the most demoralizing influences to be found in a large city, and such vigorous efforts as were recently made by a former chief of police in Chicago when he successfully cleared the streets of their presence, demonstrates that legal suppression is possible. At least this obvious temptation to young men and boys who are idly walking the streets might be avoided. . . .

A surprising number of suicides occur among girls when they discover that they have been betrayed by their lovers. . . . [Such a girl has] difficulty in finding any sort of work [and faces] the ostracism of her former friends added to her own self-accusation, the poverty and loneliness, the final ten days in the hospital . . . [which she leaves] weak and low-spirited and too broken to care what becomes of her. It is in moments such as these that many a poor girl, convinced that all the world is against her, decides to enter a disreputable house. Here at least she will find food and shelter, she will not be despised by the other inmates and she can earn money for the support of her child. Often she has received the address of such a house from one of her companions in the maternity ward where, among the fifty per cent of the unmarried mothers, at least two or three sophisticated girls are always to be found, eager to "put wise" the girls who are merely unfortunate. . . .

These discouraged girls, who so often come from domestic service to supply the vice demands of the city, are really the last representatives of those thousands of betrayed girls who for many years met the entire demand of the trade; for, while a procurer of some sort has performed his office for centuries, only in the last fifty years has the white slave market required the services of extended business enterprises in order to keep up the supply. Previously the demand had been largely met by the girls who had voluntarily entered a disreputable life because they had been betrayed. . . .

Certainly no philanthropic association, however rationalistic and suspicious of emotional appeal, can hope to help a girl once overwhelmed by desperate temptation, unless it is able to pull her back into the stream of kindly human fellowship and into a life involving normal human relations. Such an association must needs remember those wise words of Count Tolstoy: "We constantly think that there are circumstances in which a human being can be treated without affection, and there are no such circumstances." . . .

The . . . report of the Chicago Vice Commission estimates that twenty thousand of the men daily responsible for this evil in Chicago live outside of the city. They are the men who come from other towns to Chicago in order to see the sights. They are supposedly moral at home, where they are well known and subjected to the constant control of public opinion. The report goes on to state that during conventions or "show" occasions the business of commercialized vice is enormously increased. The village gossip with her vituperative tongue after all performs a valuable function both of castigation and retribution. . . .

During a recent military encampment in Chicago large numbers of young girls were attracted to it by that glamour which always surrounds the soldier. On the complaint of several mothers, investigators discovered that the girls were there without the knowledge of their parents, some of them having literally climbed out of windows after their parents had supposed them asleep. A thorough investigation disclosed not only an enormous increase of business in the restricted districts, but the downfall of many young girls who had hitherto been thoroughly respectable and able to resist the ordinary temptations of city life, but who had completely lost their heads over the glitter of a military camp. . . .

The primary difficulty of military life lies in the withdrawal of large numbers of men from normal family life, and hence from the domestic restraints and social checks which are operative upon the mass of human beings. The great peace propagandas have emphasized the unjustifiable expense involved in the maintenance of the standing armies of Europe, the social waste in the withdrawal of thousands of young men from industrial, commercial and professional pursuits into the barren negative life of the barracks. They might go further and lay stress upon the loss of moral sensibility, the destruction of romantic love, the perversion of the longing for wife and child. The very stability and refinement of the social order depend upon the preservation of these basic emotions. . . .

The great primitive instinct, so responsive to social control as to be almost an example of social docility, has apparently broken with all the restraints and decencies under two conditions: first and second, when the individual felt that he was above social control and when the individual has had an opportunity to hide his daily living. Prostitution upon a commercial basis in a measure embraces the two conditions, for it becomes possible only in a society so highly complicated that social control may be successfully evaded and the individual thus feels superior to it. When a city is so large that it is extremely difficult to fix individual responsibility, that which for centuries was considered the luxury of the king comes within the reach of every office-boy, and that lack of community control which belonged only to the overlord who felt himself superior to the standards of the people, may be seized upon by any city dweller who can evade his acquaintances. Against such moral aggression, the old types of social control are powerless. . . .

Certainly we are safe in predicting that when the solidarity of human interest is actually realized, it will become unthinkable that one class of human beings should be sacrificed to the supposed needs of another; when the rights of human life have successfully asserted themselves in contrast to the rights of property, it will become impossible to sell the young and heedless into degradation.

[1910]   The Value of Social Clubs

From the early days at Hull-House, social clubs composed of English-speaking American-born young people grew apace. So eager were they for social life that no mistakes in management could drive them away. I remember one enthusiastic leader who read aloud to a club a translation of "Antigone," which she had selected because she believed that the great themes of the Greek poets were best suited to young people. She came into the club room one evening in time to hear the president call the restive members to order with the statement, "You might just as well keep quiet for she is bound to finish it, and the quicker she gets to reading, the longer time we'll have for dancing." And yet the same club leader had the pleasure of lending four copies of the drama to four of the members, and one young man almost literally committed the entire play to memory.

On the whole we were much impressed by the great desire for self-improvement, for study and debate, exhibited by many of the young men. This very tendency, in fact, brought one of the most promising of our earlier clubs to an untimely end. The young men in the club, twenty in number, had grown much irritated by the frivolity of the girls during their long debates, and had finally proposed that three of the most "frivolous" be expelled. Pending a final vote, the three culprits appealed to certain of their friends who were members of the Hull-House Men's Club, between whom and the debating young men the incident became the cause of a quarrel so bitter that at length it led to a shooting. Fortunately the shot missed fire, or it may have been true that it was "only intended for a scare," but at any rate, we were all thoroughly frightened by this manifestation of the hot blood which the defense of woman has so often evoked. After many efforts to bring about a reconciliation, the debating club of twenty young men and the seventeen young women, who either were or pretended to be sober minded, rented a hall a mile west of Hull-House, severing their connection with us because their ambitious and right-minded efforts had been unappreciated, basing this on the ground that we had not urged the expulsion of the so-called "tough" members of the Men's Club, who had been involved in the difficulty. The seceding club invited me to the first meeting in their new quarters that I might present to them my version of the situation and set forth the incident from the standpoint of Hull-House. The discussion I had with the young people that evening has always remained with me as one of the moments of illumination which life in a Settlement so often affords. In response to my position that a desire to avoid all that was "tough" meant to walk only in the paths of smug self-seeking and personal improvement leading straight into the pit of self-righteousness and petty achievement and was exactly what the Settlement did not stand for, they contended with much justice that ambitious young people were obliged for their own reputation, if not for their own morals, to avoid all connection with that which bordered on the tough, and that it was quite another matter for the Hull-House residents who could afford a more generous judgment. . . .

In addition to these rising young people given to debate and dramatics, and to the members of the public school alumni associations which meet in our rooms, there are hundreds of others who for years have come to Hull-House frankly in search of that pleasure and recreation which all young things crave and which those who have spent long hours in a factory or shop demand as a right. For these young people all sorts of pleasure clubs have been cherished, and large dancing classes have been organized. . . .

It is but natural, perhaps, that the members of the Hull-House Woman's Club whose prosperity has given them some leisure and a chance to remove their own families to neighborhoods less full of temptations, should have offered their assistance in our attempt to provide recreation for these restless young people. In many instances their experience in the club itself has enabled them to perceive these needs. One day a Juvenile Court officer told me that a Woman's Club member, who has a large family of her own and one boy sufficiently difficult, had undertaken to care for a ward of the Juvenile Court who lived only a block from her house, and that she had kept him in the path of rectitude for six months. In reply to my congratulations upon this successful bit of reform to the club woman herself, she said that she was quite ashamed that she had not undertaken the task earlier for she had for years known the boy's mother who scrubbed a down-town office building, leaving home every evening at five and returning at eleven during the very time the boy could most easily find opportunities for wrongdoing. She said that her obligation toward this boy had not occurred to her until one day when the club members were making pillowcases for the Detention Home of the Juvenile Court, it suddenly seemed perfectly obvious that her share in the salvation of wayward children was to care for this particular boy and she had asked the Juvenile Court officer to commit him to her. She invited the boy to her house to supper every day that she might know just where he was at the crucial moment of twilight, and she adroitly managed to keep him under her own roof for the evening if she did not approve of the plans he had made. She concluded with the remark that it was queer that the sight of the boy himself hadn't appealed to her but that the suggestion had come to her in such a roundabout way.

She was, of course, reflecting upon a common trait in human nature,—that we much more easily see the duty at hand when we see it in relation to the social duty of which it is a part. When she knew that an effort was being made throughout all the large cities in the United States to reclaim the wayward boy, to provide him with reasonable amusement, to give him his chance for growth and development, and when she became ready to take her share in that movement, she suddenly saw the concrete case which she had not recognized before.

We are slowly learning that social advance depends quite as much upon an increase in moral sensibility as it does upon a sense of duty. . . .

The experiences of the Hull-House Woman's Club constantly react upon the family life of the members. Their husbands come with them to the annual midwinter reception, to club concerts and entertainments; the little children come to the May party, with its dancing and games; the older children, to the day in June when prizes are given to those sons and daughters of the members who present a good school record as graduates either from the eighth grade or from a high school. . . .

. . . The club developed many philanthropic undertakings from the humble beginnings of a linen chest kept constantly filled with clothing for the sick and poor. It required, however, an adequate knowledge of adverse city conditions so productive of juvenile delinquency and a sympathy which could enkindle itself in many others of diverse faiths and training, to arouse the club to its finest public spirit. . . . It required ability of an unusual order [in its President] to evoke a sense of social obligation from the very knowledge of adverse city conditions which the club members possessed, and to connect it with the many civic and philanthropic organizations of the city in such ways as to make it socially useful. . . .

Thus the value of social clubs broadens out in one's mind to an instrument of companionship through which many may be led from a sense of isolation to one of civic responsibility, even as another type of club provides recreational facilities for those who have had only meaningless excitements, or as a third type opens new and interesting vistas of life to those who are ambitious. . . .

The social clubs form a basis of acquaintanceship for many people living in other parts of the city. Through friendly relations with individuals, which is perhaps the sanest method of approach, they are thus brought into contact, many of them for the first time, with the industrial and social problems challenging the moral resources of our contemporary life. During our twenty years hundreds of these non-residents have directed clubs and classes, and have increased the number of Chicago citizens who are conversant with adverse social conditions and conscious that only by the unceasing devotion of each, according to his strength, shall the compulsions and hardships, the stupidities and cruelties of life be overcome. . . .

[1910]   Socialized Education

Every Thursday evening during the first years, a public lecture came to be an expected event in the neighborhood, and Hull-House became one of the early University Extension centers, first in connection with an independent society and later with the University of Chicago. One of the Hull-House trustees was so impressed with the value of this orderly and continuous presentation of economic subjects that he endowed three courses in a downtown center, in which the lectures were free to any one who chose to come. He was much pleased that these lectures were largely attended by workingmen who ordinarily prefer that an economic subject shall be presented by a partisan, and who are supremely indifferent to examinations and credits. They also dislike the balancing of pro and con which scholarly instruction implies, and prefer to be "inebriated on raw truth" rather than to sip a carefully prepared draught of knowledge.

Nevertheless Bowen Hall, which seats seven hundred and fifty people, is often none too large to hold the audiences of men who come to Hull-House every Sunday evening during the winter to attend the illustrated lectures provided by the faculty of the University of Chicago, and others who kindly give their services. These courses differ enormously in their popularity: one on European capitals and their social significance was followed with the most vivid attention and sense of participation indicated by groans and hisses when the audience was reminded of an unforgettable feud between Austria and her Slavic subjects, or when they wildly applauded a Polish hero endeared through his tragic failure. . . .

. . . A Settlement soon discovers that simple people are interested in large and vital subjects and the Hull-House residents themselves at one time, with only partial success, undertook to give a series of lectures on the history of the world, beginning with the nebular hypothesis and reaching Chicago itself in the twenty-fifth lecture! Absurd as the hasty review appears, there is no doubt that the beginner in knowledge is always eager for the general statement. . . .

When we are young we all long for those mountain tops upon which we may soberly stand and dream of our own ephemeral and uncertain attempts at righteousness. . . . A statement was recently made to me by a member of the Hull-House Boys' club, who had been unjustly arrested as an accomplice to a young thief and held in the police station for three days, that during his detention he "had remembered the way Jean Valjean behaved when he was everlastingly pursued by that policeman who was only trying to do right"; "I kept seeing the pictures in that illustrated lecture you gave about him, and I thought it would be queer if I couldn't behave well for three days when he had kept it up for years." . . .

. . . The residents of Hull-House place increasing emphasis upon the great inspirations and solaces of literature and are unwilling that it should ever languish as a subject for class instruction or for reading parties. The Shakespeare club has lived a continuous existence at Hull-House for sixteen years during which time its members have heard the leading interpreters of Shakespeare, both among scholars and players. I recall that one of its earliest members said that her mind was peopled with Shakespeare characters during her long hours of sewing in a shop, that she couldn't remember what she thought about before she joined the club, and concluded that she hadn't thought about anything at all. To feed the mind of the worker, to lift it above the monotony of his task, and to connect it with the larger world, outside of his immediate surroundings, has always been the object of art, perhaps never more nobly fulfilled than by the great English bard. Miss Starr has held classes in Dante and Browning for many years and the great lines are conned with never failing enthusiasm. I recall Miss Lathrop's Plato club and an audience who listened to a series of lectures by Dr. John Dewey on "Social Psychology," as genuine intellectual groups consisting largely of people from the immediate neighborhood, who are willing to make "that effort from which we all shrink, the effort of thought." But while we prize these classes as we do the help we are able to give to the exceptional young man or woman who reaches the college and university and leaves the neighborhood of his childhood behind him, the residents of Hull-House feel increasingly that the educational efforts of a Settlement should not be directed primarily to reproduce the college type of culture, but to work out a method and an ideal adapted to the immediate situation. They feel that they should promote a culture which will not set its possessor aside in a class with others like himself, but which will, on the contrary, connect him with all sorts of people by his ability to understand them as well as by his power to supplement their present surroundings with the historic background. . . .

. . . One of the most pitiful periods in the drama of the much-praised young American who attempts to rise in life, is the time when his educational requirements seem to have locked him up and made him rigid. He fancies himself shut off from his uneducated family and misunderstood by his friends. He is bowed down by his mental accumulations and often gets no farther than to carry them through life as a great burden, and not once does he obtain a glimpse of the delights of knowledge. . . .

Out of the fifteen hundred members of the Hull-House Boys' club, hundreds seem to respond only to the opportunities for recreation, and many of the older ones apparently care only for the bowling and the billiards. And yet tournaments and match games under supervision and regulated hours are a great advance over the sensual and exhausting pleasures to be found so easily outside the club. These organized sports readily connect themselves with the Hull-House gymnasium and with all those enthusiasms which are so mysteriously aroused by athletics.

Our gymnasium has been filled with large and enthusiastic classes for eighteen years in spite of the popularity of dancing and other possible substitutes, while the Saturday evening athletic contests have become a feature of the neighborhood. The Settlement strives for that type of gymnastics which is at least partly a matter of character, for that training which presupposes abstinence and the curbing of impulse, as well as for those athletic contests in which the mind of the contestant must be vigilant to keep the body closely to the rules of the game. . . .

Young people who work long hours at sedentary occupations, factories and offices, need perhaps more than anything else the freedom and ease to be acquired from a symmetrical muscular development and are quick to respond to that fellowship which athletics apparently afford more easily than anything else. The Greek immigrants form large classes and are eager to reproduce the remnants of old methods of wrestling, and other bits of classic lore which they still possess, and when one of the Greeks won a medal in a wrestling match which represented the championship of the entire city, it was quite impossible that he should present it to the Hull-House trophy chest without a classic phrase which he recited most gravely and charmingly. . . .

While a certain number of the residents are primarily interested in charitable administration and the amelioration which can be suggested only by those who know actual conditions, there are other residents identified with the House from its earlier years to whom the groups of immigrants make the historic appeal, and who use, not only their linguistic ability, but all the resource they can command of travel and reading to qualify themselves for intelligent living in the immigrant quarter of the city. I remember one resident lately returned from a visit in Sicily, who was able to interpret to a bewildered judge the ancient privilege of a jilted lover to scratch the cheek of his faithless sweetheart with the edge of a coin. Although the custom in America had degenerated into a knife slashing after the manner of foreign customs here, and although the Sicilian deserved punishment, the incident was yet lifted out of the slough of mere brutal assault, and the interpretation won the gratitude of many Sicilians. . . .

The Settlement casts aside none of those things which cultivated men have come to consider reasonable and goodly, but it insists that those belong as well to that great body of people who, because of toilsome and underpaid labor, are unable to procure them for themselves. Added to this is a profound conviction that the common stock of intellectual enjoyment should not be difficult of access because of the economic position of him who would approach it, that those "best results of civilization" upon which depend the finer and freer aspects of living must be incorporated into our common life and have free mobility through all elements of society if we would have our democracy endure.

The educational activities of a Settlement, as well as its philanthropic, civic, and social undertakings, are but differing manifestations of the attempt to socialize democracy, as is the very existence of the Settlement itself.

[1930]   Education by Current Events

. . . Life has a curious trick of suddenly regarding as a living moral issue, vital and unappeasable, some old outworn theme which has been kicked about for years as mere controversial material. The newly moralized issue, almost as if by accident, suddenly takes fire and sets whole communities in a blaze, lighting up human relationships and public duty with new meaning. . . . When that blaze actually starts, when the theme is heated, molten as it were with human passion and desire, the settlement can best use it in the unending effort to make culture and the issue of things go together. . . .

As an example of sudden interest, resulting in widespread education upon a given theme, the trial at Dayton, Tennessee, upon the general subject of evolution, forms a striking example. . . .

. . . What made the Tennessee incident so significant was the fact that legislative action had been taken against the teaching of the theory of evolution in tax-supported schools, by people who had a chance to express their actual desires through their government representatives. . . . The Tennessee mountaineers . . . found self-expression through the processes of local government and eagerly determined what their children should be taught upon the subject that they regarded as the most important in the world. . . .

. . . While there was no doubt that the overwhelming public opinion concerning the Tennessee trial was on the side of liberality both in politics and religion, the group of so-called narrow-minded men had made their own contribution to our national education. In the first place, they had asserted the actuality of religion. . . . Suddenly there came from a group of remote mountaineers a demonstration of a vivid and sustained interest in matters of religion, resulting in a sharp clash of doctrine between themselves and thousands of our fellow citizens, who all hung upon the issues of the trial with avid interest.

It was at times almost comic to hear the "hardboiled" city youth in his bewilderment talk about the situation. In the first place, modern economics had taught him—or he thought that it had— that a man was abjectly dependent upon the material world about him and must succumb to the iron clamp which industry imposes upon life; moreover, the youth himself gravely asserted that man's very freedom, morality and progress is determined by the material conditions which surround him and he had bodily taken over this theory into ethics and philosophy. He quoted those students of the social order who in what they considered the scientific spirit had collected and arranged data, to demonstrate the sole reaction of economic forces upon human life. These young people had for the most part lightly disregarded all teleological considerations, as they had long before renounced the theological explanations of a final cause. And yet many of them were secretly glad of this opportunity for discussion with old Jewish fathers who had never ceased to attest to the life of the spirit and who on their side caught their first glimpse in those sons hotly defending the theory of evolution, of the same zeal which they and their fathers had expended upon religion. These same young men so devoted to economic determinism as a theory of life had been already somewhat disconcerted by a recent movement in psychiatry with the emphasis upon the emotional and subconscious life versus the exclusive response to environmental stimuli. But if they were startled they were also much interested in this ardent inner life which was apparently to be found among so many different types of people who were everywhere responding to the blaze of interest started in Tennessee. . . .

Although these young Chicago intelligentsia I have been describing lived among colonies of immigrants, each one with its own history and conscious religious background, and had moreover naturally been interested in the normative sciences, they had known little about such descendants of early Americans so Anglo-Saxon and "Nordic" in background that they still had remnants of Elizabethan English in their daily speech. It was interesting to hear these young men talk of the effects of isolation whether the group were encompassed by mountains or by the invisible boundaries of a ghetto. . . .

Another instance of education through the discussion of current social developments, took place in regard to the problem of race relations when the industrial needs of war-time and the immigration restriction following the war, resulted in a great increase of Negroes in the urban populations throughout the country. This was brought to a head in Chicago as in many other places by the question of housing, when real estate values became confused as always with the subject of segregation. Whatever may be the practical solution it is still true that a complete segregation of the Negro in definite parts of the city tends in itself to put him outside the immediate action of that imperceptible but powerful social control which influences the rest of the population. Those inherited resources of civilization which are embodied in custom and kindly intercourse, make more for social restraint than does legal enactment itself.

One could easily illustrate this lack of inherited control by comparing the experience of a group of colored girls with those of a group representing the daughters of Italian immigrants or of any other South European peoples. The Italian girls very much enjoy the novelty of factory work, the opportunity to earn money and to dress as Americans do, but only very gradually do they obtain freedom in the direction of their own social affairs. Italian fathers consider it a point of honor that their daughters shall not be alone upon the street after dark, and only slowly modify their social traditions. The fathers of colored girls, on the other hand, are quite without those traditions, and fail to give their daughters the resulting protection. If colored girls yield more easily to the temptations of a city than the Italian girls do, who shall say how far the lack of social restraint is responsible for it? The Italian parents represent the social traditions which have been worked out during centuries and although such customs often become a deterrent to progress through the very bigotry of their adherents, nevertheless it is largely through a modification of these customs and manners that alien groups are assimilated into American life. The civilizations in Africa are even older than those in Italy and naturally tribal life everywhere has its own traditions and taboos which control the relations between the sexes and between parents and children. But of course these were broken up during the period of chattel slavery, for very seldom were family ties permitted to stand in the way of profitable slave sales. It was inevitable that the traditions were lost and that customs had to be built up anew. It gives an American community less justification for withholding from a colony of colored people those restraints and customs which can only be communicated through social understanding. . . .

We had discovered the use of a genuine interest in life itself by accident, in the early days of Hull-House, in such a simple matter as teaching English to our foreign-born neighbors. We were surrounded by a great many Italians in those days when unified Italy was still comparatively new and many of our neighbors had taken part in that great movement for nationalism. In our first Hull-House reading club for foreign-born students we tried to read an English translation of Mazzini's *On The Duties of Man*. It was very good reading but not always easy reading, although a shared interest that is genuine is the best possible basis for a class. When we had finished reading *On The Duties of Man*, the class with much bilingual oratory presented to Hull-House a bust of Mazzini—perhaps in gratitude that the course was over! Hull-House was opened three years before a great massacre occurred at Kishinev, Russia. A large number of Russians of Jewish origin came to this country, and hundreds of them settled in our neighborhood. Partly because of our personal contacts with some of their relatives and partly because of our knowledge of the ability of those who had been persecuted and driven away from their own country, we felt an enormous interest in the whole situation. We were also concerned with the effect upon our national existence of the sudden coming of a large number of persons who might easily be filled with hatred and a spirit of revenge. I read with a group of those Russians a book of Tolstoy's in English translation in which he works out cogently his theory of non-resistance. When I think of that group I have an impression of something very vivid. They had an intense desire to master the English language because they had something very vital to say, and could not say it unless they could find the English words. It is surprising what a stimulus such a situation provides!

[1930]   Immigrants Under the Quota

The distinct change in national policy represented by the Quota Act initiated in 1921, has been defined as the nation's massive attempt to draw its traditional forces together and to exclude the people and the influences that seemed to threaten the fierce loyalties and solidarities evoked by the war. . . .

After the war, the demand for serious restriction became widespread, arising doubtless from many causes, although the emotional content in the demand was obviously due to the fact that as a nation we had become during the war overconfident of our own nobility of purpose and had learned to distrust all foreigners as "unworthy." . . .

The sense of repression suffered during the war and after under the Quota Act was dramatized in the Chicago mayoralty campaign in 1927 when a candidate was triumphantly elected by the use of totally irrelevant slogans connected with abuse of the King of England because his majesty came to personify to the cowed citizens of foreign birth, the titular head of "the Nordics." It is said that the candidate stumbled upon the use of King George during his campaign when a jibe produced an unexpected and overwhelming response from a delighted audience composed of foreign-born citizens. The candidate had evidently hit upon one of those "vital lies" of which Vernon Lee has written so convincingly. The abuse of King George, with its implications, afforded an enormous release in a psychological sense, to those thousands of Chicago citizens who are of non-Anglo-Saxon ancestry. During the last decade such citizens had heard much about the superior Nordics, about the English foundation of our national institutions; that the Sons and Daughters of the American Revolution are alone worthy to define what constitutes acceptable patriotism. These non-Nordic citizens had sensed an uneasy fear on the part of the older stock that we may be overwhelmed from within, that we may suddenly find one day that we are no longer ourselves because our center of gravity is not securely based upon Anglo-Saxon and Puritan stock. . . .

. . . But at last a champion arose for the diverse groups living in Chicago. The abuse of King George—naturally pleasing to the Irish and inevitably highly entertaining to the Germans—embodied for the Slav, the Greek, the Latin, the Turk and all the rest, an assertion that the Anglo-Saxon was no better than he ought to be or at any rate that he would no longer be allowed to dictate what Chicago should teach its school children, whose racial background was as good as anybody's! The day of retribution had arrived! No one was ever hailed more devoutly as a champion of the misrepresented and of the oppressed, than was this valiant knight tilting at royalty. It was a curious revelation of the wide-felt need for championship that this revolt against the dominant race included the two hundred thousand colored people living in Chicago. Perhaps no one so wistfully feels the need of a champion—certainly no one can need one more —than does the Negro. King George represented for the moment the men of those dominant races who were the slave traders on the coast of Africa, who were the masters on Southern plantations, who were the shrouded night riders in the reconstruction days, the members of the Ku Klux Klan who had recently denied full high school privileges to an ambitious colored group living in the neighboring city of Gary. This call to the misrepresented also met a public response from the Chicago members of the Council Fire of American Indians, who begged to be set right in the school histories in which a successful foray of the Red Skins was invariably described as a massacre while one made by the Whites was called a victory over a savage foe. The Indians also submitted that they were the real 100 per cent Americans and that something was due them on that count as well. Of course with the allegiance of all these voters, the candidate was elected by an overwhelming majority.

Because the Quota Act went into operation so soon after the war, many families who had been separated before the war could do nothing toward getting together during the years of broken-down transportation and closed frontiers. They hoped that the end of the war would open the way, and long before normal conditions were restored thousands of people who were members of these separated families had sold all their belongings and were waiting at points of embarkation often remote from their homes. Without warning, they were placed under the operation of the Quota Acts, which often meant years of living in a strange land and country. During the first months of its operation in 1921, hundreds of distracted relatives came to Hull-House begging for information as to this new governmental regulation, and the stream has scarcely ceased since. . . .

A class of cases for which the Quota Act made scant provision were the husbands and wives, parents and children, who were being supported by members of their families living in this country but who were unable to come to America. When a group of social workers petitioned Congress to suspend the restrictions for these so-called "fireside relatives" their number was found to approximate one hundred and seventy-three thousand.

Many of the immigrants in America have faithfully sent money to their families throughout the eight years since the quota regulation was enforced, but inevitably many of them grew discouraged and others shirked their obligations altogether. . . .

One immediate consequence of the quota regulations was the withdrawals of the Latins and Slavs, who for years had performed the unskilled labor in America's industrial centers. This resulted in the arrival in the United States of a large number of Mexicans. One of the earliest colonies in Chicago was in the immediate vicinity of Hull-House. It was interesting to watch their reception in the neighborhood. At first the Italians received them almost as a group of their own countrymen. We had, for instance, a large Latin Club of young men at Hull-House, a membership fairly representative of both nationalities, but as the Mexicans in their innocence mingled freely with the Negroes from the South, who had come to Chicago in large numbers about the same time that the Mexicans themselves had come, and because many Mexicans were dark of skin they gradually became discriminated against, even by the people of Latin origins, who in Europe at least do not discriminate against the dark-skinned man. At the end of three years of a gradually less-cordial relationship between the groups, and long after the Latin Club had split upon nationalistic lines, a committee of Italians came to Hull-House with the threat that if we continued to rent Bowen Hall to the Mexicans, the Italians would discontinue to use it for their wedding receptions and other festivities. It was not that they would necessarily meet the Mexicans but that the hall would lose its prestige if it were being used by people of color! The incident afforded an example of one sorry aspect of the Americanization of immigrants, for it was quite evident that the Italians had copied their standard of social excellence from their American neighbors.

A similar example was afforded in connection with the race riots which unhappily occurred in Chicago in the summer of 1921. A colored man had been lynched in an Italian neighborhood, about half a mile from Hull-House. I had been in Europe that summer and upon my return I one evening consulted an association of Italian physicians who occasionally held their professional meetings in one of the Hull-House rooms. When I asked them why, in their opinion, such a shocking incident was possible in the United States, when the friendly attitude of the South Italian to his African neighbors is well known, the professional men replied with the utmost sincerity: "Of course this would never have happened in Italy; they are becoming Americanized." This was said in an honest effort to interpret a puzzling situation, and perhaps it did interpret it.

THE DEVIL BABY

[1930*]   . . . The knowledge of . . . [the Devil Baby's] existence burst upon the residents of Hull-House one day when three Italian women, with an excited rush through the door, demanded that the Devil Baby be shown to them. No amount of denial convinced them that he was not there, for they knew exactly what he was like with his cloven hoofs, his pointed ears and diminutive tail; the Devil Baby had, moreover, been able to speak as soon as he was born and was most shockingly profane.

* Another version of this story is in *The Long Road of Woman's Memory* (1916); the actual incident occurred in 1912.

The three women were but the forerunners of a veritable multitude; for six weeks from every part of the city and suburbs the streams of visitors to this mythical baby poured in all day long and so far into the night that the regular activities of the settlement were almost swamped. The Italian version with a hundred variations dealt with a pious Italian girl married to an atheist. Her husband in a rage had torn a holy picture from the bedroom wall saying that he would quite as soon have a devil in the house as such a thing, whereupon the devil incarnated himself in her coming child. As soon as the Devil Baby was born, he ran around the table shaking his finger at his father, who finally caught him and in fear and trembling, brought him to Hull-House. When the residents there, in spite of the baby's shocking appearance, wishing to save his soul, took him to church for baptism, they found that the shawl was empty and the Devil Baby, fleeing from the holy water, was running lightly over the backs of the pews.

The Jewish version, again with variations, was to the effect that the father of six daughters had said before the birth of a seventh child that he would rather have a devil in the family than another girl, whereupon the Devil Baby promptly appeared.

Save for a red automobile which occasionally figured in the story and a stray cigar which, in some versions, the new-born child had snatched from his father's lips, the tale might have been fashioned a thousand years ago.

Although the visitors to the Devil Baby included persons of every degree of prosperity and education, the story constantly demonstrated the power of an old wives' tale among thousands of men and women in modern society who are living with their vision fixed and their intelligence held by some iron chain of silent habit. To such primitive people the metaphor apparently is still the very stuff of life, or rather, no other form of statement reaches them; the tremendous tonnage of current writing for them has no existence. It was in keeping with their simple habits that the reputed presence of the Devil Baby should not reach the newspapers until the fifth week of his sojourn at Hull-House—after thousands of people had already been informed of his whereabouts by the old method of passing news from mouth to mouth.

For six weeks as I went about the house I would hear a voice at the telephone repeating for the hundredth time that day, "No, there is no such baby"; "No, we never had it here"; "No, he couldn't have seen it for fifty cents"; "We didn't send it anywhere, because we never had it"; "I don't mean to say that your sister-in-law lied, but there must be some mistake"; "There is no use getting up an excursion from Milwaukee, for there isn't any Devil Baby at Hull-House"; "We can't give reduced rates, because we are not exhibiting anything"; and so on and on. As I came near the front door I would catch snatches of arguments that were often acrimonious: "Why do you let so many people believe it, if it isn't here?" "We have taken three lines of cars to come and we have as much right to see it as anybody else"; "This is a pretty big place, of course you could hide it easy enough"; "What are you saying that for, are you going to raise the price of admission?"

We had doubtless struck a case of what the psychologists call the contagion of emotion added to that aesthetic sociability which impels any one of us to drag the entire household to the window when a procession comes into the street or a rainbow appears in the sky. The Devil Baby of course was worth many processions and rainbows, but I will confess that, as the empty show went on day after day, I quite revolted against such a vapid manifestation of even an admirable human trait. There was always one exception, however; whenever I heard the high eager voices of old women, I was irresistibly interested and left anything I might be doing in order to listen to them. It was a very serious and genuine matter with these old women, this story so ancient and yet so contemporaneous, and they flocked to Hull-House from every direction; those I had known for many years, others I had never known, and some whom I had supposed to be long dead. But they were all alive and eager; something in the story or in its mysterious sequences had aroused one of those active forces in human nature which does not take orders but insists only upon giving them.

During the weeks of excitement it was the old women who really seemed to have come into their own, and perhaps the most significant result of the incident was the reaction of the story upon them. It stirred their minds and memory as with a magic touch, it loosened their tongues and revealed the inner life and thoughts of those who are so often inarticulate. They are accustomed to sit at home and to hear the younger members of the family speak of affairs quite outside their own experiences, sometimes in a language they do not understand, and at best in quick glancing phrases which they cannot follow; "More than half the time I can't tell what they are talking about," is an oft-repeated complaint.

Perhaps my many conversations with these aged visitors crystallized thoughts and impressions I had been receiving through years, or the tale itself may have ignited a fire, as it were, whose light illumined some of my darkest memories of neglected and uncomfortable old age, of old peasant women who had ruthlessly probed into the ugly depths of human nature in themselves and others. Many of them who came to see the Devil Baby had been forced to face tragic experiences, the powers of brutality and horror had had full scope in their lives and for years they had had acquaintance with disaster and death. Such old women do not shirk life's misery by feeble idealism, for they are long past the stage of make-believe. They relate without flinching the most hideous experiences: "My face has had this queer twist for now nearly sixty years; I was ten when it got that way, the night after I saw my father do my mother to death with his knife." "Yes, I had fourteen children; only two grew to be men and both of them were killed in the same explosion. I was never sure they brought home the right bodies." But even the most hideous sorrows which the old women related had apparently subsided into the paler emotion of ineffectual regret, and they seemed, in some unaccountable way, to lose all bitterness and resentment against life, or rather to be so completely without it that they must have lost it long since.

None of them had a word of blame for undutiful children or heedless grandchildren, because apparently the petty and transitory had fallen away from their austere old age, the fires were burned out. Perhaps because they had come to expect nothing more of life and had perforce ceased from grasping and striving, they had obtained, if not renunciation, at least that quiet endurance which allows the wounds of the spirit to heal. Some of these old women had struggled for weary years with poverty and much childbearing, had known what it was to be bullied and beaten by their husbands, neglected and ignored by their prosperous children, and burdened by the support of the imbecile and the shiftless ones. They had literally gone "Deep written all their days with care."

One old woman actually came from the poorhouse, having heard of the Devil Baby "through a lady from Polk Street visiting an old lady who has a bed in our ward." It was no slight achievement for the penniless and crippled old inmate to make her escape. She had asked "a young bar-keep in a saloon across the road" to lend her ten cents, offering as security the fact that she was an old acquaintance at Hull-House who could not be refused so slight a loan. She marveled at some length over the goodness of the young man, for she had not had a dime to spend for a drink for the last six months, and he and the conductor had been obliged to lift her into the street car by main strength. She was naturally much elated over the achievement of her escape. To be sure, from the men's side, they were always walking off in the summer and taking to the road, living like tramps they did, in a way no one from the woman's side would demean herself to do; but to have left in a street car like a lady, with money to pay her own fare, was quite a different matter, although she was indeed "clean wore out" by the effort. However, it was clear that she would consider herself well repaid by a sight of the Devil Baby and that not only the inmates of her own ward, but those in every other ward in the house would be made to "sit up" when she got back; it would liven them all up a bit, and she hazarded the guess that she would have to tell them about that baby at least a dozen times a day.

As she cheerfully rambled on, we weakly postponed telling her there was no Devil Baby, first that she might have a cup of tea and rest, and then through a sheer desire to withhold a blow from one who had received so many throughout a long, hard life.

Our guest recalled with great pride that her grandmother had possessed second sight; that her mother had heard the banshee three times, and that she, herself, had heard it once. All this gave her a certain proprietary interest in the Devil Baby and I suspected she cherished a secret hope that when she should lay her eyes upon him, her inherited gifts might be able to reveal the meaning of the strange portent. At the least, he would afford a proof that her family-long faith in such matters was justified. Her misshapen hands lying on her lap fairly trembled with eagerness.

But even that was easier than my experience with an old woman, long since bed-ridden, who had doggedly refused to believe that there was no Devil Baby at Hull-House, unless "herself" came and told her so. Because of her mounting irritation with the envoys who one and all came back to her to report "they say it ain't there," it seemed well that I should go promptly before "she fashed herself into the grave." As I walked along the street, and even as I went up the ramshackle outside stairway of the rear tenement and through the dark corridor to the "second floor back" where she lay in her untidy bed, I was assailed by a veritable temptation to give her a full description of the Devil Baby, which by this time I knew so accurately (for with a hundred variations to select from I could have made a monstrous infant almost worthy of his name), and also to refrain from putting too much stress on the fact that he had never been really and truly at Hull-House. I found my mind hastily marshalling arguments for not disturbing her belief in the story which had so evidently brought her a vivid interest long denied her. She lived alone with her young grandson who went to work every morning at seven o'clock and save for the short visits made by the visiting nurse and by kind neighbors, her long day was monotonous and undisturbed. But the story of a Devil Baby, with his existence officially corroborated as it were, would give her a lodestone which would attract the neighbors far and wide and exalt her once more into the social importance she had had twenty-four years before when I had first known her. She was then the proprietor of the most prosperous secondhand store on a street full of them, her shiftless, drinking husband and her jolly good-natured sons doing exactly what she told them to do. This however was long past, for "owing to the drink," in her own graphic phrase, "the old man, the boys, and the business, too, were clean gone" and there was "nobody left but little Tom and me, and nothing for us to live on."

I remember how well she used to tell a story when I once tried to collect some folklore for Mr. Yeats to prove that an Irish peasant does not lose his faith in the little people nor his knowledge of Gaelic phrases simply because he is living in a city. She had at that time told me a wonderful tale concerning a red cloak worn by an old woman to a freshly dug grave. The story of the Devil Baby would give her material worthy of her powers, but of course she must be able to believe it with all her heart. She could live only a few months at the very best, I argued to myself; why not give her this vivid interest and through it awake those earliest recollections of that long-accumulated folklore with its magic power to trans-figure and eclipse the sordid and unsatisfactory surroundings in which life is actually spent? I solemnly assured myself that the imagination of old people needs to be fed and probably has quite as imperious a claim as that of childhood, which levies upon us so remorselessly with its "I want a fairy story, but I don't like you to begin by saying that it isn't true." Impatiently I found myself chal-lenging the educators who had given us no pedagogical instructions for the treatment of old age, although they had fairly overinformed us as to the use of the fairy tale with children.

The little room was stuffed with a magpie collection, the usual odds and ends which compose an old woman's treasures, augmented in this case by various articles which a secondhand store, even of the most flourishing sort, could not sell. In the picturesque con-fusion, if anywhere in Chicago, an urbanized group of the little people might dwell; they would certainly find the traditional atmos-phere which they strictly require, marveling faith, and unalloyed reverence. At any rate, an eager old woman aroused to her utmost capacity of wonder and credulity was the very soil, prepared to a nicety, for planting the seed-thought of the Devil Baby. If the object of my errand had been an hour's reading to a sick woman, it would have been accounted to me for philanthropic righteousness and if the chosen reading had lifted her mind from her bodily discomforts and harassing thoughts so that she forgot them all for one fleeting moment, how pleased I should have been with the success of my effort. But here I was with a story at my tongue's end, stupidly hesitating to give it validity, although the very words were on my lips. I was still arguing the case with myself when I stood on the threshold of her room and caught the indomitable gleam of her eye, fairly daring me to deny the existence of the Devil Baby, her slack dropsical body so responding to her overpowering excitement that for the moment she looked positively menacing.

But, as in the case of many another weak soul, the decision was taken out of my hands, my very hesitation was enough, for nothing is more certain than that the bearer of a magic tale never stands dawdling on the doorstep. Slowly the gleam died out of the expectant old eyes, the erect shoulders sagged and pulled forward, and I saw only too plainly that the poor old woman had accepted one more disappointment in a life already overflowing with them. She was violently thrown back into all the limitations of her personal experience and surroundings, and that larger life she had anticipated so eagerly was as suddenly shut away from her as if a door had been slammed in her face.

The vivid interest of so many old women in the story of the Devil Baby may have been an unconscious, although powerful, testimony that tragic experiences gradually become dressed in such trappings in order that their spent agony may prove of some use to a world which learns at the hardest; and that the strivings and sufferings of men and women long since dead, their emotions no longer connected with flesh and blood, are thus transmuted into legendary wisdom. The young are forced to heed the warning in such a tale, although for the most part it is so easy for them to disregard the words of the aged. That the old women who came to visit the Devil Baby believed that the story would secure them a hearing at home was evident, and as they prepared themselves with every detail of it, their old faces shone with a timid satisfaction. Their features, worn and scarred by harsh living, as effigies built into the floor of an old church become dim and defaced by roughshod feet, grew poignant and solemn.

Sometimes in talking to a woman who was "but a hair's breadth this side of darkness," I realized that old age has its own expression for the mystic renunciation of the world. The impatience with all non-essentials, the craving to be free from hampering bonds and soft conditions, recalled Tolstoy's last impetuous journey, and I was once more grateful to his genius for making clear another unintelligible impulse of bewildered humanity. Often, in the midst of a conversation, one of those touching old women would quietly express a longing for death, as if it were a natural fulfillment of an inmost desire, with a sincerity and anticipation so genuine that I would feel abashed in her presence, ashamed to "cling to this strange thing that shines in the sunlight and to be sick with love for it."

From our visitors to the Devil Baby it gradually became evident that the simpler women were moved not wholly by curiosity, but that many of them prized the story as a valuable instrument in the business of living. From them and from the surprising number of others who had been sent by the aged and the bed-ridden to secure an exact history and description of the child, the suggestion finally became quite irresistible that such a story, outlining a great abstraction, may once have performed the high service of tradition and discipline in the beginnings of a civilized family life. The legend exhibited all the persistence of one of those tales which has doubtless been preserved through the centuries because of its taming effects upon recalcitrant husbands and fathers. Shamefaced men brought to Hull-House by their womenfolk to see the baby, but ill concealed their triumph when there proved to be no such visible sign of retribution for domestic derelictions. On the other hand, numbers of men came by themselves, one group from a neighboring factory on their "own time" offered to pay twenty-five cents, a half dollar, two dollars apiece to see the child, insisting that it must be at Hull-House because "the women had seen it." To my query as to whether they supposed we would, for money, exhibit a poor little deformed baby, if one had been born in the neighborhood, they replied: "Sure, why not?" and "it teaches a good lesson, too," they added as an afterthought, or perhaps as a concession to the strange moral standards of a place like Hull-House. All the members in this group of hardworking men, in spite of a certain swagger toward one another and a tendency to bully the derelict showman, wore a hangdog look betraying that sense of unfair treatment which a man is so apt to feel when his womankind makes an appeal to the supernatural. In their determination to see the child, the men recklessly divulged much more concerning their motives than they had meant to do. Their talk confirmed my impression that such a story may still act as a restraining influence in the sphere of marital conduct which, next to primitive religion, has always afforded the most fertile field for irrational taboos and savage punishments.

What story could be better than this to secure sympathy for the mother of too many daughters and contumely for the irritated father; the touch of mysticism, the supernatural sphere in which it was placed, would render a man quite helpless.

The story of the Devil Baby, evolved in response to the imperative needs of anxious wives and mothers, recalls the theory that woman first fashioned the fairy story, that combination of wisdom and romance, in an effort to tame her mate and to make him a better father to her children, until such stories finally became a crude creed for domestic conduct, softening the treatment men accorded to women. Because such stories, expressing the very essence of human emotion, did not pretend to imitate the outside of life, they were careless of verisimilitude and absolutely indifferent to the real world. Possibly the multitude of life's failures, the obscure victims of unspeakable wrong and brutality, have embodied their memories in a literature of their own, of which the story of the Devil Baby is a specimen, crude and ugly in form, as would be inevitable, but still bringing relief to the supercharged heart.

During the weeks that the Devil Baby drew multitudes of visitors to Hull-House, my mind was opened to the fact that new knowledge derived from concrete experience is continually being made available for the guidance of human life; that humble women are still establishing rules of conduct as best they may, to counteract the base temptations of a man's world. I saw a new significance in the fact that thousands of women, for instance, make it a standard of domestic virtue that a man must not touch his pay envelope, but bring it home unopened to his wife. High praise is contained in the phrase, "We have been married twenty years and he never once opened his own envelope," or covert blame in the statement, "Of course he got to gambling; what can you expect from a man who always opens his own pay." The women were so fatalistically certain of this relation of punishment to domestic sin, of reward to domestic virtue, that when they talked about them, as they so constantly did in connection with the Devil Baby, it often sounded as if they were using the words of a widely known ritual. Among the visitors to the Devil Baby were many foreign-born peasant women who, when they had come to America, had been suddenly subjected to the complicated and constantly changing environment of city life, and, finding no outlet for many habits and tendencies, might easily have been thrown into that state described by psychologists as one of baulked disposition. To them this simple tale with its direct connection between cause and effect, between wrongdoing and punishment, brought soothing and relief, and restored a shaken confidence as to the righteousness of the universe. Because the Devil Baby embodied an undeserved wrong to a poor mother whose tender child had been claimed by the forces of evil, his merely reputed presence had power to attract to Hull-House hundreds of women who had been humbled and disgraced by their children; mothers of the feeble-minded, of the vicious, of the criminal, of the prostitute. In their talk it was as if their long role of maternal apology and protective reticence had at last broken down, as if they could speak out freely because for once a man responsible for an ill-begotten child had been "met up with" and had received his deserts. Their sinister version of the story was that the father of the Devil Baby had married without confessing a hideous crime committed years before, thus basely deceiving both his innocent young bride and the good priest who performed the solemn ceremony; that the sin had become incarnate in his child which, to the horror of the young and trusting mother, had been born with all the outward aspects of the devil himself.

As if drawn by a magnet, these forlorn women issued forth from the many homes in which dwelt "the two unprofitable goddesses, Poverty and Impossibility." Occasionally it seemed to me that the women were impelled by a longing to see one good case of retribution before they died, as a bullied child hopes to deal at least one crushing blow at his tormentor when he "grows up," but I think, on the whole, such an explanation was a mistake; it is more probable that the avidity of the women demonstrated that the story itself, like all interpretative art, was one of those free, unconscious attempts to satisfy, outside of life, those cravings which life itself leaves unsatisfied. At moments, however, baffled desires, sharp cries of pain, echoes of justices unfulfilled, the original material from which such tales are fashioned, would break through the rigid restraints imposed by all Art, even that unconscious of itself.

With an understanding quickened, perhaps, through my own acquaintance with the mysterious child, I listened to many tragic reminiscences from the visiting women; of premature births, "because he kicked me in the side"; of children maimed and burnt because "I had no one to leave them with when I went to work"; women had seen the tender flesh of growing little bodies given over to death because "he wouldn't let me send for the doctor," or because "there was no money to pay for the medicine." But even these mothers, rendered childless through insensate brutality, were less pitiful than some of the others, who might well have cried aloud of their children as did a distracted mother of her child centuries ago:

> That God should send this one thing more
> Of hunger and of dread, a door
> Set wide to every wind of pain!

Such was the mother of a feeble-minded boy, who said: "I didn't have a devil baby myself, but I bore a poor 'innocent' who made me fight devils for twenty-three years." She told of her son's experiences from the time the other little boys had put him up to stealing that they might hide in safety and leave him to be found with "the goods on him," until grown into a huge man he fell into the hands of professional burglars; he was evidently the dupe and stool-pigeon of the vicious and criminal until the very day he was locked into the state penitentiary. "If people played with him a little, he went right off and did anything they told him to, and now he's been sent up for life. We call such innocents 'God's Fools' in the old country, but over here the Devil himself gets them. I've fought off bad men and boys from the poor lamb with my very fists; nobody ever came near the house except such-like and the police officers, who were arresting him."

There were a goodly number of visitors to the Devil Baby of the type of those to be found in every large city, who are on the verge of nervous collapse, or who exhibit many symptoms of mental aberration, and yet are sufficiently normal to be at large most of the time, and to support themselves by drudgery which requires little mental effort although the exhaustion resulting from the work they are able to do, is the one thing from which they should be most carefully protected. One such woman, evidently obtaining inscrutable comfort from the story of the Devil Baby even after she had become convinced that we harbored no such creature, came many times to tell of her longing for her son, who had joined the army eighteen months before and was now stationed in Alaska. She always began with the same words:

"When Spring comes and the snow melts so that I know he could get out, I can hardly stand it. You know I was once in the insane asylum for three years at a stretch, and since then I haven't had much use of my mind except to worry with. Of course I know that it is dangerous for me, but what can I do? I think something like this: 'The snow is melting, now he could get out, but his officers won't let him off and if he runs away he will be shot for a deserter —either way I'll never see him again; I'll die without seeing him'— and then I'll begin all over again with the snow." After a pause, she said: "The recruiting officer ought not to have taken him, he's my only son and I'm a widow. It's against the rules, but he was so crazy to go that I guess he lied a little—at any rate, the government has him now and I can't get him back. Without this worry about him my mind would be all right; if he were here he would be earning money and keeping me and we would be happy all day long."

Recalling the vagabondish lad, who had never earned much money and had certainly never "kept" his hardworking mother, I ventured to suggest that, even if he were at home he might not have work these hard times, that he might get into trouble and be arrested—I did not need to remind her that he had been already arrested twice—that he was now fed and sheltered and under discipline, and I added hopefully something about his seeing the world. She looked at me out of her withdrawn harried eyes, as if I were speaking a foreign tongue. "That wouldn't make any real difference to me—the work, the money, his behaving well and all that, if I could cook and wash for him. I don't need all the money I earn scrubbing that factory. I only take bread and tea for supper, and I choke over that, thinking of him."

She ceased to speak, overcome by a thousand obscure emotions which could find no outlet in words. She dimly realized that the facts in the case, to one who had known her boy from childhood, were far from creditable, and that no one could understand the eternally unappeased idealism which, for her, surrounded her son's return. She was even afraid to say much about it, lest she should be overmastered by her subject and be considered so irrational as to suggest a return to the hospital for the insane.

Those mothers who have never resisted fate nor buffeted against the black waters but have allowed the waves to close over them, worn and bent as they are by hard labor, subdued and misshapen by the brutality of men, are at least unaffrighted by the melodramatic coarseness of life, which Stevenson more gently describes as "the uncouth and outlandish strain in the web of the world." The story of the Devil Baby may have made its appeal through its frank presentation of this very demoniac quality, to those who live under the iron tyranny of that poverty which threatens starvation, and under the dread of a brutality which may any dark night bring them or their children to extinction; to those who have seen both virtue and vice go unrewarded and who have long since ceased to complain.

A sorrowful woman, clad in heavy black, who came one day, exhibited such a capacity for prolonged weeping that it was evidence in itself of the truth of at least half her statement, that she had cried herself to sleep every night of her life for fourteen years in fulfillment of a "curse" laid upon her by an angry man that "her pillow would be wet with tears as long as she lived." Her respectable husband had a shop in the red light district because he found it profitable to sell to the men and women who lived there. She had kept house in the room over the store from the time she was a bride newly come from Russia, and her five daughters had been born there, but never a son to gladden her husband's heart.

She took such a feverish interest in the Devil Baby that, when I was obliged to disillusion her, I found it hard to take away her comfort in the belief that the Powers that Be are on the side of the woman when her husband resents too many daughters. But, after all, the birth of daughters was but an incident in her unmitigated woe, for the scoldings of a disappointed husband were as nothing to the curse of a strange enemy, although she doubtless had a confused impression that if there were retribution for one in the general scheme of things, there might be for the other. When the weeping woman finally put the events of her disordered life in some sort of sequence, it became clear that about fifteen years ago she had reported to the police a vicious house whose back door opened into her own yard. Her husband had forbidden her to do anything about it and had said that it would only get them into trouble, but she had been made desperate one day when she saw her little girl, then twelve years old, come out of the door, gleefully showing her younger sister a present of money. Because the poor woman had tried for ten years without success to induce her husband to move from the vicinity of such houses, she was certain that she could save her child only by forcing out "the bad people" from her own door yard. She therefore made her one frantic effort, found her way to the city hall and there reported the house to the chief himself. Of course, "the bad people stood in with the police" and nothing happened to them save, perhaps, a fresh levy of blackmail, but the keeper of the house, beside himself with rage, made the dire threat and laid the curse upon her. In less than a year from that time he had enticed her daughter into a disreputable house in another part of the district. The poor woman, ringing one doorbell after another, had never been able to find her, but her sisters, who in time came to know where she was, had been dazzled by her mode of life. The weeping mother was quite sure that two of her daughters, while still outwardly respectable and "working downtown," earned money in the devious ways which they had learned all about when they were little children, although for the past five years the now prosperous husband had allowed the family to live in a suburb where the two younger daughters were "growing up respectable."

Certain of the visitors, although confronted by those mysterious and impersonal wrongs which are apparently inherent in the very nature of things, gave us glimpses of another sort of wisdom than that expressed in the assumptions that the decrees of Fate are immutable. Such a glimpse came to me through conversation with a woman whose fine mind and indomitable spirit I had long admired; I had known her for years, and the recital of her sufferings added to those which the Devil Baby had already induced other women to tell me, pierced me afresh.

"I had eleven children, some born in Hungary and some born here, nine of them boys; all of the children died when they were little but my dear Liboucha. You know all about her. She died last winter in the insane asylum. She was only twelve years old when her father, in a fit of delirium tremens, killed himself after he had chased us around the room, trying to kill us first. She saw it all, the blood splashed on the wall stayed in her mind the worst; she shivered and shook all that night through, and the next morning she had lost her voice, couldn't speak out loud for terror. After a while she went to school again and her voice came back, although it was never very natural. She seemed to do as well as ever and was awful pleased when she got into high school. All the money we had, I earned scrubbing in a public dispensary although sometimes I got a little more by interpreting for the patients, for I know three languages, one as well as the other. But I was determined that whatever happened to me, Liboucha was to be educated. My husband's father was a doctor in the old country, and Liboucha was always a clever child. I wouldn't have her live the kind of life I had, with no use for my mind except to make me restless and bitter. I was pretty old and worn out for such hard work, but when I used to see Liboucha on a Sunday morning ready for church in her white dress, with her long yellow hair braided round her beautiful pale face, lying there in bed to rest my aching bones for the next week's work, I'd feel almost happy, in spite of everything. But of course no such peace could last in my life; the second year at high school Liboucha began to seem different and to do strange things. You know the time she wandered away for three days and we were all wild with fright, although a kind woman had taken her in and no harm came to her. I could never be easy after that; she was always gentle, but she was awful sly about running away and at last I had to send her to the asylum. She stayed there off and on for five years, but I saw her every week of my life and she was always company for me, what with sewing for her, washing and ironing her clothes, cooking little things to take out to her, and saving a bit of money to buy fruit for her. At any rate, I had stopped feeling so bitter, and got some comfort out of seeing the one thing that belonged to me on this side of the water, when all of a sudden she died of heart failure and they never took the trouble to send for me until the next day."

She stopped as if wondering afresh that the Fates could have been so casual, but with a sudden illumination, as if she had been awakened out of the burden and intensity of her restricted personal interests into a consciousness of those larger relations that are, for the most part, so strangely invisible. It was as if the young mother of the grotesque Devil Baby—that victim of wrongdoing on the part of others—had revealed to this tragic woman much more clearly than soft words had ever done, that the return of a deed of violence upon the head of the innocent is inevitable; as if she had realized that, although she was destined to walk all the days of her life with the piteous multitude who bear the undeserved wrongs of the world, she would walk henceforth with a sense of companionship.

At moments it seemed possible that these simple women, representing an earlier development, eagerly seized upon this story because it was so primitive in form and substance. Certainly, one evening, a long-forgotten ballad made an unceasing effort to come to the surface of my mind as I talked to a feeble woman who, in the last stages of an incurable disease from which she soon afterwards died, had been helped off the street car in front of Hull-House. The ballad tells how the lover of a proud and jealous mistress, who demanded as a final test of devotion that he bring her the heart of his mother, had quickly cut the heart from his mother's breast and impetuously returned to his lady, bearing it upon a salver; and how, when stumbling in his gallant haste, he stooped to replace upon the silver plate his mother's heart which had rolled to the ground, the heart, still beating with tender solicitude, whispered the hope that her child was not hurt. The ballad itself was scarcely more exaggerated than the story of our visitor that evening, who was carried through the door of Hull-House in a desperate effort to see the Devil Baby. I was familiar with her vicissitudes; the shiftless, drinking husband and the large family of children, all of whom had brought her sorrow and disgrace, and I knew that her heart's desire was to see again, before she died, her youngest son, who was a life prisoner in the penitentiary. She was confident that the last piteous stage of her disease would secure him a week's parole, founding this forlorn hope upon the fact that "they sometimes let them out to attend a mother's funeral, and perhaps they'd let Joe come a few days ahead; he could pay his fare afterwards from the insurance money. It wouldn't take much to bury me." Again we went over the hideous story: Joe had violently quarreled with a woman, the proprietor of the house in which his disreputable wife was living, because she had withheld from him a part of his wife's "earnings," and in the altercation had killed her—a situation, one would say, which it would be difficult for even a mother to condone. But not at all. Her thin gray face worked with emotion, her trembling hands restlessly pulled at her shabby skirt as the hands of the dying pluck at their sheets, but she put all the vitality she could muster into his defense. She told us he had legally married the girl, who supported him, "although Lily had been so long in that life that few men would have done it. Of course such a girl must have a protector or everybody would fleece her. Poor Lily said to the day of her death that he was the kindest man she ever knew, and treated her the whitest; that she herself was to blame for the murder, because she told on the old miser, and Joe was so hot-headed she might have known that he would draw a gun for her." The gasping mother concluded: "He was always that handsome and had such a way. One winter when I was scrubbing in an office building, I'd never get home much before twelve o'clock, but Joe would open the door for me just as pleasant as if he hadn't been waked out of a sound sleep." She was so triumphantly unconscious of the incongruity of a sturdy son in bed while his mother earned his food, that her auditors said never a word, and in silence we saw a hero evolved before our eyes, a defender of the oppressed, the best beloved of his mother, who was losing his high spirits and eating his heart out behind prison bars. He could well defy the world even there, surrounded as he was by that invincible affection which assures both the fortunate and unfortunate alike that we are loved, not according to our deserts, but in response to some profounder law.

This imposing revelation of maternal solicitude was an instance of what continually happened in connection with the Devil Baby. In the midst of the most tragic reminiscences there remained that which has been called the great revelation of tragedy, or sometimes the great illusion of tragedy; that which has power in its own right to make life palatable and at rare moments even beautiful.

THE DEMAND FOR SOCIAL JUSTICE

[1899]   The Subtle Problem of Charity

For most of the years during a decade of residence in a settlement, my mind was sore and depressed over the difficulties of the charitable relationship. The incessant clashing of ethical standards, which had been honestly gained from widely varying industrial experience,—the misunderstandings inevitable between people whose conventions and mode of life had been so totally unlike,— made it seem reasonable to say that nothing could be done until industrial conditions were made absolutely democratic. The position of a settlement, which attempts at one and the same time to declare its belief in this eventual, industrial democracy, and to labor toward that end, to maintain a standard of living, and to deal humanely and simply with those in actual want, often seems utterly untenable and preposterous. Recently, however, there has come to my mind the suggestion of a principle, that while the painful condition of administering charity is the inevitable discomfort of a transition into a more democratic relation, the perplexing experiences of the actual administration have a genuine value of their own. The economist who treats the individual cases as mere data, and the social reformer who labors to make such cases impossible, solely because of the appeal to his reason, may have to share these perplexities before they feel themselves within the grasp of a principle of growth, working outward from within; before they can gain the exhilaration and uplift which come when the individual sympathy and intelligence are caught into the forward, intuitive movement of the mass. This general movement is not without its intellectual aspects, but it is seldom apprehended by the intellect alone. The social reformers who avoid the charitable relationship with any of their fellow men take a certain outside attitude toward this movement. They may analyze it and formulate it; they may be most valuable and necessary, but they are not essentially within it. The mass of men seldom move together without an emotional incentive, and the doctrinaire, in his effort to keep his mind free from the emotional quality, inevitably stands aside. He avoids the perplexity, and at the same time loses the vitality.

[1910]   At any rate the residents at Hull-House discovered that while their first impact with city poverty allied them to groups given over to discussion of social theories, their sober efforts to heal neighborhood ills allied them to general public movements which were without challenging creeds. But while we discovered that we most easily secured the smallest of much needed improvements by attaching our efforts to those of organized bodies, nevertheless these very organizations would have been impossible, had not the public conscience been aroused and the community sensibility quickened by these same ardent theorists.

[1910]   Charity and Social Justice*

In an attempt to review the recent trend in the development of charity, that which has appeared most striking to your President is a gradual coming together of two groups of people, who have too often been given to a suspicion of each other and sometimes to actual vituperation. One group who have traditionally been moved to action by "pity for the poor" we call the Charitable; the other, larger or smaller in each generation, but always fired by a "hatred of injustice," we designate as the Radicals.

These two groups, as the result of a growing awareness of distress and of a slowly deepening perception of its causes, are at last uniting into an effective demand for juster social conditions. The Charitable have been brought to this combination through the conviction that the poverty and crime with which they constantly deal are often the result of untoward industrial conditions, while the Radicals have been slowly forced to the conclusion that if they would make an effective appeal to public opinion they must utilize carefully collected data as to the conditions of the poor and criminal. It is as if the Charitable had been brought, through the care of the individual, to a contemplation of social causes, and as if the Radical had been forced to test his social doctrine by a sympathetic observation of actual people. . . .

It would be easy from the records of this Conference to trace the gradual steps by which charitable folk were irresistibly led from Cure to Prevention, as it would also be possible to demonstrate from contemporaneous records that we are now being led in the same gradual but unresting manner from Prevention to a consideration of Vital Welfare. The negative policy of relieving destitution, or even the more generous one of preventing it, is giving way to the positive idea of raising life to its highest value.

If at times the moral fire seems to be dying out of the good old words Relief and Charity, it has undoubtedly filled with a new

* President's address, National Conference of Charities and Correction.

warmth certain words which belong distinctively to our own times; such words as Prevention, Amelioration, and Social Justice. It is also true that those for whom these words contain most of hope and warmth are those who have been long mindful of the old tasks and obligations, as if the great basic emotion of human Compassion had more than held its own. After all, sympathetic knowledge is the only way of approach to any human problem. The line of least resistance into the jungle of human wretchedness must always be through that region which is most thoroughly explored, not only by the information of the statistician, but by the understanding of the Charitable. . . .

Many illustrations are possible of social advance due to sanitary science pushed by the Charitable, but for our purpose nothing illustrates this more rapidly and graphically than the changes arising from the movement to control and eradicate tuberculosis. We can quite honestly instance the demand for more generous feeding of the healthful members of the family, which is arising from the proper feeding of the tuberculosis patient; better tenements for the entire population will doubtless result from those tenements of no dark rooms and no hallways, which have been built for incipient cases of tuberculosis; we may also claim that more rest and leisure for all will follow the demand which is made for it on behalf of the tuberculosis patient. This latter will quickly bring us back to the social movement itself, for the effort to adjust a man's work to his powers is largely at the base of the entire labor struggle. . . .

. . . The Committee on "Occupational Standards," newly appointed this year, . . . has to do with that . . . function of the State by which it seeks to protect its workers from their own weakness and degradation, and insists that the livelihood of the manual laborer shall not be beaten down below the level of efficient citizenship. This undertaking of the State assumes new forms almost daily. What have the Charitable people contributed to the movement for the State control over industrial diseases or the protection of machinery? What have they done in collecting data which illustrates pro and con the necessity for old age pensions, industrial insurance, employer's liability acts, the "regulation of the hours of labor," the control of "the sweated trades," the prohibition of the sale of intoxicants? Perhaps the charity of the past may have claimed a share only in the last two, and yet where could trustworthy data for the use of the State Legislators be so easily collected as in the State institutions for the criminal and defective, and in the orphanges and hospitals of private philanthropy? Although the connection is so obvious, it was never made until recently, and it is only contemporaneous charity that is taking a leading part in the establishment of the various safeguards against premature disablement and dependence of the manual worker. It is perhaps significant that the most drastic survey [Pittsburgh Survey] of industrial conditions ever made in America was inaugurated and carried out by the editors of a paper called "Charities." . . .

Is it because our modern industrialism is so new that we have been slow to connect it with the poverty all about us? The socialists talk constantly of the relation of economic wrong to destitution and point out the connection between industrial maladjustment and individual poverty, but the study of social conditions, the obligation to eradicate poverty, cannot belong to one political party nor to one economic school, and after all it was not a socialist, but that ancient friend of the poor, St. Augustine, who said "thou givest bread to the hungry, but better were it that none hungered and thou hadst no need to give to him." . . .

. . . The part America shall take in this . . . crusade of the compassionate, in this standing army of humanity's self-pity suddenly mobilized for a new conquest, . . . lies largely with the members of this Conference to determine. For is it not true that out of the most persistent and intelligent efforts to alleviate poverty will arise the most successful efforts to eradicate poverty?

[1913]   The Call of the Social Field

It requires an unfaltering courage to act year after year upon the belief that the hoary abominations of society can only be done away with through the "steady impinging of fact on fact, of interest on interest, and of will on will." It requires skill as well as loving kindness to be able to say this to an ardent young person so that the statement, even although it contains the implication that these hideous conditions will at last be changed, shall not come as a dash of cold water to his ardent hopes. It requires tact and training to make it clear that because each of us can do so little in the great task of regenerating society, it is therefore more necessary that each should dedicate his powers and add his individual will to the undertaking.

[1911]   . . . What is it that we would put before eager young people to make them feel the stir, and the pull and the stress of this life in the city wilderness as something worthy of their steel, of their very finest endeavor? . . .

A young person possessed with a fine enthusiasm for a new social program may work side by side with the most careful social workers, who are also pushing it forward. But he must do it all with his feet on the ground. He must not do it from an *a priori* conception of what society might and ought to be. He must know his congested neighborhood and give reasons for the faith which is in him. He need not mount a box on the street corner and preach a new social order, but he must be able to say to the people about him, in regard to the tenement house which needs to be reconstructed and in regard to the street which needs to be cleaned, that he knows the best method of procedure in order to bring about these reforms. And with that backing of careful neighborhood understanding and with definite relations to the city or state or Federal Government he may be as radical as he likes on the economic side. . . .

Then if an educated young person cares more for the other side of life, for that human history which has to do with its gentler aspects, for that poesy which has been embodied in literature, for those softer human qualities which have grown when cherished by similarity of belief or social solidarity, he too can be made most useful in this social field.

Much as we need economic study and forceful as is the student of sociology in the problems pressing for solution in the depressed quarters of the city, personally I have discovered that some of the best things are found and put forward by the man or woman who looks at life from this humanistic point of view. Such a young person sees the newly arrived immigrant, for instance, in relation to his past and to the things which his nationality and his race have brought into life; he tries to restore the immigrant to the framework from which he was torn when he came to America. The mind of such a young person nurtures and brings to fruit a certain beauty and culture and human development which would otherwise go to waste. But no one can undertake this humanistic task unless he is willing to bring the fruits of his own culture to bear upon the situation. So to any young person who wishes to go into the social . . . field, . . . I would say bring with you all that you can that softens life, all the poesy, all the sympathetic interpretation. You will need it all; and every scrap of history and language that you know, all of that which has made your own life rich, will be fairly torn off your back as you pass through those crowded city quarters.

Then there is the scientific mind which would apply to the old social problems of the household, to the care and nurture of children, to the prolongation of human life and the alleviation of old age, the scientific knowledge of our time. Thus far most of this valuable data has been lavished upon our industries. Our factories estimate to a fraction the amount of power which a certain machine requires; they use every scrap of material, because waste is not only bad business but disgraceful; and when one goes into a tenement house quarter, one longs for a sign that such care is about to be bestowed upon the culture of human beings. . . . Why all this care for the product and so little concern for the producers? The business man everywhere is using the best appliances that he may preserve his product and make it valuable. On the other side, what have we, the social workers, done for the producers? If we had the business man's enthusiasm and his ability, if we had adequately asserted the claims of the producers, the community would have been obliged at length to recognize them. Let us not blame the business man for his success, but see to it that he shall act as a spur to the rest of us. Will we belittle human fellowship by having it appear that business enterprise is more powerful? Our deepest morality says we must stand by the weak and the wretched and bring them into some sort of decency of life and of social order.

[1930]   Social Service and the Progressive Party

By 1909, the beginning of the third decade at Hull-House, we had already discovered that our intellectual interests, our convictions and activities were all becoming parts of larger movements and that research into social conditions was gradually being developed in the universities and by the great foundations. Based therefore on a more careful knowledge of the situation to be remedied, the five years to 1914 were filled with a veritable zeal for social reform throughout the United States. The efforts both in volume and type were differentiated from those of the preceding two decades. The immediate influence was the Pittsburgh Survey which, financed by the new Russell Sage Foundation and begun as early as 1907, was the first of the community surveys. It was described as

An appraisal of how far human engineering has kept pace with the mechanical developments in the American steel districts. . . .

The Pittsburgh Survey aroused the entire country to conditions of work in the great American industries. The report challenged the belief that it was primarily an employer's business to produce goods and that he was not expected to discover and prevent social waste and injury. . . .

In this same year of 1909, President Roosevelt called together in Washington people from all parts of the country to consider the best type of care to be given to dependent children. It brought the entire subject before the country as a whole and gave to social work a dignity and a place in the national life which it had never had before. We did not realize this at the moment, however, for during the conference itself we were all absorbed in the hope that the gathering might solidify the movement for home-placing versus institutional care for dependent children which at that moment was being discussed throughout the country. President Roosevelt was much amused by a small incident. As the evening speakers were waiting to file upon the platform, the young man in charge, a little overcome by his responsibilities, said, "Are we all here? Yes, here is my Catholic speaker, my Jewish speaker, the Protestant, the colored man, and the woman. Let's all go on." I remarked to Booker T. Washington, "You see, I am last; that is because I have no vote." He replied: "I am glad to know the reason. I have always before been the end of such a procession myself." . . .

In spite of the success of many of these detached efforts, I cannot tell just when we began to have a sense of futility and came to feel that what was needed was a great cause which should pull together the detached groups in the various states that they might not only work simultaneously for the same things, each group in its own state, but that they might have the help and backing of the Federal Government itself. . . .

It was during the campaign to obtain backing for the establishment of the Children's Bureau and also at three Congressional hearings in its behalf, that we constantly encountered the familiar argument of states rights and the insistence that states alone were concerned in such matters. It became clear that the Federal Government could interest itself in agriculture and fisheries, but not in childhood. There was evidently confusion in the minds of many of our fellow countrymen between self-government and local government. . . . We forget that politics are largely a matter of adjusted human relations through any unit of government which best serves the purpose. More and more, social workers, with thousands of other persons throughout the nation, had increasingly felt the need for a new party which should represent "the action and passion of the times," which should make social reform a political issue of national dimensions, which should inaugurate an educational campaign with leaders advocating its measures to the remotest parts of the country, which should send representatives to Congress and to the state legislatures who had been publicly committed to social reform and who were responsible to constituents for specific measures.

It was at the Conference of Social Work [formerly National Conference of Charities and Corrections] in 1912 that a group of social workers after a spirited discussion agreed that if the groups in America who were filled with similar social compunctions and who knew that our social legislation was falling behind the rest of the world, really hoped to secure the help of intelligent and conscientious people, it would be necessary to place these questions before the entire country as a coherent political program. The group was convinced that it was not the social workers alone, but many others, who believed that industry should be subjected to certain tests of social efficiency and should measure up to standards necessary for public health and safety.

The final report of the committee [on Occupational Standards] appointed by the [1909] Conference of Social Work was written after much discussion with physicians, employers and labor leaders.

It presented as components of the standard of living, first, wages; second, hours; third, safety and health; fourth, housing; fifth, terms of working life; sixth, compensation or insurance and ended with the statement that "The conservation of our human resources contributes the most substantial asset to the welfare of the future." The National Conference adopts no resolutions, but the section meeting on occupational standards adjourned as such, reconvened as individuals and adopted a program of industrial minimums which was subscribed to in this fashion by representatives of twenty national organizations. . . .

We were gradually learning that new ideas can never gain wide acceptance unless the persons who hold them confess them openly and give them an honest and effective adherence. It was only later we discovered that when the idea and measure become part of a political campaign we command an unrivaled method for their understanding. . . .

From various directions, therefore, people were drawing toward a new political party. It was at first as if one heard in the distance the grave and measured tread of history, but the pace increased during the first half of 1912 and became absolutely breathless by midsummer. It was in August, 1912, that the Progressive Party was organized.

Suddenly, as if by magic, the city of Chicago became filled with men and women from every state in the Union who were evidently haunted by the same social compunctions and animated by like hopes; they revealed to each other mutual sympathies and memories. They urged methods which had already been tried in other countries, for righting old wrongs and for establishing standards in industry. For three days together they defined their purposes and harmonized their wills into gigantic coöperation. Among the members of the Platform Committee for the new Progressive Party were the social workers who had approved three successive reports at the National Conference conventions, others who had been closely identified with the Men and Religion Forward Movement who thus felt the challenge to give political expression to the religious motive, and still others who embodied largely the standpoint of the scholar. One sub-committee would seem to me like a session of the National Conference of Charities and Corrections; another, like a session of the American Sociological Society, with a liberal sprinkling of American Authors in both. . . . The dean of a university law school acted as chairman of the Resolution Committee, and men conversant with the later developments in social legislation supplied nomenclature and information concerning similar legislation abroad; but these men, with the so-called practical members of the committee, were not representing the opinion of any individual nor the philosophy of any group. They were trying, as conscientious American citizens, to meet that fundamental obligation of adapting the legal order to the changed conditions of national life. . . .

They believed that the program of social legislation placed before the country by the Progressive Party was of great significance to the average voter quite irrespective of the party which might finally claim his allegiance. . . .

The real interest in the measures advocated in the party platform came however during the campaign itself when it was possible to place them before many groups throughout the country. Sometimes the planks in our platform were sharply challenged, but more often regarded with approval and occasionally with enthusiasm. I recall a meeting in Leadville, Colorado, made up altogether of miners who were much surprised to find that politics had anything to do with such affairs. They had always supposed that hours of labor were matters to be fought for and not voted upon. It was very exhilarating to talk to them, and it seemed to me that I had never before realized how slow we had been to place the definite interests of the workingmen in such shape that they could be voted upon. . . .

The Progressive Party campaign remains in my mind as a wonderful opportunity for education not only on the social justice planks in the platform but on the history of the ideology back of them. Aristotle is reported to have said that politics is a school wherein questions are studied not for the sake of knowledge but for the sake of action. Out of his wisdom he might have added, that politics is most valuable as a school because the average man has an inveterate tendency not to study at all, unless he sees the prospect of action ahead of him. During the Progressive campaign, measures of social amelioration were discussed up and down the land as only party politics can be discussed, in the remotest farmhouse to which the rural free delivery brought the weekly newspaper; certain economic principles became current talk and new phrases entered permanently into popular speech. Certainly those of us identified with the campaign were convinced that people are ready to grapple with social problems whenever a well considered program is laid before them. . . .

The campaign renewed one's convictions that if the community as a whole were better informed as to the ethical implications of industrial wrongs whole areas of life could be saved from becoming brutalized or from sinking into hard indifference. We craved the understanding support which results from a widespread and sincere discussion of a given subject by thousands of our fellow citizens before any attempt should be made to secure legislative action. At moments we believed that we were witnessing a new pioneering of the human spirit, that we were in all humility inaugurating an exploration into the moral resources of our fellow citizens. . . .

Perhaps the Progressive Party once more demonstrated what political history has many times made evident, that new parties ultimately write the platforms for all parties; that a cause which a new party has the courage to espouse is later taken up by existing political organizations to whom direct appeal has previously proved fruitless.

[1930]   Social Workers and Other Professions

It is perhaps all too customary for social workers to count up their achievements and to call upon the community for due appreciation. Such a custom has been in fact inherent in the situation itself, for while the doctor and the lawyer quietly and unobtrusively collect their fees from the individual upon whom their services have been bestowed, the social worker from necessity must collect his fees not from the people he has served whose pockets are perforce empty, but from the prosperous members of the community who are convinced that those services in the first place were necessary and in the second place have been well performed. Sometimes the social worker has to insist that the given services were both necessary to the social good and were well done in individual cases, against the very denials and shrill outcries of the recipients themselves. . . .

In spite of the fact that you may detect traces of boastfulness superinduced by these dilemmas—habits we have not yet outgrown in spite of our acknowledged professional standard—I should like to point out that social workers were the pioneers in certain movements afterwards taken over by medicine and law.

Let us take as our first example that astonishing achievement of our own time, that brilliant success in social engineering, the campaign against the spread of tuberculosis. It inevitably came at last into the hands of physicians and from the first they gave help and advice, but the investigation into the "lung block" of New York, the discovery that successive inhabitants of certain tenements inevitably developed tuberculosis, the piling up of the grisly percentage of tuberculosis connected with certain industries, the insistence that tuberculosis is especially a disease of poverty, so that a tuberculosis map of a given city superimposed upon a poverty map of the same city will almost exactly coincide, was done in large part by social workers. . . .

The National Safety Council for Prevention of Accidents and Diseases in Industry is an organization of laymen which antedates by some years the organization of Industrial Physicians and Surgeons. In fact, the entrance of medical science in industry has been a very late development in this country and the prevention of occupational diseases is still largely in the hands of laymen. . . . The campaign for the prevention of venereal diseases, certainly on its educational side, has been very largely in lay hands, and even the actual treatment of the disease in Chicago is promoted on the largest scale by an institution which was founded by laymen. The bitter opposition of the medical profession [to the Public Health Institute in Chicago] has been difficult for a layman to respect. . . .

It was a physician acting for the Children's Bureau who first revealed to the public the extent of the maternity death rate in the United States. Compared to other nations whose statistics are trustworthy, the United States in this regard was nineteenth on the list, comparable to Chile and Spain. No medical body had ever troubled itself to discover these facts and the American Medical Association bitterly resented their publication by a lay organization, even a governmental one. Since that time, obstetricians the country over have accepted these figures and constantly quote them, but the opposition of organized medicine to the work of the Children's Bureau does not abate. . . .

We will all admit that the founding of mental hygiene societies was due more to Clifford Beers, a layman, than to anyone else. There is perhaps no organization to which the perplexed social worker appeals with a greater sense of relief. If the mental hygiene nurse can adjust a border line case to a family situation, the achievement is certainly one in which every good citizen rejoices. . . .

In a sense these early efforts were the pioneers, as it were, of the widespread work in psychiatry . . . although the very first formal effort to apply careful study to delinquent children was proposed and financed by a woman who through long service on the board of an organization dealing with delinquent children had been much distressed by the lack of careful appraisal of their physical and mental possibilities. It was a typical case of the social worker fumbling for modes of prevention not yet fully established as a recognized part of the social structure. . . .

Let us turn to the legal profession for some illustrations: The social workers may, I think, claim the juvenile court. . . . The probation officer of the juvenile court is still considered a social worker, and the court itself, while conducted by a judge, has to a considerable extent that coördinating and organizing function, that mobilizing of the curative and preventive services provided in astonishing variety for the assistance of those in distress, which we have come to define as social work.

May I also instance in relation to the law, the establishment of legal aid societies, which are so important in the lives of the poor and those most easily discriminated against. In many cities these societies are being utilized for clinical practice to law students, somewhat analogous to the clinical training of young physicians. And yet everywhere this attempt to extend the benefits of the legal profession has been urged and organized by those outside of the profession. The largest one I know is connected with a family welfare society.

It would be easy to give many instances in the field of education, such as vocational guidance.

I do not claim any perspicacity on the part of the social worker. I should say that if he has at times seen the need, before the profession involved saw it, it may be due to the fact that, when we face a social situation in which certain values are but dimly emergent, a socially unified group may fail to tap its resources simply because they all see alike. By the same token it may be possible for the social worker, living in the midst of divers groups whose history, language and customs show the tremendous variability of human nature, to find clues to a new life pattern in such a situation because each group sees it differently although all feel alike that something should be done about it.

A state of tension when old values are at hazard may be the very moment when the groups realize that the whole situation calls for new adjustments and are driven to utilize half formed purposes for experimental action. If I may be permitted to use a mixed metaphor, in the midst of a storm they scramble out of a welter of broken boats and cling together to a new safety device which the passengers in sounder boats profoundly distrust. But the device itself may be the beginning of a new method of transportation destined to replace and to transcend the comfortable boat in which the careful passengers sit tight.

Position of Women

Introduction by ASHLEY MONTAGU

Anthropologist, social biologist, author of
The Natural Superiority of Women

Extracts selected and arranged by
Margaret E. Dungan

Jane Addams was in her twentieth year, and still an undergraduate at Rockford Seminary, when the first of the pieces which appears in this section, "Bread Givers," was written, spoken, and published. It luminously states the course which was to be realized in Jane Addams' lifework. The nobility and beauty of her character shine through her words with the brilliance of a new star that has made its permanent appearance in the heavens. That light was to shine with undiminished vigor for the next half-century, casting a healing beam into the dark areas of our industrial society, and bringing the warmth of its glow into the lives of thousands who would otherwise have remained in darkness and sorrow in a society seemingly utterly indifferent to human need.

In this, among the earliest of her writings, Jane Addams programmatically plots the course which she was to follow for the rest of her life. How beautifully she expresses herself! And how consistently thereafter she did so in everything she said, wrote, and did. She was a woman of genius, and her genius lay in her humanity.

It is a conviction soon developed in anyone who reads Jane Addams that here is a human being who is spiritually the kin of Emerson and Thoreau, one who wrote quite as beautifully as they did, but who felt even more strongly than they, that words must be supported by acts. Great literature came out of Concord, Massachusetts, ennobling many a life with high sentiment and nobler aims, but out of Jane Addams came not only great literature—and I regard her writings as such—but a great life beautifully and actively lived in the unremitting service of her fellow human beings. The settlement movement throughout the world—not forgetting the indebtedness to Samuel Barnett's English university settlements, on which she based her own work—largely owes its existence and development to the influence of Jane Addams. It was the personal influence of this irresistibly magnetic woman which drew to herself and to her ideas the interest and support of so many women and men throughout the world. In this Jane Addams once more exemplified the fact that it is personal influence that determines the size of a person's life, not simply words, nor yet even deeds. Never, however, let us underestimate the influence of words, and still less of deeds in a life such as that of Jane Addams. These were of paramount importance. In the case of Jane Addams, words, deeds, and influence were all of a piece. The meaning of a word for her was the action it produced. Her writings are clarion calls to action.

The essence of Jane Addams' success lay in her profound interest and involvement in human beings, and her sense of responsibility to others. If she was intolerant of anything, it was of injustice. But even here her gentle spirit invariably succeeded in getting wrongs righted without the least friction being generated in the process.

Besides pioneer work in amelioration of the conditions of life for the working classes and the foreign born, outstanding is the contribution Jane Addams made in awakening women to a sense of their own nature and the rights and obligations which should follow from this recognition. It was abundantly clear to her that in the male-dominated world of America, and elsewhere, there was too much of what the Greeks (or at any rate Aeschylus) called *aperotos eros,* unloving love, and that it lay within the power of women to ameliorate, and, perhaps, to correct this condition. As a woman she understood the nature of the profound difference which exists between the sexes, and saw that far from acting to separate them, the very qualities possessed by women were needed to complement, inform, and enlarge those of the male in order to realize an approximation to a full-rounded human being and a more healthily functioning society.

Jane Addams was, of course, not the only woman who perceived this, but she was undoubtedly one of the most persuasive voices in helping both women and men to understand the soundness of this view. Her effectiveness lay especially in the manner with which she placed the role of women squarely within the matrix of a badly creaking industrial society, and in pointing out to women the extent to which they were avoiding their obligations by failing to fulfill themselves as persons. Her plea for fuller participation of women in civic housekeeping, that is, civic government, has not gone altogether unheeded, but it needs to be repeated again and again until women are represented in at least as great numbers as men in every aspect of civic government. And not only in civic government, but in the state and national governments, and on every international council and governmental body.

"As we believe that woman has no right to allow what really belongs to her to drop away from her, so we contend that the ability to perform an obligation comes largely in proportion as that obligation is conscientiously assumed." Women, the world over, still need to attend to the full meaning of these words of Jane Addams.

Jane Addams, being the realist she was, did not for a moment deceive herself that because women were women they could do better in politics than men. On the contrary, she was justly critical of many women in politics, and urged them to be less conventional, less fearful of men, and to have more faith in their own judgment. In our own time we have observed the sad fact that some women can be as narrow and as reactionary as the most narrow and reactionary of men. Jane Addams' appeal, however, was not directed to the moribund but to those capable of growth and of life, to those whose "human urgings to foster life and to protect the helpless" would not be stilled.

ASHLEY MONTAGU

BREAD GIVERS

[1880]   Friends and Citizens of Rockford:—The class of 1881 has invited you this evening to the First Junior Exhibition ever given within the walls of Rockford Seminary. The fact of its being the first, seems to us a significant one, for it undoubtedly points more or less directly to a movement which is gradually claiming the universal attention. We mean the change which has taken place during the last fifty years in the ambition and aspirations of woman; we see this change most markedly in her education. It has passed from accomplishments and the arts of pleasing, to the development of her intellectual force, and her capabilities for direct labor. She wishes not to be a man, nor like a man, but she claims the same right to independent thought and action. Whether this movement is tending toward the ballot-box, or will gain simply equal intellectual advantages, no one can predict, but certain it is that woman has gained a new confidence in her possibilities, and a fresher hope in her steady progress.

We then, the class of 1881, in giving this our Junior Exhibition, are not trying to imitate our brothers in college; we are not restless and anxious for things beyond us, we simply claim the highest privileges of our time and avail ourselves of its best opportunities.

But while on the one hand, as young women of the 19th century, we gladly claim these privileges, and proudly assert our independence, on the other hand we still retain the old ideal of womanhood—the Saxon lady whose mission it was to give bread unto her household. So we have planned to be "Bread-givers" throughout our lives; believing that in labor alone is happiness, and that the only true and honorable life is one filled with good works and honest toil, we have planned to idealize our labor, and thus happily fulfil Woman's Noblest Mission. But if at any time we should falter in our trust, if under the burden of years, we should for the moment doubt the high culture which comes from giving, then may be the memory of this evening when we were young and strong, when we presented to our friends a portion of the work already accomplished, and told them of the further labor we had planned for the future, then, I say, the memory of our Junior Exhibition may come to us as an incentive to renewed effort. It may prove to us a vow by which we pledged ourselves unto our high calling; and if through some turn of fortune we should be confined to the literal meaning of our words, if our destiny throughout our lives should be to give good, sweet, wholesome bread unto our loved ones, then perchance we will do even that the better, with more of conscious energy and innate power for the memory of our Junior Exhibition.

WHY WOMEN SHOULD VOTE

[1910]   For many generations it has been believed that woman's place is within the walls of her own home, and it is indeed impossible to imagine the time when her duty there shall be ended or to forecast any social change which shall release her from that paramount obligation.

This paper is an attempt to show that many women to-day are failing to discharge their duties to their own households properly simply because they do not perceive that as society grows more complicated it is necessary that woman shall extend her sense of responsibility to many things outside of her own home if she would continue to preserve the home in its entirety. One could illustrate in many ways. A woman's simplest duty, one would say, is to keep her house clean and wholesome and to feed her children properly. Yet if she lives in a tenement house, as so many of my neighbors do, she cannot fulfill these simple obligations by her own efforts because she is utterly dependent upon the city administration for the conditions which render decent living possible. Her basement will not be dry, her stairways will not be fireproof, her house will not be provided with sufficient windows to give light and air, nor will it be equipped with sanitary plumbing, unless the Public Works Department sends inspectors who constantly insist that these elementary decencies be provided. Women who live in the country sweep their own dooryards and may either feed the refuse of the table to a flock of chickens or allow it innocently to decay in the open air and sunshine. In a crowded city quarter, however, if the street is not cleaned by the city authorities no amount of private sweeping will keep the tenement free from grime; if the garbage is not properly collected and destroyed a tenement-house mother may see her children sicken and die of diseases from which she alone is powerless to shield them, although her tenderness and devotion are unbounded. She cannot even secure untainted meat for her household, she cannot provide fresh fruit, unless the meat has been inspected by city officials, and the decayed fruit, which is so often placed upon sale in the tenement districts, has been destroyed in the interests of public health. In short, if woman would keep on with her old business of caring for her house and rearing her children she will have to have some conscience in regard to public affairs lying quite outside of her immediate household. The individual conscience and devotion are no longer effective. . . .

If women follow only the lines of their traditional activities here are certain primary duties which belong to even the most conservative women, and which no one woman or group of women can adequately discharge unless they join the more general movements looking toward social amelioration through legal enactment.

The first of these, of which this article has already treated, is woman's responsibility for the members of her own household that they may be properly fed and clothed and surrounded by hygienic conditions. The second is a responsibility for the education of children: (a) that they may be provided with good schools; (b) that they may be kept free from vicious influences on the street; (c) that when working they may be protected by adequate child-labor legislation.

(a) The duty of a woman toward the schools which her children attend is so obvious that it is not necessary to dwell upon it. But even this simple obligation cannot be effectively carried out without some form of social organization as the mothers' school clubs and mothers' congresses testify, and to which the most conservative women belong because they feel the need of wider reading and discussion concerning the many problems of childhood. It is, therefore, perhaps natural that the public should have been more willing to accord a vote to women in school matters than in any other, and yet women have never been members of a Board of Education in sufficient numbers to influence largely actual school curricula. If they had been, kindergartens, domestic science courses and school playgrounds would be far more numerous than they are. . . .

(b) But women are also beginning to realize that children need attention outside of school hours; that much of the petty vice in cities is merely the love of pleasure gone wrong, the overrestrained boy or girl seeking improper recreation and excitement. It is obvious that a little study of the needs of children, a sympathetic understanding of the conditions under which they go astray, might save hundreds of them. Women traditionally have had an opportunity to observe the play of children and the needs of youth, and yet in Chicago, at least, they had done singularly little in this vexed problem of juvenile delinquency until they helped to inaugurate the Juvenile Court movement a dozen years ago. The Juvenile Court Committee, made up largely of women, paid the salaries of the probation officers connected with the court for the first six years of its existence, and after the salaries were cared for by the county the same organization turned itself into a Juvenile Protective League, and through a score of paid officers are doing valiant service in minimizing some of the dangers of city life which boys and girls encounter.

This Protective League, however, was not formed until the women had had a civic training through their semi-official connection with the Juvenile Court. This is, perhaps, an illustration of our inability to see the duty "next to hand" until we have become alert through our knowledge of conditions in connection with the larger duties. We would all agree that social amelioration must come about through the efforts of many people who are moved thereto by the compunction and stirring of the individual conscience, but we are only beginning to understand that the individual conscience will respond to the special challenge largely in proportion as the individual is able to see the social conditions because he has felt responsible for their improvement. . . . The more extensively the modern city endeavors on the one hand to control and on the other hand to provide recreational facilities for its young people the more necessary it is that women should assist in their direction and extension. . . .

(c) . . . If woman's sense of obligation had enlarged as the industrial conditions changed she might naturally and almost imperceptibly have inaugurated the movements for social amelioration in the line of factory legislation and shop sanitation. That she has not done so is doubtless due to the fact that her conscience is slow to recognize any obligation outside of her own family circle, and because she was so absorbed in her own household that she failed to see what the conditions outside actually were. . . . After all, we see only those things to which our attention has been drawn, we feel responsibility for those things which are brought to us as matters of responsibility. If conscientious women were convinced that it was a civic duty to be informed in regard to these grave industrial affairs, and then to express the conclusions which they had reached by depositing a piece of paper in a ballot-box, one cannot imagine that they would shirk simply because the action ran counter to old traditions. . . .

. . . Woman's traditional function has been to make her dwelling-place both clean and fair. Is that dreariness in city life, that lack of domesticity which the humblest farm dwelling presents, due to a withdrawal of one of the naturally cooperating forces? If women have in any sense been responsible for the gentler side of life which softens and blurs some of its harsher conditions, may they not have a duty to perform in our American cities?

IF MEN WERE SEEKING THE FRANCHISE

[1913]   Let us imagine throughout this article, if we can sustain an absurd hypothesis so long, the result upon society if the matriarchal period had held its own; if the development of the State had closely followed that of the Family until the chief care of the former, as that of the latter, had come to be the nurture and education of children and the protection of the weak, sick and aged. In short let us imagine a hypothetical society organized upon the belief that "there is no wealth but life." With this Ruskinian foundation let us assume that the political machinery of such a society, the franchise and the rest of it, were in the hands of women because they had always best exercised those functions. Let us further imagine a given moment when these women, who in this hypothetical society had possessed political power from the very beginnings of the State, were being appealed to by the voteless men that men might be associated with women in the responsibilities of citizenship.

Plagiarizing somewhat upon recent suffrage speeches let us consider various replies which these citizen women might reasonably make to the men who were seeking the franchise; the men insisting that only through the use of the ballot could they share the duties of the State.

First, could not the women say: "Our most valid objection to extending the franchise to you is that you are so fond of fighting— you always have been since you were little boys. You'd very likely forget that the real object of the State is to nurture and protect life, and out of sheer vainglory you would be voting away huge sums of money for battleships, not one of which could last more than a few years, and yet each would cost ten million dollars; more money than all the buildings of Harvard University represent, although it is the richest educational institution in America. Every time a gun is fired in a battleship it expends, or rather explodes, seventeen hundred dollars, as much as a college education costs many a country boy, and yet you would be firing off these guns as mere salutes, with no enemy within three thousand miles, simply because you so enjoy the sound of shooting.

"Our educational needs are too great and serious to run any such risk. Democratic government itself is perilous unless the electorate is educated; our industries are suffering for lack of skilled workmen; more than half a million immigrants a year must be taught the underlying principles of republican government. Can we, the responsible voters, take the risk of wasting our taxes by extending the vote to those who have always been so ready to lose their heads over mere military display?"

Second, would not the hypothetical women, who would have been responsible for the advance of industry during these later centuries, as women actually were during the earlier centuries when they dragged home the game and transformed the pelts into shelter and clothing, say further to these disenfranchised men: "We have carefully built up a code of factory legislation for the protection of the workers in modern industry; we know that you men have always been careless about the house, perfectly indifferent to the necessity for sweeping and cleaning; if you were made responsible for factory legislation it is quite probable that you would let the workers in the textile mills contract tuberculosis through needlessly breathing the fluff, or the workers in machine shops through inhaling metal filings, both of which are now carried off by an excellent suction system which we women have insisted upon, but which it is almost impossible to have installed in a man-made State because the men think so little of dust and its evil effects. In many Nations in which political power is confined to men, and this is notably true in the United States of America, there is no protection even for the workers in white lead, although hundreds of them are yearly incapacitated from lead poisoning, and others actually die.

"We have also heard that in certain States, in order to save the paltry price of a guard which would protect a dangerous machine, men legislators allow careless boys and girls to lose their fingers and sometimes their hands, thereby crippling their entire futures. These male legislators do not make guarded machinery obligatory, although they know that when the heads of families are injured at these unprotected machines the State must care for them in hospitals, and when they are killed, that if necessary the State must provide for their widows and children in poorhouses."

These wise women, governing the State with the same care they had always put into the management of their families, would further place against these men seeking the franchise the charge that men do not really know how tender and delicate children are, and might therefore put them to work in factories, as indeed they have done in man-made States during the entire period of factory production. We can imagine these women saying: "We have been told that in certain States children are taken from their beds in the early morning before it is light and carried into cotton mills, where they are made to run back and forth tending the spinning frames until their immature little bodies are so bent and strained that they never regain their normal shapes; that little children are allowed to work in canneries for fifteen and seventeen hours until, utterly exhausted, they fall asleep among the debris of shells and husks."

Would not these responsible women voters gravely shake their heads and say that as long as men exalt business profit above human life it would be sheer folly to give them the franchise; that, of course, they would be slow to make such matters the subject of legislation?

Would not the enfranchised women furthermore say to these voteless men: "You have always been so eager to make money; what assurance have we that in your desire to get the largest amount of coal out of the ground in the shortest possible time you would not permit the mine supports to decay and mine damp to accumulate, until the percentage of accidents among miners would be simply heartbreaking? Then you are so reckless. Business seems to you a mere game with big prizes, and we have heard that in America, where the women have no vote, the loss of life in the huge steel mills is appalling; and that the number of young brakemen, fine young fellows, every one of them the pride of some mother, killed every year is beyond belief; that the average loss of life among the structural-iron workers who erect the huge office buildings and bridges is as disastrous in percentages as was the loss of life in the Battle of Bull Run. When the returns of this battle were reported to President Lincoln he burst into tears of sorrow and chagrin; but we have never heard of any President, Governor or Mayor weeping over the reports of this daily loss of life, although such reports have been presented to them by Governmental investigators; and this loss of life might easily be reduced by protective legislation."

Having thus worked themselves into a fine state of irritation, analogous to that ever-recurrent uneasiness of men in the presence of insurgent women who would interfere in the management of the State, would not these voting women add: "The trouble is that men have no imagination, or rather what they have is so prone to run in the historic direction of the glory of the battlefield, that you cannot trust them with industrial affairs. Because a crew in a battleship was once lost under circumstances which suggested perfidy the male representatives of two great Nations voted to go to war;

yet in any day of the year in one of these Nations alone—the United States of America—as many men are killed through industrial accidents as this crew contained. These accidents occur under circumstances which, if not perfidious, are at least so criminally indifferent to human life as to merit Kipling's characterization that the situation is impious."

Certainly these irritated women would designate such indifference to human life as unpatriotic and unjustifiable, only to be accounted for because men have not yet learned to connect patriotism with industrial affairs.

These conscientious women responsible for the State in which life was considered of more value than wealth would furthermore say: "Then, too, you men exhibit such curious survivals of the mere savage instinct of punishment and revenge. The United States alone spends every year five hundred million dollars more on its policemen, courts and prisons than upon all its works of religion, charity and education. The price of one trial expended on a criminal early in life might save the State thousands of dollars and the man untold horrors. And yet with all this vast expenditure little is done to reduce crime. Men are kept in jails and penitentiaries where there is not even the semblance of education or reformatory measure; young men are returned over and over again to the same institution until they have grown old and gray, and in all of that time they have not once been taught a trade, nor have they been in any wise prepared to withstand the temptations of life.

"A homeless young girl looking for a lodging may be arrested for soliciting on the streets, and sent to prison for six months, although there is no proof against her save the impression of the policeman. A young girl under such suspicion may be obliged to answer the most harassing questions put to her by the city attorney, with no woman near to protect her from insult; she may be subjected to the most trying examination conducted by a physician in the presence of a policeman, and no matron to whom to appeal. At least these things happen constantly in the United States—in Chicago, for instance—but possibly not in the Scandinavian countries where juries of women sit upon such cases, women whose patience has been many times tested by wayward girls and who know the untold moral harm which may result from such a physical and psychic shock."

Then these same women would go further, and, because they had lived in a real world and had administered large affairs and were therefore not prudish and affected, would say: "Worse than anything which we have mentioned is the fact that in every man-ruled city the world over a great army of women are so set aside as outcasts that it is considered a shame to speak the mere name which designates them. Because their very existence is illegal they may be arrested whenever any police captain chooses; they may be brought before a magistrate, fined and imprisoned. The men whose money sustains their houses, supplies their tawdry clothing and provides them with intoxicating drinks and drugs, are never arrested, nor indeed are they even considered lawbreakers."

Would not these fearless women, whose concern for the morals of the family had always been able to express itself through State laws, have meted out equal punishment to men as well as to women, when they had equally transgressed the statute law?

Did the enfranchised women evoked by our imagination speak thus to the disenfranchised men, the latter would at least respect their scruples and their hesitation in regard to an extension of the obligation of citizenship. But what would be the temper of the masculine mind if the voting women representing the existing State should present to them only the following half-dozen objections, which are unhappily so familiar to many of us: If the women should say, first, that men would find politics corrupting; second, that they would doubtless vote as their wives and mothers did; third, that men's suffrage would only double the vote without changing results; fourth, that men's suffrage would diminish the respect for men; fifth, that most men do not want to vote; sixth, that the best men would not vote?

I do no believe that women broadened by life and its manifold experiences would actually present these six objections to men as real reasons for withholding the franchise from them, unless indeed they had long formed the habit of regarding men not as comrades and fellow-citizens, but as a class by themselves, in essential matters really inferior although always held sentimentally very much above them.

Certainly no such talk would be indulged in between men and women who had together embodied in political institutions the old affairs of life which had normally and historically belonged to both of them. If woman had adjusted herself to the changing demands of the State as she did to the historic mutations of her own household she might naturally and without challenge have held the place in the State which she now holds in the family.

When Plato once related his dream of an ideal Republic he begged his fellow-citizens not to ridicule him because he considered the cooperation of women necessary for its fulfillment. He contended that so far as the guardianship of the State is concerned there is no distinction between the powers of men and women save those which custom has made.

UTILIZATION OF WOMEN IN CITY GOVERNMENT

[1907]   As the city itself originated for the common protection of the people and was built about a suitable centre of defense which formed a citadel such as the Acropolis at Athens or the Kremlin at Moscow, so we can trace the beginning of the municipal franchise to the time when the problems of municipal government were still largely those of protecting the city against rebellion from within and against invasion from without. A voice in city government, as it was extended from the nobles, who alone bore arms, was naturally given solely to those who were valuable to the military system. . . . It was fair that only those who were liable to a sudden call to arms should be selected to decide as to the relations which the city should bear to rival cities, and that the vote for war should be cast by the same men who would bear the brunt of battle and the burden of protection. . . .

But rival cities have long since ceased to settle their claims by force of arms, and we shall have to admit, I think, that this early test of the elector is no longer fitted to the modern city. . . .

It has been well said that the modern city is a stronghold of industrialism, quite as the feudal city was a stronghold of militarism, but the modern city fears no enemies, and rivals from without, and its problems of government are solely internal. Affairs for the most part are going badly in these great new centres in which the quickly congregated population has not yet learned to arrange its affairs satisfactorily. Insanitary housing, poisonous sewage, contaminated water, infant mortality, the spread of contagion, adulterated food, impure milk, smoke-laden air, ill-ventilated factories, dangerous occupations, juvenile crime, unwholesome crowding, prostitution, and drunkenness are the enemies which the modern city must face and overcome would it survive. Logically, its electorate should be made up of those who can bear a valiant part in this arduous contest, of those who in the past have at least attempted to care for children, to clean houses, to prepare foods, to isolate the family from moral dangers, of those who have traditionally taken care of that side of life which, as soon as the population is congested, inevitably becomes the subject of municipal consideration and control.

To test the elector's fitness to deal with this situation by his ability to bear arms, is absurd. A city is in many respects a great business corporation, but in other respects it is enlarged housekeeping. If American cities have failed in the first, partly because office holders have carried with them the predatory instinct learned in competitive business, and cannot help "working a good thing" when they have an opportunity, may we not say that city housekeeping has failed partly because women, the traditional housekeepers, have not been consulted as to its multiform activities? The men of the city have been carelessly indifferent to much of this civic housekeeping, as they have always been indifferent to the details of the household. They have totally disregarded a candidate's capacity to keep the streets clean, preferring to consider him in relation to the national tariff or to the necessity for increasing the national navy, in a pure spirit of reversion to the traditional type of government which had to do only with enemies and outsiders.

It is difficult to see what military prowess has to do with the multiform duties, which, in a modern city, include the care of parks and libraries, superintendence of markets, sewers, and bridges, the inspection of provisions and boilers, and the proper disposal of garbage. Military prowess has nothing to do with the building department which the city maintains to see to it that the basements be dry, that the bedrooms be large enough to afford the required cubic feet of air, that the plumbing be sanitary, that the gas-pipes do not leak, that the tenement-house court be large enough to afford light and ventilation, and that the stairways be fireproof. The ability to carry arms has nothing to do with the health department maintained by the city, which provides that children be vaccinated, that contagious diseases be isolated and placarded, that the spread of tuberculosis be curbed, and that the water be free from typhoid infection. Certainly the military conception of society is remote from the functions of the school boards, whose concern it is that children be educated, that they be supplied with kindergartens and be given a decent place in which to play. The very multifariousness and complexity of a city government demands the help of minds accustomed to detail and variety of work, to a sense of obligation for the health and welfare of young children, and to a responsibility for the cleanliness and comfort of others.

Because all these things have traditionally been in the hands of women, if they take no part in them now, they are not only missing the education which the natural participation in civic life would bring to them, but they are losing what they have always had. From the beginning of tribal life women have been held responsible for the health of the community, a function which is now represented by the health department; from the days of the cave dwellers, so far as the home was clean and wholesome, it was due to their efforts, which are now represented by the bureau of tenement-house inspection; from the period of the primitive village, the only public sweeping performed was what they undertook in their own dooryards, that which is now represented by the bureau of street cleaning. Most of the departments in a modern city can be traced to woman's traditional activity, but in spite of this, so soon as these old affairs were turned over to the care of the city, they slipped from woman's hands, apparently because they then became matters for collective action and implied the use of the franchise. Because the franchise had in the first instance been given to the man who could fight, because in the beginning he alone could vote who could carry a weapon, the franchise was considered an improper thing for a woman to possess. . . .

. . . It is so easy to believe that things that used to exist still go on long after they are passed; it is so easy to commit irreparable blunders because we fail to correct our theories by our changing experience. So many of the stumbling-blocks against which we fall are the opportunities to which we have not adjusted ourselves. Because it shocks an obsolete ideal, we keep hold of a convention which no longer squares with our genuine insight, and we are slow to follow a clue which might enable us to solace and improve the life about us.

Why is it that women do not vote upon the matters which concern them so intimately? Why do they not follow these vital affairs and feel responsible for their proper administration, even though they have become municipalized? What would the result have been could women have regarded the suffrage, not as a right or a privilege, but as a mere piece of governmental machinery without which they could not perform their traditional functions under the changed conditions of city life? Could we view the whole situation as a matter of obligation and of normal development, it would be much simplified. We are at the beginning of a prolonged effort to incorporate a progressive developing life founded upon a response to the needs of all the people, into the requisite legal enactments and civic institutions. To be in any measure successful, this effort will require all the intelligent powers of observation, all the sympathy, all the common sense which may be gained from the whole adult population. . . .

It is questionable whether women to-day, in spite of the fact that there are myriads of them in factories and shops, are doing their full share of the world's work in the lines of production which have always been theirs. Even two centuries ago they did practically all the spinning, dyeing, weaving, and sewing. They carried on much of the brewing and baking and thousands of operations which have been pushed out of the domestic system into the factory system. But simply to keep on doing the work which their grandmothers did, was to find themselves surrounded by conditions over which they have no control.

Sometimes when I see dozens of young girls going into the factories of a certain biscuit company on the West Side of Chicago, they appear for the moment as a mere cross-section in the long procession of women who have furnished the breadstuffs from time immemorial, from the savage woman who ground the meal and baked a flat cake, through innumerable cottage hearths, kitchens, and bake ovens, to this huge concern in which they are still carrying on their traditional business. But always before, during the ages of this unending procession, women themselves were able to dictate concerning the hours and the immediate conditions of their work; even grinding the meal and baking the cake in the ashes was diversified by many other activities. But suddenly, since the application of steam to the processes of kneading bread and of turning the spindle, which really means only a different motor power and not in the least an essential change in her work, she has been denied the privilege of regulating the conditions which immediately surround her. . . .

. . . Practically one-half of the workingwomen in the United States are girls—young women under the age of twenty-five years. This increase in the number of young girls in industry is the more striking when taken in connection with the fact that industries of to-day differ most markedly from those of the past in the relentless speed which they require. This increase in speed is as marked in the depths of sweat-shop labor as in the most advanced New England mills, where the eight looms operated by each worker have increased to twelve, fourteen, and even sixteen looms. This speed, of course, brings a new strain into industry and tends inevitably to nervous exhaustion. Machines may be revolved more and more swiftly, but the girl workers have no increase in vitality responding to the heightened pressure. An ampler and more far-reaching protection than now exists, is needed in order to care for the health and safety of woman in industry. Their youth, their helplessness, their increasing numbers, the conditions under which they are employed, all call for uniform and enforceable statutes. The elaborate regulations of dangerous trades, enacted in England and on the Continent for both adults and children, find no parallel in the United States. The injurious effects of employments involving the use of poisons, acids, gases, atmospheric extremes, or other dangerous processes, still await adequate investigation and legislation in this country. How shall this take place, save by the concerted efforts of the women themselves, those who are employed, and those other women who are intelligent as to the worker's needs and who possess a conscience in regard to industrial affairs? . . .

So far as women have been able, in Chicago at least, to help the poorest workers in the sweatshops, it has been accomplished by women organized into trades unions. The organization of Special Order Tailors found that it was comparatively simple for an employer to give the skilled operatives in a clothing factory more money by taking it away from the wages of the seam-sewer and button-holer. The fact that it resulted in one set of workers being helped at the expense of another set did not appeal to him, so long as he was satisfying the demand of the union without increasing the total cost of production. But the Special Order Tailors, at the sacrifice of their own wages and growth, made a determined effort to include even the sweat-shop workers in the benefits they had slowly secured for themselves. By means of the use of the label they were finally able to insist that no goods should be given out for home-finishing save to women presenting union cards, and they raised the wages from nine and eleven cents a dozen for finishing garments, to the minimum wage of fifteen cents. They also made a protest against the excessive subdivision of the labor upon garments, a practice which enables the manufacturer to use children and the least skilled adults. Thirty-two persons are commonly employed upon a single coat, and it is the purpose of the Special Order Tailors to have all the machine work performed by one worker, thus reducing the number working on one coat to twelve or fourteen. As this change will at the same time demand more skill on the part of the operator, and will increase the variety and interest in his work, these garment-makers are sacrificing both time and money for the defence of Ruskinian principles—one of the few actual attempts to recover the "joy of work." . . . The poorest women are often but uncomprehending victims of this labor movement of which they understand so little, and which has become so much a matter of battle that helpless individuals are lost in the conflict.

A complicated situation occurs to me in illustration. A woman from the Hull-House Day Nursery came to me two years ago asking to borrow twenty-five dollars, a sum her union had imposed as a fine. She gave such an incoherent account of her plight that it was evident that she did not in the least understand what it was all about. A little investigation disclosed the following facts: The "Nursery Mother," as I here call her for purposes of identification, had worked for a long time in an unorganized overall factory, where the proprietor, dealing as he did in goods purchased exclusively by workingmen, found it increasingly difficult to sell his overalls because they did not bear the union label. He finally made a request to the union that the employees in his factory be organized. This was done, he was given the use of the label, and upon this basis he prospered for several months.

Whether the organizer was "fixed" or not, the investigation did not make clear; for, although the "Nursery Mother," with her fellow-workers, had paid their union dues regularly, the employer was not compelled to pay the union scale of wages, but continued to pay the same wages as before. At the end of three months his employees discovered that they were not being paid the union scale, and demanded that their wages be raised to that amount. The employer, in the meantime having extensively advertised his use of the label, concluded that his purpose had been served, and that he no longer needed the union. He refused, therefore, to pay the union scale, and a strike ensued. The "Nursery Mother" went out with the rest, and within a few days found work in another shop, a union shop doing a lower grade of manufacturing. At that time there was no uniform scale in the garment trades, and although a trade unionist working for union wages, she received lower wages than she had under the non-union conditions in the overall factory. She was naturally much confused and, following her instinct to get the best wages possible, she went back to her old place. Affairs ran smoothly for a few weeks, until the employer discovered that he was again losing trade because his goods lacked the label, whereupon he once more applied to have his shop unionized. The organizer, coming back, promptly discovered the recreant "Nursery Mother," and, much to her bewilderment, she was fined twenty-five dollars. She understood nothing clearly, nor could she, indeed, be made to understand so long as she was in the midst of this petty warfare. Her labor was a mere method of earning money quite detached from her European experience, and failed to make for her the remotest connection with the community whose genuine needs she was supplying. No effort had been made to show her the cultural aspect of her work, to give her even the feeblest understanding of the fact that she was supplying a genuine need of the community, and that she was entitled to respect and a legitimate industrial position. It would have been necessary to make such an effort from the historic standpoint, and this could be undertaken only by the community as a whole and not by any one class in it. Protective legislation would be but the first step toward making her a more valuable producer and a more intelligent citizen. The whole effort would imply a closer connection between industry and government, and could be accomplished intelligently only if women were permitted to exercise the franchise.

A certain healing and correction would doubtless ensue could we but secure for the protection and education of industrial workers that nurture of health and morals which women have so long reserved for their own families and which has never been utilized as a directing force in industrial affairs.

When the family constituted the industrial organism of the day, the daughters of the household were carefully taught in reference to the place they would take in that organism, but as the household arts have gone outside the home, almost nothing has been done to connect the young women with the present great industrial system. This neglect has been equally true in regard to the technical and cultural sides of that system.

The failure to fit the education of women to the actual industrial life which is carried on about them has had disastrous results in two directions. First, industry itself has lacked the modification which women might have brought to it had they committed the entire movement to that growing concern for a larger and more satisfying life for each member of the community, a concern which we have come to regard as legitimate. Second, the more prosperous women would have been able to understand and adjust their own difficulties of household management in relation to the producer of factory products, as they are now utterly unable to do.

As the census of 1900 showed that more than half of the women employed in "gainful occupations" in the United States are engaged in households, certainly their conditions of labor lie largely in the hands of women employers. At a conference held at Lake Placid by employers of household labor, it was contended that future historical review may show that the girls who are to-day in domestic service are the really progressive women of the age; that they are those who are fighting conditions which limit their freedom, and although they are doing it blindly, at least they are demanding avenues of self-expression outside their work; and that this struggle from conditions detrimental to their highest life is the ever-recurring story of the emancipation of first one class and then another. It was further contended that in this effort to become sufficiently educated to be able to understand the needs of an educated employer from an independent standpoint, they are really doing the community a great service, and did they but receive co-operation instead of opposition, domestic service would lose its social ostracism and attract a more intelligent class of women. And yet this effort, perfectly reasonable from the standpoint of historic development and democratic tradition, receives little help from the employing housekeepers, because they know nothing of industrial development. . . .

. . . If American women could but obtain a liberating knowledge of that history of industry and commerce which is so similar in every country of the globe, the fact that so much factory labor is performed by immigrants would help to bring them nearer to the immigrant woman. Equipped with "the informing mind" on the one hand and with experience on the other, we could then walk together through the marvelous streets of the human city, no longer conscious whether we are natives or aliens, because we have become absorbed in a fraternal relation arising from a common experience.

And this attitude of understanding and respect for the worker is necessary, not only to appreciate what he produces, but to preserve his power of production, again showing the necessity for making that substitute for war—human labor—more aggressive and democratic. We are told that the conquered races everywhere, in their helplessness, are giving up the genuine practise of their own arts. In India, for instance, where their arts have been the blossom of many years of labor, the conquered races are casting them aside as of no value in order that they may conform to the inferior art, or rather, lack of art, of their conquerors. Morris constantly lamented that in some parts of India the native arts were quite destroyed, and in many others nearly so; that in all parts they had more or less begun to sicken. This lack of respect and understanding of the primitive arts found among colonies of immigrants in a modern cosmopolitan city, produces a like result in that the arts languish and disappear. We have made an effort at Hull-House to recover something of the early industries from an immigrant neighborhood, and in a little exhibit called a labor museum, we have placed in historic sequence and order methods of spinning and weaving from a dozen nationalities in Asia Minor and Europe. The result has been a striking exhibition of the unity and similarity of the earlier industrial processes. Within the narrow confines of one room, the Syrian, the Greek, the Italian, the Russian, the Norwegian, the Dutch, and the Irish find that the differences in their spinning have been merely putting the distaff upon a frame or placing the old hand-spindle in a horizontal position. A group of women representing vast differences in religion, in language, in tradition, and in nationality, exhibit practically no difference in the daily arts by which, for a thousand generations, they have clothed their families. When American women come to visit them, the quickest method, in fact almost the only one of establishing a genuine companionship with them, is through this same industry, unless we except that still older occupation, the care of little children. Perhaps this experiment may claim to have made a genuine effort to find the basic experiences upon which a cosmopolitan community may unite at least on the industrial side. . . .

Can we learn our first lesson in modern industry from these humble peasant women who have never shirked the primitive labors upon which all civilized life is founded, even as we must obtain our first lessons in social morality from those who are bearing the brunt of the overcrowded and cosmopolitan city which is the direct result of modern industrial conditions? If we contend that the franchise should be extended to women on the ground that less emphasis is continually placed upon the military order and more upon the industrial order of society, we should have to insist that, if she would secure her old place in industry, the modern woman must needs fit her labors to the present industrial organization as the simpler woman fitted hers to the more simple industrial order. It has been pointed out that woman lost her earlier place when man usurped the industrial pursuits and created wealth on a scale unknown before. Since that time women have been reduced more and more to a state of dependency, until we see only among the

European peasant women as they work in the fields, "the heavy, strong, enduring, patient, economically functional representative of what the women of our day used to be."

Cultural education as it is at present carried on in the most advanced schools, is to some extent correcting the present detached relation of women to industry but a sense of responsibility in relation to the development of industry would accomplish much more. As men earned their citizenship through their readiness and ability to defend their city, so perhaps woman, if she takes a citizen's place in the modern industrial city, will have to earn it by devotion and self-abnegation in the service of its complex needs.

The old social problems were too often made a cause of war in the belief that all difficulties could be settled by an appeal to arms. But certainly these subtler problems which confront the modern cosmopolitan city, the problems of race antagonisms and economic adjustments, must be settled by a more searching and genuine method than mere prowess can possibly afford. The first step toward their real solution must be made upon a past experience common to the citizens as a whole and connected with their daily living. As moral problems become more and more associated with our civic and industrial organizations, the demand for enlarged activity is more exigent. If one could connect the old maternal anxieties, which are really the basis of family and tribal life, with the candidates who are seeking offices, it would never be necessary to look about for other motive powers, and if to this we could add maternal concern for the safety and defence of the industrial worker, we should have an increasing code of protective legislation.

We certainly may hope for two results if women enter formally into municipal life. First, the opportunity to fulfill their old duties and obligations with the safeguard and the consideration which the ballot alone can secure for them under the changed conditions, and, second, the education which participation in actual affairs always brings. As we believe that woman has no right to allow what really belongs to her to drop away from her, so we contend that ability to perform an obligation comes very largely in proportion as that obligation is conscientiously assumed.

ASPECTS OF THE WOMAN'S MOVEMENT

[1930]   There are certain days which remain in our memories in the light of *species aeternitatis*, days which seem to break through into the reality which lies beneath the outward seeming. I spent such a day on the Danube in the summer of 1913, with delegates to the International Suffrage Alliance, meeting that year in Buda-Pest. These women from many nations, sitting upon the deck of the river steamer, felt that curious stimulus which comes from the discovery of like-mindedness between people of varied cultures, for there is something of the same interest in discovering the underlying likenesses as there is in the patriotic cherishing of distinctive national traits. Not a breath, not a tremor of the future, ruffled the polished surface of the Danube on that summer day. There was no haunting apprehension that these bordering states within a year's time would be firing the opening shots of the most terrible war recorded in history. Did the day acquire its curious significance later? Did the glamor come in retrospect after we had realized that the end of this peaceful scene had been so near? Was it etched upon our memories as the aspect of a friend whom we have seen for the last time becomes unforgettable, not less, but more impressive if we do not know that death is coming so soon?

The stories of the river told by our hostesses increased in romantic content as we approached the beautiful old cities of Buda and Pest. Their tales extolled the Hungarian prowess which through the years of the Turkish wars had saved Europe from Asiatic control. Such wars seemed as the Crusades or the Conquest of Alexander, fit subjects for poetic recital. It was the poetry of a past grown tranquil because it was apart from life. The heroes belonged to other centuries, not our own. We did not anticipate the rough measures and poignant reproach with which contemporary poets would deal with war, nor could we then understand that it is "only the living poets who express a feeling that is actually being made and torn out of us at the moment. We do not recognize it as poetry in the first place; too often, for some reason, we fear it."

That convention in the summer of 1913, in the old Hungarian capital, was the first I had attended of the International Suffrage Alliance, although for several years I had served as vice-president of the National American Women's Suffrage Association when Dr. Anna Shaw was its brilliant president. I recall her vivid personality in many striking situations, but one in Buda-Pest remains most clearly in my mind. The old city on the Danube had long been a stronghold of Calvinism, with the result that one of the most beautiful churches belonged to the Presbyterians. It had been decided that Dr. Shaw was to give the "Congress sermon" there, but when the day arrived there was great difficulty as to a woman occupying the pulpit. The matter was finally arranged by placing a platform, with a reading desk upon it, in what had been at one time the junction of the transept and the nave of the stately old church, while the audience was seated around the platform in four different directions. In scholastic cap and gown, she stood on her raised dais and with the eloquence of which she had been past master since her early days as a pioneer Methodist preacher, she filled the vast arches with a valiant plea for the rights of women based on the old historic pleas for the rights of the individual, so dear to Calvin's heart.

The status of equal suffrage reported at the Congress by the delegates from twenty-six parliamentary nations not only gave a world-wide view of the movement, but strikingly presented various evolutionary stages. The very earliest stage was doubtless represented by the women of Asia, who were making the first struggle against their traditional barriers and customs rooted in primitive times. The resolution, therefore, admitting the Chinese Woman's Suffrage Society to the International Alliance, was carried with tremendous applause. None of the Chinese women were present, although they sent their greetings upon a beautiful banner which bore the words: "Helping each other. All of one mind." The convention was told that certain Chinese women had been decapitated for the truths they told while fighting their battle for freedom, and that at any day the men might find a reason to silence the leaders of the movement when, in their enthusiasm, they made too many converts. Be that as it may, in spite of the somber implications of the report, the entire convention agreed with the thrilling words of Mrs. Catt, the International President, that even as we review "the slow tragic struggle upward of the women of the west, we know that there is no escape for these eastern women, that they must follow the vision in their souls as we have done and as other women have done before us." It was the northern women who more than any others represented the final stage of the movement. Three members of parliament sat in the fine delegation from Finland and public servants were also found in the imposing delegation from Sweden and Norway. A most encouraging report came from Turkey where, in spite of eastern customs, the new constitution had given women a political status, due to that tendency of each revolution to incorporate into its program the most advanced features of existing governments.

The final impression of the convention at Buda-Pest was that the movement for equal suffrage was growing, pushing and developing in all the countries upon the face of the earth, that the coming together of its representatives was no perfunctory matter, but the free exchange of new experiences and untrammeled hopes. The movement was everywhere surprisingly spontaneous, manifesting itself in widely separated groups within the same nation; sometimes it was sectarian and dogmatic, at others philosophic and grandiloquent; it was both amorphous and sporadic, or carefully organized and consciously directed, but it was always vital and constantly becoming more widespread.

Here in the United States our efforts for social reform continued to move forward during the years immediately preceding the outbreak of the World War in 1914; but as I look back at this pre-war period of "social engineering"—to use a phrase which was then new —I am, however, surprised to find how much time was given by various social workers to securing the franchise for women because the movement seemed perfectly germane to the main issue. These efforts at social engineering, which were municipal, state, national, and international in scope, were often illustrated by huge exhibits, one on child welfare, in Chicago, filling the Coliseum with throngs of visitors for a fortnight. The energy fluctuated, of course, but the movement pushed on almost as if it were suspected that all efforts for social progress would not only be suddenly interrupted by a world war but that the revolutions following the war, especially the one in Russia, would so terrorize good men and women throughout the world that the mildest of propositions looking toward social change of any sort still in some quarters suggests Bolshevism. Quite as the French revolution, in its time, had held up all reform measures for two decades, even in the English parliament, because the very word liberalism connoted the guillotine.

Through all my experiences in the woman's movement and in the stirring conventions held every year, there remained in my mind certain stories of simple women who could not do otherwise than make an effort for the franchise because they needed it so bitterly. There was a sanction quite outside of the organized movement. In the suffrage campaign during which I had spoken in five of the western states I had come away with a tremendous admiration for western women. I recall an outdoor meeting on the steps of a county building in a Kansas town. A man in the crowd ventured one of the cheap jibes to which women suffragists had been so long subjected. An old lady who had come from Wisconsin to help in the campaign suddenly mounted the seat of the automobile in which she was sitting and begged leave to reply to him. To our surprise she evidently knew his name and the very county in Kansas from which he came. She told of her experiences in Kansas fifty years earlier when she had campaigned there to secure the school vote for women, and had then known the speaker's mother, who was living in a remote part of the new state. This pioneer mother had borne six children without medical attendance or the ministrations of any woman, and had buried two without the benefit of clergy. She had been eager for the school vote because she wanted a school for her growing family, and in the midst of her cares had worked hard in the campaign. The simple tale of courageous living and high thinking was unfolded before her son and ended with the question directed to him: "Who can better vote on the needs of this state of yours or on the needs of this great country of ours than a woman like that?" He had of course no reply, and sheepishly disappeared in the crowd.

I had seen the vivid interest among the Italian women of our neighborhood in their insistence upon a bond issue for a contagious disease hospital, their excitement over the demand that more attendants be provided for the lake bathing beaches to which their adventurous young sons repaired every hot night. Was there an instinctive wisdom behind their high-handed demand that political

action should concern itself with genuine human needs? How necessary to human existence, to its very survival, the occupations of
primitive women had been. From a journey to Egypt made in 1913
I had carried away an unforgettable impression of the unremitting
efforts of countless women to water parched fields that their children might be fed. The stately Egyptian women constantly carrying
water from the Nile was an epitome of the endless labor of mothers
to keep their children alive—that unchanging demand of the race
life. I recall an evening at Luxor, when my friend and I sat on the
wall outside the city just at the moment the women in their tiny
mud huts below were lighting the fires that they might cook the
chief meal of the day. We knew that the primitive clay houses were
lifted high above the level of the fields because they rested on the
ruins of villages which had crumbled there from time immemorial.
We also came to realize with a sudden pang that the mothers
feeding their children under these smoking roofs were clutched by
the old fear that there was not enough for each to have his portion,
and that the simple scene before us with all its implication was but
part of that unceasing struggle carried on by hard pressed women
all over the world. . . .

The instinctive reaction of simple women to the human factors
in a given situation was illustrated for me at the beginning of the
second Balkan war, which now seems so remote. About two hundred
Greeks who had held a meeting in our gymnasium marched from
there to the train on the first lap of their long journey to the seat
of war. Only a few hours afterward approximately the same number of Bulgarians from neighboring parts of the city, marched by
Hull-House, proud of the fact that they too were starting forth to
defend the fatherland from enemies which included the Greeks. A
Hull-House neighbor, a shrewd and able woman, remarked to me
as the last stalwart form disappeared: "I look at these young men
here and at those who marched by this morning. Both sets of them
fine upstanding young fellows, that some mother has brought up
through the measles and whooping cough and all that, and here they
are, going away to kill each other. Why not stand up right here in
Halsted Street, and pair off as they do in Parliament; and it's the
strange thing for me to be recommending the English Parliament as
a model for anybody!" she concluded.

I thought of this incident sometimes when I was in Europe during the first year of the Great War. A young soldier had sent a letter to the Women's Congress at The Hague in which he asked why women had not made long before, the protest against war which is denied to men: "Ever since I have been in the trenches," he wrote, "I have been wondering what is the matter with the women. They would not be called cowards, and they need not be afraid. Why are they holding back? It is clear why the men are holding back, but why do not women make a statement so many of us are longing for?" That same year, a statesman of another nation and in another language expressed his surprise that women had been silent so long. All the censorships which ingenious minds later evolved did not exist in the beginning of the war, and women came to possess knowledge of the actual state of affairs. Perhaps never before in the history of war had there been such a solidarity among women as their organizations had achieved during the last century. Women in response to their new training availed themselves of wider knowledge concerning the relation of war to the civilian population than had ever been possible before.

At the very beginning of the World War, I was among the suffragists who had protested against the "throw back" in the scientific sense to the conception of patriotism gradually built up during thousands of years. Europe had had one revolution after another in which women as well as men had taken part, in order that a patriotism might be established guaranteeing with loyalty to the state liberty for the individual to carry on his own vocation and his own conception of the good life. In these genuine democracies, war and revolution were growing obsolete and inadequate, for democracy is a system of life depending upon a system of work which can only be carried forward through times of uninterrupted peace. When war is declared, however, all this is lost; thousands of men march to their death under compulsion of a tribal conception of patriotism. They respond to a basic appeal of self-defense and fight because they have been told they must thus save their homes from destruction. There is undoubtedly a fine primitive spirit which quickly responds to this appeal, but it is unworthy of modern civilization to utilize such instincts at so fearful a cost. . . .

During the decade of suffrage women have learned that ideas

change less rapidly than events, with the result that much political thought is always out of date and inappropriate to changed conditions. Perhaps their most important duty is making this adjustment of the popular mind, and because they envisage the political situation afresh, they may enable the average citizen to escape from the deadening effects of worn-out conventional phrases which so largely dominate political life. When Jeannette Rankin interrupted the roll call in the House of Representatives on April 5th, 1917, to say: "I want to stand by my country—but I cannot vote for war," the feminist movement was supposed to have received a knockout blow. The patriots cried aloud that women would infect politics with pacifism, an alarm, however, which the situation in Congress twelve years later unfortunately proved unfounded. There were then eight women who were members of the lower house. They were said to "disagree on the tariff, prohibition and farm relief, but to be united on the issue of national defense," which is interpreted into more cruisers and higher appropriations for military purposes.

I am quite sure that women in politics thus far have been too conventional, too afraid to differ with the men, too unused to trust to their own judgment, too skeptical of the wisdom of the humble, to release the concern of simple women into the ordering of political life, too inclined to narrow their historic perspective to the experience of the formal woman's movement and thus unwittingly have restricted women's role in the racial development. On the whole I am quite inclined to agree with Chesterton when he wrote, "Many people have imagined that feminine politics would be merely pacifist or humanitarian or sentimental. The real danger of feminine politics is too much of a masculine policy."

THE WORLD'S FOOD SUPPLY
AND WOMAN'S OBLIGATION

[1918]   During the last three years [1915-1918] every sympathetic man and woman in the United States has been at times horribly oppressed with the consciousness that widespread famine had once more returned to the world.

At moments there seemed to be no spot upon which to rest one's mind with a sense of well being.

One recalled Servia, where three-fourths of a million people out of the total population of three million had perished miserably of typhus and other diseases superinduced by long continued privations; Armenia, where, in spite of her heart-breaking history, famine and pestilence have never stalked so unchecked; Palestine, where the old horrors of the Siege of Jerusalem, as described by Josephus, have been revived; and perhaps the crowning horror of all the "Way of the Cross"—so called by the Russians because it is easily traced by the continuous crosses raised over the hastily dug graves—beginning with the Galician thoroughfares, and stretching south and east for fourteen hundred miles, upon which a distracted peasantry ran breathlessly until stopped by the Caspian Sea, or crossed the Ural Mountains into Asia, only to come back again because there was no food there.

There is no doubt that many Americans experienced a great sense of relief therefore when Congress finally established a Department of Food Administration for the United States and when Mr. Hoover, who had spent two and a half years in Europe in intimate contact with the backwash of war, made his first appeal to his fellow countrymen in the name of the food shortage of the entire world, insisting that "the situation is more than war, it is a problem of humanity." We were relieved to know that there was something we could actually do about it, and we received the instructions for our intelligent action and guidance with gratitude. I firmly believe that thousands of people are striving every day to carry out those instructions in a spirit of humility, and cherish the hope that their efforts may prove to be of genuine human service. . . .

We all know that practically every nation in Europe is living on rations, and is destined to suffer privation for a long time. Our best efforts will no more than relieve them.

The question is, can we, the United States, produce enough for ourselves and enough more to make up the most bitter deficiencies?

If we ask what has been done before when there seemed to be too little food in the world, we shall find that the deficiency has always been corrected by the application of human intelligence and human labor to the soil. . . .

From the time we were little children we have all of us, at moments at least, cherished overwhelming desires to be of use in the great world, to play a conscious part in its progress. The difficulty has always been in attaching our vague purposes to the routine of our daily living, in making a synthesis between our ambitions to cure the ills of the world on the one hand and the need to conform to household requirements on the other.

It is a very significant part of the situation, therefore, that at this world's crisis the two have become absolutely essential to each other. A great world purpose cannot be achieved without our participation founded upon an intelligent understanding—and upon the widest sympathy; at the same time the demand can be met only if it is attached to our domestic routine, its very success depending upon a conscious change and modification of our daily habits.

It is no slight undertaking to make this synthesis; it is probably the most compelling challenge which has been made upon woman's constructive powers for centuries. They must exert all their human affection and all their clarity of mind in order to make the great moral adjustment which the situation demands.

But what have women's clubs done for us, of what worth is the comradeship and study carried on through so many years, if they cannot serve us in a great crisis like this? Through the earlier years of the Women's Club movement there was much abstract study of history, literature, science and the arts, as if both those women who had been deprived of the stimulus which collective intellectual effort brings and those women who had sadly missed their old college companionships were equally determined to find it through the widely organized clubs. It was rather the fashion in those earlier days to make fun of this studious effort, it was called foolish and superficial and a woman was sometimes told that it would be much better for her to study the art of darning her husband's stockings and the science of cooking his meals.

Nevertheless the women kept on with a sound instinct, perhaps, for what they needed most—a common background and a mutual understanding, in short the very cultivation which has so wonderfully illumined and unified the practical affairs which they have undertaken during these later years. And because thousands of women made a sustained effort to comprehend the world in which we live it may now be possible to summon to the aid of women everywhere an understanding of woman's traditional relation to food, of her old obligation to nurture the world. . . .

. . . We are told that when the crops of grain and roots so painstakingly produced by primitive women began to have a commercial value their production and exchange was taken over by men, as they later took over the manufacturing of pottery and other of woman's early industries. Such a history, of course, but illustrates that the present situation may be woman's opportunity if only because foods at this moment are no longer being regarded from their money-making value but from the point of view of their human use.

In these dark years, so destructive of the old codes, the nations, forced back to their tribal function of producing and conserving food, are developing a new concern for the feeding of their peoples. All food supplies have long been collected and distributed through the utilization of the commercial motive. When it was commercially valuable to a man, to a firm, or a nation, food was shipped; when it was not commercially valuable, food was withheld or even destroyed. At the present moment, however, just as the British government has undertaken the responsibility of providing the British Isles with imported food, so other belligerent and neutral nations have been obliged to pursue the same course in order to avert starvation. Commercial competition has been suppressed, not in response to any theory, but because it could not be trusted to feed the feeble and helpless. There is no doubt that even after Peace is declared the results of starvation arising from the world's shortage of food, will compel these governments to continue and even extend their purchasing in other lands. But such a state of affairs will itself indicate a new order—the substitution of the social utility motive for that of commercial gain. The nations in their official relations to each other totally lack that modification which has come in their internal politics by the increasing care of the poor, the concern for the man at the bottom, which has led to all sorts of ameliorative legislation, including the protection and education of children. In international affairs the nations have still dealt almost exclusively with political and commercial affairs considered as matters of "rights," consequently they have never been humanized in their relations to each other as they have been in their internal affairs.

It is quite understandable that there was no place for woman and her possible contribution in these international relationships; they were indeed not "woman's sphere." But is it not quite possible that as women entered into city politics when clean milk and sanitary housing became matters for municipal legislation, as they have consulted state officials when the premature labor of children and the tuberculosis death rate became factors in a political campaign, so they may normally be concerned with international affairs when these are dealing with such human and poignant matters as food for the starving and the rescue of women and children from annihilation?

There are unexpected turnings in the paths of moral evolution and it would not be without precedent if, when the producing and shipping of food was no longer a commercial enterprise but had been gradually shifted to a desire to feed the hungry, a new and powerful force in international affairs would have to be reckoned with.

The instinct to feed those with whom we have made alliances certainly bears an analogy to those first interchanges between tribe and tribe, when a shortage of food became the humble beginning of exchange. At the present moment the Allied Nations are collecting and conserving a common food supply and each nation is facing the necessity of making certain concessions to the common good that the threat of famine for all may be averted. A new internationalism is being established day by day; the making of a more reasonable world order, so cogently urged by the President of the United States, is to some extent already under way, the war itself forming its matrix. An English economist has recently pointed out that in Europe generally the war has thus far thrown the custom tariffs flat. Are they, perhaps, disappearing under this onslaught of energized pity for world-wide needs? And is a motive power, new in the relations between nations, being evolved in response to hunger and love, as the earlier domestic ethics had been? Under this new standard of measurement, preferential tariffs inevitably disappear because the nation denied the open door must suffer in its food supplies; the control of strategic waterways or interstate railroad lines by any one nation who might be tempted to consider only the interest of its own commerce becomes unthinkable.

It is possible that the more sophisticated questions of national grouping and territorial control will gradually adjust themselves if the paramount human question of food for the hungry be fearlessly and drastically treated upon an international basis. The League of Nations, destined to end wars, upon which the whole world, led by President Wilson, is fastening its hopes, may be founded not upon broken bits of international law, but upon ministrations to primitive human needs, as all the really stable political institutions in the world have been.

In this great undertaking women may bear a valiant part if they but stretch their minds to comprehend what it means in this world crisis to produce food more abundantly and to conserve it with wisdom.

Child Welfare

Introduction by KATHARINE F. LENROOT

Former chief of the Children's Bureau, U.S. Department of Labor

Extracts selected and arranged by

Kathleen Lowrie

Jane Addams "is incomprehensible to the observer except as she is seen against the background of the period which produced her"—a time that showed the remarkable growth of our great cities, when the competitive economic struggle was at its height. So spoke her friend Frances Perkins, in the memorial service held for her in 1935 by the National Conference of Social Work. She lived and died in another age than ours, though well remembered by all of us who are now in life's later years. Her spirit, her interpretations of human experience, and her example are more important today than when her physical presence was with us, for our need is greater and our vision is less clear.

The family, the child, and the youth, and the problems created for them by the industrialization of our economy and the congestion and neglect of our great cities, were matters of primary concern to Jane Addams. The high lights of her thought on these problems, as brought together here, are of great value to us, as we face the basic issues of our time. Underlying what she wrote is the way in which she related her life fully to the great minds and spirits of the past and to the manifestations of truth, beauty, and goodness in the teeming and poverty-stricken neighborhoods of her city. She illuminated and became a part of the lives of all who came within her influence. She was firm in the faith that the affection of man for woman, of parents for children, even in the hardest circumstances could flower and bear fruit in domestic happiness and child welfare.

The great changes that have come since Jane Addams died make it imperative that we give full recognition to the power inherent within the family and the generation and nurture of children—a power for good or for ill exceeding the forces set in motion by nuclear fission and by man's mental prowess in discovering the secrets of matter, energy, and outer space. Far more than material wealth or scientific education, the character of family life will determine the future—for us, for the Communist nations, and for the whole world.

We are giving too little attention to the evaluation of this force and of the efficacy of the means devised by a previous generation for strengthening the home. Financial assistance, for example, has been divorced, largely, from service, in spite of heroic efforts by case-work staffs, and service to families from the practical means of giving them that lift toward self-achievement and mutual help that would revitalize the apathetic, the hurt, the bewildered, and the lonely. Our efforts to wipe out slums and rehouse those with limited incomes have been too impersonal, too much dominated by other considerations, and sometimes too impractical, to achieve the best results. Too often our concepts of the standards and values inherent in family living have been unclear, our attitude toward youth and its problems negative, our faith weak.

Jane Addams clearly appraised evils which still persist, whose removal now seems as far off as when she was alive. There have been gains in material standards of living, in leisure and the means for its enjoyment, and in educational opportunity which she would not have ventured to predict, but far too many families still live in crowded, dirty, rat-infested tenements, on streets where there is little to challenge and much to corrupt youth. How descriptive of the gang life of a great city today is her plea to "make safe the street in which the majority of our young people find their recreation and their permanent relationships . . . through influences of which each participant is unconscious as he struggles alone and unaided in the strength of a current which seizes him and bears him along with myriads of others, a current which may so easily wreck the very foundations of domesticity."

The overstimulation of the senses without a corresponding stir of the higher imagination, of which Jane Addams spoke in *The Spirit of Youth and the City Streets,* has now been brought into the homes of rich and poor alike through radio, television, and the daily press. How much of youthful crime is aggravated by the violence the young see or read about is difficult to measure but needs our serious consideration. For many adolescents idleness in out-of-school hours and boredom in school have been substituted for the early employment which often sapped the energies of previous generations and deprived them of an education. Young people need, above all, constructive outlets for their restlessness and spirit of adventure, the contagion of high ideals, opportunity to feel that they have a place in society, an obligation toward it, and something worth while to give. For all our knowledge of the psychology and the pathology of youth, our means for dealing with its problems are, for the most part, almost as crude and as confused as in Jane Addams' time.

Above all, we need to remember her commitment to freedom, her love of justice, and her unquenchable faith in people. "The variation from the established type," she said, "is at the root of all change . . . all that keeps life from growing unprofitably stale and repetitious." As "our court of last appeal" against the materialism of the age, she named "the wonderful and inexplicable instinct for justice which resides in the hearts of men, . . . which is never so irresistible as when the heart is young."

KATHARINE F. LENROOT

FAMILY AFFECTION

[1909]   To one who has lived for years in a crowded quarter where men, women and children constantly jostle each other and press upon every inch of space in shop, tenement and street, nothing is more impressive than the strength, the continuity, the varied and powerful manifestations, of family affection. . . . Every tenement house contains women who for years spend their hurried days in preparing food and clothing and pass their sleepless nights in tending and nursing their exigent children, . . . every shop is crowded with workingmen who year after year spend all of their wages upon the nurture and education of their children, reserving for themselves but the shabbiest clothing and a crowded place at the family table.

    . . . The familiar and the constant manifestations of family affection . . . are so intimate a part of life that we scarcely observe them.

    . . . "These are the five children of my brother. He and his wife, my father and mother, were all done for in the bad time at Kishinef. It's up to me all right to take care of the kids, and I'd no more go back on them than I would on my own." Or, again: "Yes, I have seven children of my own. My husband died when Tim was born. The other three children belong to my sister, who died the year after my husband. I get on pretty well. I scrub in a factory every night from six to twelve, and I go out washing four days a week. So far the children have all gone through the eighth grade before they quit school," she concludes, beaming with pride and joy.

    That wonderful devotion to the child seems at times, in the midst of our stupid social and industrial arrangements, all that keeps society human, the touch of nature which unites it. . . . The devotion to the child is "the inevitable conclusion of the two premises of the practical syllogism, the devotion of man to woman." It is, of course, this tremendous force which makes possible the family, that bond which holds society together and blends the experience of generations into a continuous story. The family has been called "the fountain of morality," "the source of law," "the necessary prelude to the state" itself; but while it is continuous historically, this dual bond must be made anew a myriad times in each generation, and the forces upon which its formation depend must be powerful and unerring. . . .

It is inevitable that a force which is enduring enough to withstand the discouragements, the suffering and privation of daily living, strenuous enough to overcome and rectify the impulses which make for greed and self-indulgence, should be able, even under untoward conditions, to lift up and transfigure those who are really within its grasp and set them in marked contrast to those who are merely playing a game with it or using it for gain.

[1932]   It is hard to even associate death with the eager, flame-like spirit of our beloved [Jenny Dow Harvey, first kindergarten teacher at Hull-House], and yet she made the only possible preparation for it—that of free and joyous right-living. The minds of all of us here are crowded with sweet memories of her; let us draw together through them and comfort one another as best we may.

Almost exactly fifteen years ago I first saw her when she came to offer her services in connection with the House which we were planning. In the midst of my precocupation I was conscious that I had no right to hope for such quality and charm as this eager young girl was offering. There was something of such exquisite enthusiasm, of desire to know the life of the poor in order to serve them without reservation, of a touching humility in regard to her own powers with a certain proud consciousness that they were too fine to be wasted, such an impatience to know of the larger experience, that she carried with her the very aroma of the Spirit of Youth, to whom the world is wide and for whom all things are possible.

During the next three years we saw her almost daily with the little children of humble people. Her varied gifts, her willingness and her ability to become as a little child among them, her abandon to their interests, her merriment over the discovery made one day quite accidentally that the children thought she was a little girl in a white apron and had never dreamed that she was a "grown lady," all combined to produce the most successful following I have ever known of Froebel's command "to live with the children." . . .

We can all recall those busy days of preparation which came after the kindergarten days; the frank and joyous acceptance of the highest gift which life can offer to a woman. It seems to me that I have never seen a more simple, high-bred acceptance of life's joys, a more confident going forward to meet them, than was revealed in the establishment of that first home. It was to many of us a revelation of time-old experiences lifted up to their highest possibility, and lived out with ardor and inspiration.

Of the later years filled with the duties and the cares of a devoted wife and mother, it is impossible to speak. She traveled the happy road which has been trodden by the willing feet of many women, but I am confident that I speak for most of us in this room when I say that we have never seen more absolute welcome to life's obligations, a more exquisite comradeship between parents and children, a more complete devotion and even gratitude to all that a household of little children implies. The most persistent image of her which has come into my mind during the last sad weeks has been that of a young mother playing a game with an imperious boy of three, not in the abstracted half-hearted manner in which most adults play with children, but with a vividness and gayety almost equal to his own, and yet the game was a mere vehicle for the exquisite affection and appeal with which she enveloped him, dropping it at length in sheer despair because it became overweighted with her love and devotion, and she must seek a more direct expression. I shall always carry that impression of her as she caught the child in her arms against a background of blue sky reflected in the smooth flowing river.

And yet, although her life was so rich in all the noblest affections, she did not become wholly absorbed in them. She had from girlhood an insatiable hunger of mind which constantly fed itself with high thoughts and good books. We can all recall the keen relish with which she read aloud the pages which had brought her solace or inspiration. Sometimes she would offer gentle apology because

the reading was so long, and regret that the books she found satisfying were always "so thick." I remember old discussions in which
I pitted Marcus Aurelius against her beloved Emerson, her early
enthusiasm over Frederick Harrison's "Meanings of History," with
her wonder over the stupidity of a world which learns so hardly
the lesson of the past, her quick finding of the best book lying upon
one's table, and her instinct for the kernel of its message. She had
above all the open mind, the untrammeled, searching, ample spirit.

> This was my lady's birth,
> God gave her charm and mirth
> And laid His whole sweet earth
> Between her hands.

She was of those called "the once born," and carried from her
childhood a sense of harmony with life, of the joyousness and righteousness of it all; she was not of dual nature, and yet she was no
shallow optimist who thinks that all things work together for good
without our sincere and unceasing effort. She was quick to be
touched by the misery and the grotesqueness of life, and never
failed in her gallant effort to make things better. With something of
the noble simplicity and naïveté of a fine child she was undismayed
by the most complicated situations, and in her enthusiasm for the
best educational methods and belief in the reality of social force,
she brought to bear not only a clear mind, but that charm and
ardor which often attain results when colder methods fail. Her
outer behavior but revealed the inner life, for she kept to the end
her animation, her elasticity. She was ever a reminder, an earnest,
of all that is essential youth.

[1902]   Our democracy is making inroads upon the family, the
oldest of human institutions, and a claim is being advanced which
in a certain sense is larger than the family claim. The claim of the
state in time of war has long been recognized, so that in its name the
family has given up sons and husbands and even the fathers of
little children. If we can once see the claims of society in any such
light, if its misery and need can be made clear and urged as an
explicit claim, as the state urges its claims in the time of danger,
then for the first time the daughter who desires to minister to that
need will be recognized as acting conscientiously. . . .

The family as well as the state we are all called upon to maintain as the highest instititutions which the race has evolved for its safe-guard and protection. But merely to preserve these institutions is not enough. There come periods of reconstruction, during which the task is laid upon a passing generation, to enlarge the function and carry forward the ideal of a long-established institution. . . . It is im-possible to bring about the higher development by any self-assertion or breaking away of the individual will. The new growth in the plant swelling against the sheath, which at the same time im-prisons and protects it, must still be the truest type of progress. The family in its entirety must be carried out into the larger life. Its various members together must recognize and acknowledge the validity of the social obligation. . . . We have all seen parental con-trol and the family claim assert their authority in fields of effort which belong to the adult judgment of the child and pertain to activity quite outside the family life. . . .

Such glimpses remind us of that tragedy enacted centuries ago in Assisi, when the eager young noble cast his very clothing at his father's feet, dramatically renouncing his filial allegiance, and for-mally subjecting the narrow family claim to the wider and more universal duty. All the conflict of tragedy ensued which might have been averted, had the father recognized the higher claim, and had he been willing to subordinate and adjust his own claim to it. The father considered his son disrespectful and hard-hearted, yet we know St. Francis to have been the most tender and loving of men, responsive to all possible ties, even to those of inanimate nature. We know that by his affections he freed the frozen life of his time. The elements of tragedy lay in the narrowness of the father's mind; in his lack of comprehension and his lack of sympathy with the power which was moving his son. . . . The notion of a larger obligation can only come through the response to an enlarged interest in life and in the social movements around us.

EDUCATION

[1902]   As democracy modifies our conception of life, it con-stantly raises the value and function of each member of the com-munity, however humble he may be. We have come to believe that the most "brutish man" has a value in our common life, a function to perform which can be fulfilled by no one else. We are gradually requiring of the educator that he shall free the powers of each man and connect him with the rest of life. We ask this not merely because it is the man's right to be thus connected, but because we have become convinced that the social order cannot afford to get along without his special contribution. Just as we have come to resent all hindrances which keep us from untrammelled comradeship with our fellows, and as we throw down unnatural divisions, not in the spirit of the eighteenth-century reformers, but in the spirit of those to whom social equality has become a necessity for further social development, so we are impatient to use the dynamic power residing in the mass of men, and demand that the educator free that power. We believe that man's moral idealism is the constructive force of progress, as it has always been; but because every human being is a creative agent and a possible generator of fine enthusiasm, we are sceptical of the moral idealism of the few and demand the education of the many, that there may be greater freedom, strength, and subtilty of intercourse and hence an increase of dynamic power. We are not content to include all men in our hopes, but have become conscious that all men are hoping and are part of the same movement of which we are a part.

Many people impelled by these ideas have become impatient with the slow recognition on the part of the educators of their manifest obligation to prepare and nourish the child and the citizen for social relations. The educators should certainly conserve the learning and training necessary for the successful individual and family life, but should add to that a preparation for the enlarged social efforts which our increasing democracy requires. The democratic ideal demands of the school that it shall give the child's own experience a social value; that it shall teach him to direct his own activities and adjust them to those of other people. We are not willing that thousands of industrial workers shall put all of their activity and toil into services from which the community as a whole reaps the benefit, while their mental conceptions and code of morals are narrow and untouched by any uplift which the consciousness of social value might give them.

We are impatient with the schools which lay all stress on reading and writing, suspecting them to rest upon the assumption that the ordinary experience of life is worth little, and that all knowledge and interest must be brought to the children through the medium of books. Such an assumption fails to give the child any clew to the life about him, or any power to usefully or intelligently connect himself with it. . . .

If we admit that in education it is necessary to begin with the experiences which the child already has and to use his spontaneous and social activity, then the city streets begin this education for him in a more natural way than does the school. . . .

. . . If a boy is once thoroughly caught in these excitements, nothing can save him from over-stimulation and consequent debility and worthlessness. . . .

. . . There are hundreds of boys of various nationalities who conscientiously remain in school and fulfill all the requirements of the early grades, and at the age of fourteen are found in factories, painstakingly performing their work year after year. These later are the men who form the mass of the population in every industrial neighborhood of every large city; but they carry on the industrial processes year after year without in the least knowing what it is all about. . . . Both in the school and in the factory, in proportion as his work grows dull and monotonous, his recreation must become more exciting and stimulating. The hopelessness of adding evening classes and social entertainments as a mere frill to a day filled with monotonous and deadening drudgery constantly becomes more apparent to those who are endeavoring to bring a fuller life to the industrial members of the community. . . . If the army of school children who enter the factories every year possessed thoroughly vitalized faculties, they might do much to lighten this incubus of dull factory work which presses so heavily upon so large a number of our fellow-citizens. . . . The business man . . . has sometimes said, "Teach the children to write legibly and to figure accurately and quickly; to acquire habits of punctuality and order; to be prompt to obey; and you will fit them to make their way in the world as I have made mine." Has the workingman been silent as to what he desires for his children, and allowed the business man to decide for him there, as he has allowed the politician to manage his municipal affairs, or has the workingman so far shared our universal optimism that he has really believed that his children would never need to go into industrial life at all, but that all of his sons would become bankers and merchants? . . .

It is at last on behalf of the average workingman that our increasing democracy impels us to make a new demand upon the educator. . . . A code of social ethics is now insisting that he shall be a conscious member of society, having some notion of his social and industrial value. . . .

. . . The schools do . . . little really to interest the child in the life of production, or to excite his ambition in the line of industrial occupation. . . .

. . . The children of the working people learn many useful things in the public schools, but the commercial arithmetic, and many other studies, are founded on the tacit assumption that a boy rises in life by getting away from manual labor. . . .

Apparently we have not yet recovered manual labor from the deep distrust which centuries of slavery and the feudal system have cast upon it. . . . To do obviously little with one's hands, is still the desirable status. . . .

. . . We assume that all men are searching for "puddings and power," to use Carlyle's phrase, and furnish only the schools which help them to those ends. . . .

Among the many disappointments which the settlement experiment has brought to its promoters, perhaps none is keener than the fact that they have as yet failed to work out methods of education . . . adapted to the needs of adult working people. . . . They leave quite untouched the great mass of the factory population, the ordinary workingman of the ordinary workingman's street, whose attitude is best described as that of "acquiescence," who lives through the aimless passage of the years without incentive "to imagine, to design, or to aspire." . . .

It will certainly be embarrassing to have our age written down triumphant . . . in that our factories were filled with intricate machines, . . . but defeated in that it lost its head over the achievement and forgot the men, . . . that the machine tenders . . . walked about in the same streets with us, . . . but that we were absolutely indifferent and made no genuine effort to supply to them the artist's perception or student's insight, which alone could fuse them into social consciousness, . . . that the scholars among us continued with yet more research, that the educators were concerned only with the young and the promising, and the philanthropists with the criminals and helpless. . . .

. . . If the shop constantly tends to make the workman a specialist, then the problem of the educator in regard to him is quite clear: it is to give him what may be an offset from the overspecialization of his daily work, to supply him with general information and to insist that he shall be a cultivated member of society with a consciousness of his industrial and social value. . . .

. . . If a workingman is to have a conception of his value at all, he must see industry in its unity and entirety; he must have a conception that will include not only himself and his immediate family and community, but the industrial organization as a whole. . . . To make the moral connection it would be necessary to give him a social consciousness of the value of his work, and at least a sense of participation and a certain joy in its ultimate use; to make the intellectual connection it would be essential to create in him some historic conception of the development of industry and the relation of his individual work to it.

Workingmen themselves have made attempts in both directions, which it would be well for moralists and educators to study. It is a striking fact that when workingmen formulate their own moral code, and try to inspire and encourage each other, it is always a large and general doctrine which they preach. They were the first class of men to organize an international association, and the constant talk at a modern labor meeting is of solidarity and of the identity of the interests of workingmen the world over. It is difficult to secure a successful organization of men into the simplest trades organization without an appeal to the most abstract principles of justice and brotherhood. As they have formulated their own morals by laying the greatest stress upon the largest morality, so if they could found their own schools, it is doubtful whether they would be of the mechanic institute type. Courses of study arranged by a group of workingmen are most naïve in their breadth and generality. They will select the history of the world in preference to that of any period or nation. The "wonders of science" or "the story of evolution" will attract workingmen to a lecture when zoölogy or chemistry will drive them away. The "outlines of literature" or "the best in literature" will draw an audience when a lecturer in English poetry will be solitary. . . .

It is easy to indict the educator, to say that he has gotten entangled in his own material, and has fallen a victim to his own methods; but granting this, what has the artist done about it—he who is supposed to have a more intimate insight into the needs of his contemporaries, and to minister to them as none other can? . . .

As the poet bathes the outer world for us in the hues of human feeling, so the workman needs some one to bathe his surroundings with a human significance—some one who shall teach him to find that which will give a potency to his life. His education, however simple, should tend to make him widely at home in the world, and to give him a sense of simplicity and peace in the midst of the triviality and noise to which he is constantly subjected. He, like other men, can learn to be content to see but a part, although it must be a part of something.

It is because of a lack of democracy that we do not really incorporate him in the hopes and advantages of society, and give him the place which is his by simple right. We have learned to say that the good must be extended to all of society before it can be held secure by any one person or any one class; but we have not yet learned to add to that statement, that unless all men and all classes contribute to a good, we cannot even be sure that it is worth having.

ADOLESCENCE

[1909]   Nothing is more certain than that each generation longs for a reassurance as to the value and charm of life, and is secretly afraid lest it lose its sense of the youth of the earth. . . .

. . . It can come to him [the average man] only through the chance embodiment of joy and youth which life itself may throw in his way. . . . One generation after another has depended upon its young to equip it with gaiety and enthusiasm, to persuade it that living is a pleasure, until men everywhere have anxiously provided

channels through which this wine of life might flow, and be preserved for their delight. The classical city promoted play with careful solicitude, building the theater and stadium as it built the
market place and the temple. . . . In the medieval city the knights
held their tourneys, the guilds their pageants, the people their
dances, and the church made festival for its most cherished saints
with gay street processions. . . . Only in the modern city have men
concluded that it is no longer necessary for the municipality to provide for the insatiable desire for play . . . and this at the very moment
when the city has become distinctly industrial. . . .

. . . This industrialism has gathered together multitudes of eager
young creatures from all quarters of the earth as a labor supply. . . .

This stupid experiment of organizing work and failing to organize play has, of course, brought about a fine revenge. The love of
pleasure will not be denied, and when it has turned into all sorts
of malignant and vicious appetites, then we, the middle aged, grow
quite distracted and resort to all sorts of restrictive measures . . . but
almost worse than the restrictive measures is our apparent belief that
the city itself has no obligation in the matter, an assumption upon
which the modern city turns over to commercialism practically all
the provisions for public recreation.

. . . Coarse and illicit merrymakings . . . [confuse] joy with lust,
and gaiety with debauchery. . . .

. . . The most precious moment in human development is the
young creature's assertion that he is unlike any other human being,
and has an individual contribution to make to the world. The variation from the established type is at the root of all change, the only
possible basis for progress, all that keeps life from growing unprofitably stale and repetitious.

Is it only the artists who really see these young creatures as they
are—the artists who are themselves endowed with immortal youth?
Is it our disregard of the artist's message which makes us so blind
and so stupid, or are we so under the influence of our Zeitgeist that
we can detect only commercial values in the young as well as in the
old? It is as if our eyes were holden to the mystic beauty, the re-
demptive joy, the civic pride which these multitudes of young people might supply to our dingy towns.

. . . Vividly there appeared to my mind the delicately tinted piece of wall in a Roman catacomb where the early Christians, through a dozen devices of spring flowers, skipping lambs and a shepherd tenderly guiding the young, had indelibly written down that the Christian message is one of inexpressible joy. Who is responsible for forgetting this message delivered by the "best Christian people" two thousand years ago? Who is to blame that the lambs, the little ewe lambs, have been so caught upon the brambles?

. . . The spontaneous joy, the clamor for pleasure, the desire of the young people to appear finer and better and altogether more lovely than they really are, the idealization not only of each other but of the whole earth which they regard but as a theater for their noble exploits, the unworldly ambitions, the romantic hopes, . . . what might they not do to make our sordid cities more beautiful, more companionable? . . .

. . . Permit me to quote . . . that ancient and wonderful conversation between Socrates and the wise woman Diotima. Socrates asks: "What are they doing who show all this eagerness and heat which is called love? And what is the object they have in view? Answer me." Diotima replies: "I will teach you. The object which they have in view is birth in beauty, whether of body or soul. . . . For love, Socrates, is not as you imagine, the love of the beautiful only . . . but the love of birth in beauty, because to the mortal creature generation is a sort of eternity and immortality."

. . . The trivial and obscene words, the meaningless and flippant airs run through the heads of hundreds of young people for hours. . . . We totally ignore that ancient connection between music and morals which was so long insisted upon by philosophers as well as poets. . . .

Our attitude towards music is typical of our carelessness towards all those things which make for common joy. . . .

To the Greeks virtue was not a hard conformity to a law felt as alien to the natural character, but a free expression of the inner life. To treat thus the fundamental susceptibility of sex . . . would mean to loosen it from the things of sense and to link it to the affairs of the imagination . . . to fit to this gross and heavy stuff the wings of the mind, . . . and thus bring charm and beauty to the prosaic city and connect it subtly with the arts of the past as well as with the vigor and renewed life of the future. . . .

. . . The youth's power for appreciating is far ahead of his ability for expression. "The inner traffic fairly obstructs the outer current," and it is nothing short of cruelty to over-stimulate his senses as does the modern city . . . without a corresponding stir of the higher imagination. . . .

. . . Every high school boy and girl . . . will declare one of their companions to be "in love" if his fancy is occupied by the image of a single person about whom all the newly found values gather, and without whom his solitude is an eternal melancholy. But if the stimulus does not appear as a definite image, and the values evoked are dispensed over the world, the young person suddenly seems to have discovered a beauty and significance in many things—he responds to poetry, he becomes a lover of nature, he is filled with religious devotion or with philanthropic zeal. Experience, with young people, easily illustrates the possibility and value of diffusion.

It is neither a short nor an easy undertaking to substitute the love of beauty for mere desire, to place the mind above the senses; but is not this the sum of the immemorial obligation which rests upon the adults of each generation if they would nurture and restrain the youth, and has not the whole history of civilization been but one long effort to substitute psychic impulsion for the driving force of blind appetite? . . .

. . . There would seem to be but one path open to us in America. That path implies freedom for the young people made safe only through their own self-control . . . based upon knowledge and habits of clean companionship. . . . No course between the two is safe in a modern city, . . . in the most crowded quarters the young people themselves are working out a protective code which reminds one of the instinctive protection that the free-ranging child in the country learns in regard to poisonous plants and "marshy places," or of the cautions and abilities that the mountain child develops in regard to ice and precipices. . . .

The mothers who are of most use to . . . normal city working girls are the mothers who develop a sense of companionship with the changing experiences of their daughters, who are willing to modify ill-fitting social conventions into rules of conduct which are of actual service to their children in their daily lives of factory work and of city amusements. Those mothers, through their sympathy and adaptability, substitute keen present interests and activity for solemn warnings and restraint, self-expression for repression. . . .

By all means let us preserve the safety of the home, but let us also make safe the street in which the majority of our young people find their recreation and form their permanent relationships . . . through influences of which each participant is unconscious as he struggles alone and unaided in the strength of a current which seizes him and bears him along with myriads of others, a current which may so easily wreck the very foundations of domesticity. . . .

A certain number of the outrages upon the spirit of youth may be traced to degenerate or careless parents who totally neglect their responsibilities; a certain other large number of wrongs are due to sordid men and women who deliberately use the legitimate pleasure-seeking of young people as lures into vice. There remains, however, a third very large class of offenses . . . traceable to a dense ignorance on the part of the average citizen as to the requirements of youth, and to a persistent blindness on the part of educators as to youth's most obvious needs. . . .

. . . We are told that all the activities of primitive man and even those of his more civilized successors may be broadly traced to the impulsion of two elemental appetites. The first drove him to the search for food, the hunt developing into war with neighboring tribes and finally broadening into barter and modern commerce; the second urged him to secure and protect a mate, developing into domestic life, widening into the building of homes and cities, into the cultivation of the arts and a care for beauty. . . .

. . . If we would minimize the temptations of the struggle and free the boy from the constant sense of the stupidity and savagery of life . . . it may give us a clue for the undertaking to trace his misdeeds to the unrecognized and primitive spirit of adventure corresponding to the old activity of the hunt, of warfare, and of discovery. . . .

There are many of these adventurous boys who exhibit a curious incapacity for any effort which requires sustained energy. They show an absolute lack of interest in the accomplishment of what they undertake, so marked that if challenged in the midst of their activity, they will be quite unable to tell you the end they have in view. . . .

There is an entire series of difficulties directly traceable to the foolish and adventurous persistence of carrying loaded firearms. . . .

Then there are those piteous cases due to a perfervid imagination which fails to find material suited to its demands. I can recall misadventures of children living within a few blocks of Hull-House which may well fill with chagrin those of us who are trying to administer to their deeper needs. I remember a Greek boy of fifteen who was arrested for attempting to hang a young Turk, stirred by some vague notion of carrying on a traditional warfare, and of adding another page to the heroic annals of Greek history. When sifted, the incident amounted to little more than a graphic threat and the lad was dismissed by the court, covered with confusion and remorse that he had brought disgrace upon the name of Greece when he had hoped to add to its glory. . . .

. . . The desire to jump out of the humdrum experience of life also induces boys to experiment with drinks and drugs to a surprising extent. For several years the residents of Hull-House struggled with the difficulty of prohibiting the sale of cocaine to minors under a totally inadequate code of legislation, which has at last happily been changed to one more effective and enforcible. The long effort brought us into contact with dozens of boys who had become victims of the cocaine habit. . . .

May we not assume that this love of excitement, this desire for adventure, is basic, and will be evinced by each generation of city boys as a challenge to their elders? . . .

Possibly . . . the adult population . . . believed that youth could thus early become absorbed in a hand to mouth existence, and so entangled in materialism that there would be no reaction against it. It is as though we were deaf to the appeal of these young creatures, claiming their share of the joy of life, flinging out into the dingy city their desires and aspirations after unknown realities, their unutterable longings for companionship and pleasure. Their very demand for excitement is a protest against the dullness of life, to which we ourselves instinctively respond.

LABOR

[1907]   . . . There are, in the United States, according to the latest census [1900], 580,000 children between the ages of ten and four- teen years, who cannot read nor write. They are not the immigrant children. They are our own native-born children. . . .

We have two millions . . . under the age of sixteen years who are earning their own livings. . . .

May we not . . . trace some of this national indifference to the disposition of the past century to love children without really know- ing them? We refuse to recognize them as the great national asset and are content to surround them with a glamour of innocence and charm. . . .

. . . It is only through the elaborated inventions of our own age that skill as well as strength has been so largely eliminated that, for example, a little child may "tend the thread" in a textile mill almost as well as an adult. This is true of so many industries that the temp- tation to exploit premature labor has become peculiar to this indus- trial epoch and we are tempted as never before to use the labor of little children.

. . . How deeply are we concerned that this labor shall not result to the detriment of the child, and what excuses are we making to ourselves for thus prematurely using up the strength which really belongs to the next generation? . . .

How far are we responsible when we allow custom to blind our eyes to the things that are wrong? In spite of the enormous growth in charitable and correctional agencies designed for children, are we really so lacking in moral insight and vigor that we fail even to perceive the real temptation of our age and totally fail to grapple with it? An enlightened State which regarded the industrial sit- uation seriously would wish to conserve the ability of its youth, to give them valuable training in relation to industry, quite as the old- fashioned State carefully calculated the years which were the most valuable for military training. . . .

The municipal lodging-house in Chicago in addition to housing vagrants, makes an intelligent effort to put them into regular industry. A physician in attendance makes a careful examination of each man who comes to the lodging-house, and one winter we tried to see what connection could be genuinely established between premature labor and worn-out men. It is surprising to find how many of them are tired to death of monotonous labor, and begin to tramp in order to get away from it—as a business man goes to the woods because he is worn out with the stress of business life. This inordinate desire to get away from work seems to be connected with the fact that the men started to work very early, before they had the physique to stand up to it, or the mental vigor with which to overcome its difficulties, or the moral stamina which makes a man stick to his work whether he likes it or not. But we cannot demand any of these things from the growing boy. They are all traits of the adult. A boy is naturally restless, his determination easily breaks down, and he runs away. . . .

We have made public education our great concern in America, and perhaps the public-school system is our most distinctive achievement; but there is a certain lack of consistency in the relation of the State to the child after he leaves the public school. At great expense the State has provided school buildings and equipment, and other buildings in which to prepare professional teachers. It has spared no pains to make the system complete, and yet as rapidly as the children leave the schoolroom, the State seems to lose all interest and responsibility in their welfare. . . .

At no point does the community say to the employer, We are allowing you to profit by the labor of these children whom we have educated at great cost, and we demand that they do not work so many hours that they shall be exhausted. Nor shall they be allowed to undertake the sort of labor which is beyond their strength, nor shall they spend their time at work that is absolutely devoid of educational value. The preliminary education which they have received in school is but one step in the process of making them valuable and normal citizens, and we cannot afford to have that intention thwarted. . . .

Uniform compulsory education laws in connection with uniform child labor legislation are the important factors in securing educated producers for the nation. . . . The new pedagogy holds that it is a child's instinct and pleasure to exercise all his faculties and to make discoveries in the world around him. It is the chief business of the teacher merely to direct his activity and to feed his insatiable curiosity. . . . The educators . . . are endeavoring to supply [this need] by manual arts in the school, by courses in industrial history, and by miniature reproductions of industrial processes, thus constantly coming into better relations with the present factory system. . . .

. . . There is another side to the benefits of child-labor legislation represented by the time element, the leisure which is secured to the child for the pursuit of his own affairs, quite aside from the opportunity afforded him to attend school. Helplessness in childhood, the scientists tell us, is the guarantee of adult intellect, but they also assert that play in youth is the guarantee of adult culture. It is the most valuable instrument the race possesses to keep life from becoming mechanical.

The child who cannot live life is prone to dramatize it, and the very process is a constant compromise between imitation and imagination, as the over-mastering impulse itself which drives him to incessant play is both reminiscent and anticipatory. In proportion as the child in later life is to be subjected to a mechanical and one-sided activity, and as a highly subdivided labor is to be demanded from him, it is therefore most important that he should have his full period of childhood and youth for this play expression in order that he may cultivate within himself the root of a culture which alone can give his later activity a meaning [*The Play of Man*, Groos, page 394]. This is true whether or not we accept the theory that the aesthetic feelings originate in the play impulse, with its corollary that the constant experimentation found in the commonest forms of play are to be looked upon as "the principal source of all kinds of art." . . .

Quite aside also from the problem of individual development and from the fact that play, in which the power of choice is constantly presented and constructive imagination required, is the best corrective of the future disciplinary life of the factory, there is another reason why the children who are to become producers under the present system should be given their full child-life period. . . .

. . . Somewhere they must learn to carry on an orderly daily life —that life of mutual trust, forbearance, and help which is the only real life of civilized man. Play is the great social stimulus, and it is the prime motive which unites children and draws them into comradeship. A true democratic relation and ease of acquaintance is found among the children in a typical factory community because they more readily overcome differences of language, tradition, and religion than do the adults. "It is in play that nature reveals her anxious care to discover men to each other," and this happy and important task, children unconsciously carry forward day by day with all the excitement and joy of co-ordinate activity. . . . We have not as yet utilized this joy of association in relation to the system of factory production which is so preëminently one of large bodies of men working together for hours at a time. . . .

. . . By regarding each producer as a solitary unit, a tremendous power is totally unutilized. In the case of children who are prematurely put to work under such conditions, an unwarranted nervous strain is added as they make their effort to stand up to the individual duties of life while still in the stage of group and family dependence. . . .

We have already democratized education in the interests of the entire community; but recreation and constructive play, which afford the best soil for establishing genuine and democratic social relations, we have left untouched, although they are so valuable in emotional and dynamic power. . . . The city that refrains from educating the play motive is obliged to suppress it. . . .

. . . Industry at the present moment, as represented by masses of men in the large factories, is quite as chaotic as the early armies were. We have failed to apply our education to the real life of the average factory producer. He works without any inner coherence or sense of comradeship. Our public education has done little as yet to release his powers or to cheer him with the knowledge of his significance to the State.

JUSTICE

[1930]   We have been impressively told by one of our contemporaries that the love of justice which exists in the heart of man is the distinguishing mark of his humanity and should be respected as such. He also regards it as the supreme obligation of each generation to find the means by which it may be purified and still further increased. He warns us that this undertaking is made difficult by all which we do not perceive, or perceive incompletely, and by all that we question too superficially. It is at the mercy of every error of reason and of every ambush laid by personal interest. Hedged around by the most insidious dangers, it falls a victim to the strangest of oblivions and the most inconceivable blunders. Of all our spiritual efforts, it is the one that we should watch with the greatest care and anxiety, with the most passionate eagerness and solicitude. . . .

. . . Obtaining a more intelligent justice, is illustrated by the establishment of a clinic in connection with the Juvenile Court in Chicago for the psychiatric study of delinquent children. . . .

In 1909, the opening year of the second twenty years at Hull-House, the Juvenile Court in Chicago, which at that time was housed opposite the settlement, became the scene of the first psychopathic clinic ever established for the systematic study of children in an effort to discover the causes of their so-called delinquency. . . .

. . . We all felt that in addition to the study of conditions responsible for the delinquency of the child, there should be added the study of the child himself, not only that a scientific estimate of his abnormality might be placed at the disposal of the judge, but also that the child's full coöperation might be secured in the task of his own rehabilitation. . . .

. . . Later the state of Illinois founded the Institute for Juvenile Research, carried on in one of the Chicago buildings of the University of Illinois but holding schools and clinics in various part of the state. . . .

Partly as a result of this increasing study throughout the country, . . . I think we have all become more or less conscious that it is possible to trace in all of our courts at the present moment, what has been called "dual philosophies in the treatment of crime." Acting upon one theory, the crime itself is punished, according to a well-established code, so many years in the penitentiary for this crime and so many years for that. On the other hand there is a growing tendency to individualize punishment, to find out what is fitted to a given criminal in order to deter him from further crimes and if possible to reëducate him.

There is much evidence that we are caught at this moment between these two theories. . . .

While this challenge to existing court procedure was in an earlier stage of development and in the first years of the psychopathic clinic, we were already conscious of a curious reaction sweeping over the country in favor of severity of punishment, leaning even to the revival of old punishments which had been largely given up because of their brutality. The public . . . ignorantly believed that severity of punishment was in itself a deterrent to crime. . . . In 1911 . . . the city was horrified by a very brutal murder committed by six young men and boys, apparently without any object, not even that of petty theft, as the truck gardener whom they killed early one morning as he was driving into the city, had in his possession but a few dollars which he vainly offered in exchange for his life. . . . Four of the young men suffered the extreme penalty of the law. . . . The boys confessed to the revolting crime, which was apparently without mitigating circumstances, and throughout the trial bore themselves with unbroken bravado. Although a protest was made by many citizens against the brutalizing effect upon the community of such a wholesale execution, . . . it was evident that public sentiment as a whole upheld the drastic punishment. A fair discussion might have brought out the fact that the hanging of four young men must have a sadistic influence on the community as a whole and affect especially the reveries of adolescents, each one of whom easily imagines himself "the stoical hero who mounts the gallows without flinching"—a picture which is a thousand times more intriguing than a prosaic life in prison. . . . These boys had all been brought up in Chicago's most congested area, where the housing is the worst in the city, and where the only amusements within walking distance were connected with saloons and designed primarily to lure their earnings from them. The challenge they met at home from the overworked, harassed parents was, "How much money on Saturday?" The father of two of the boys said, less than a week before the day set for the execution: "I don't care what they do with them; it is nothing to me"; adding, with a shrug of his shoulders: "Neither of those boys ever brought home a penny." In one of the other homes, where eleven people lived in two dark, unsanitary, rear-basement rooms, the old father, who was a ragpicker, discussed the probable hanging, saying that if Philip "swung," John, a younger brother, would have to bear alone the expense of the insurance on the life of the mother, and "she might die any day." The mother of the youngest boy, crying over the tub as she bent to the family washing, said that he had "always been a good boy at home." She was much distressed that his little sister, twelve years old, who was suffering from tuberculosis, had become so excited over the news of her brother's fate that she had had a hemorrhage. . . .

Who that has ever studied such sordid conditions, can believe that what the situation needs is more brutality? . . .

The newspapers bring us every morning, information concerning many crimes. We ardently wish that the psychiatrists could add to their analysis of individual minds a study of the social situation. We should like to have them tell us what the effect upon the community is, for instance, of a case of capital punishment. Does it deter crime, as so many newspaper editors seem to think it does, or does it actually increase it? Perhaps the historians could tell us whether in those places wherein witches were executed others were deterred from becoming witches.

As Adler, the great Viennese psychologist, has been recently pointing out, there is in fact a morbid but very real attraction in the horrible, a sort of unescapable hypnosis. . . . One result of the reaction in favor of severity of punishment was to arouse a great admiration for the use of drastic measures on the part of the public officials; a state's attorney received great acclaim and many votes when he could boast of the large number of men he had "sent over the road" or "sent to the chair."

In the midst of a period of shocking lawlessness, the Chicago chief of police announced that he was ready to promote an officer who killed a criminal resisting his arrest. The chief is quite willing that the police officer should be judge, jury and executioner all in one. . . .

In the midst of these divided counsels, the treatment of the young criminal proceeds with the unsatisfactory results divided aims always entail. It is impossible to carry out either line of procedure with vigor for it is doubtless true that "while the fear of hanging does not deter men from crime, the fear of inflicting death deters many a jury from finding a just verdict and favors the escape of criminals." . . .

On the other hand, a boy who has been brought before the Juvenile Court, studied by a psychiatrist, and at last sent to a correctional institution, may be there subjected to a brutality of punishment which is unbelievable and typical of the worst of the old regime. In this period of transition, when neither side has its way, the young criminals continue to increase in numbers.

Slowly through the years one is forced to recognize that the increase of crime is connected with the general state of political corruption throughout the community as a whole, for "no social institution can escape from the community which gives it birth and which either promotes or retards its operation." . . . The lawyers who defend Chicago boys love to give them the impression that . . . acquittal is merely a question of the cleverness of the lawyer. What startles me many times about these boys is their amazing lack of moral feeling. . . . They like to perform the courageous act. . . . The unnatural state of boasting in which the young criminal lives seems to inhibit his higher faculties. It is as if the spirit of thwarted adventure and the bravado of cheap achievement were the factors which carried him into a life of criminality. . . . The policeman himself—promoted according to the number of arrests he had made—embodies the use of violence although he might be the greatest possible aid in the effort to substitute intelligent good will. . . .

. . . If success in maintaining order . . . with a minimum of force entitled him to promotion, this would in itself go far to change the entire psychology of the situation. . . .

That our present methods are ineffective is obvious since all the surveys show a large number of repeaters in the penal institutions. . . . If our legal procedure cannot do better than that in dealing with criminals we certainly have a right to challenge the whole process for there is rank failure somewhere. . . .

Is the entire conception of the police founded upon military discipline? Is the policeman in reality a survival of the soldier in the midst of a civilian population, and does the official conduct required from him conform to standards alien to the rest of the community? . . .

We are of necessity dependent upon the police for the first steps in humanizing justice so far as these boys are concerned. . . . The policeman on the beat ought to be a valuable source of evidence as he is naturally the only man who has been exposed, as it were, to the habitat of the criminal and who gives the neighborhood standards and temptations somewhat in the humbled ways of a father whose son has disgraced him. Instead of this we get the triumphant spirit of a thief catcher determined to justify himself for having made an arrest. This attitude of self-justification is perhaps more responsible for third-degree methods than we realize.

Is the attempt to secure a more intelligent justice which the psychiatric study of delinquents typifies, still in its very beginning because we are so entangled with the older theories of crime and punishment? . . . What we all really demand is an immunity from fear. Is the incessant insistence upon more severe punishment a result of a state of panic which inhibits our intelligence?

ART AND RECREATION

[1909]   . . . [The] tendency to slake the thirst for adventure by viewing the drama is, of course, but a blind and primitive effort in the direction of culture. . . .

. . . Many young people go to the theater . . . to hear discussed the themes which seem to them so tragically important. . . . An English playwright [states] that "The theater is literally making the minds of our urban populations today. It is a huge factory of sentiment, of character, of points of honor, of conceptions of conduct, of everything that finally determines the destiny of a nation. The theater is not only a place of amusement, it is a place of culture, a place where people learn how to think, act, and feel." Seldom, however, do we associate the theater with our plans for civic righteousness. . . .

The few attempts which have been made in this direction are astonishingly rewarding to those who regard the power of self-expression as one of the most precious boons of education. . . . The Hull-House Theater is constantly besieged by children clamoring to "take part" in the plays of Schiller, Shakespeare, and Molière, although they know it means weeks of rehearsal and the complete memorizing of "stiff" lines. The audiences sit enthralled by the final rendition. . . . Quite aside from its educational possibilities one never ceases to marvel at the power of even a mimic stage to afford to the young a magic space in which life may be lived in efflorescence. . . . It would also be easy to illustrate youth's eagerness for artistic expression from the recitals given by the pupils . . . of the Hull-House Music School. . . .

In so far as the illusions of the theater succeed in giving youth the rest and recreation which comes from following a more primitive code of morality, it has a close relation to the function performed by public games. It is, of course, less valuable because the sense of participation is largely confined to the emotions and the imagination, and does not involve the entire nature. . . .

Well considered public games . . . might both fill the mind with the imaginative material constantly supplied by the theater, and also afford the activity which the cramped muscles of the town dweller so sorely need. Even the unquestioned ability which the theater possesses to bring men together into a common mood and to afford them a mutual topic of conversation, is better accomplished with the one national game which we already possess, and might be infinitely extended through the organization of other public games.

. . . Boston has its municipal gymnasiums, cricket fields, and golf grounds. Chicago has seventeen parks with playing fields, gymnasiums and baths, which at present enroll thousands of young people. . . .

We are only beginning to understand what might be done through the festival, the street procession, the band of marching musicians, orchestral music in public squares or parks, with the magic power they all possess to formulate the sense of companionship and solidarity. The experiments which are being made in public schools . . . may in time work out into pageants of genuine beauty and significance. No other nation has so unparalleled an opportunity to do this through its schools as we have, for no other nation has so widespreading a school system. . . .

The city schools of New York have effected the organization of high school girls into groups for folk dancing. These old forms of dancing which have been worked out in many lands and through long experiences, safeguard unwary and dangerous expression and yet afford a vehicle through which the gaiety of youth may flow. Their forms are indeed those which lie at the basis of all good breeding, forms which at once express and restrain, urge forward and set limits.

One may also see another center of growth for public recreation and the beginning of a pageantry for the people in the many small parks and athletic fields which almost every American city is hastening to provide for its young. . . .

The many foreign colonies which are found in all American cities afford an enormous reserve of material for public recreation and street festival. . . . From the gay celebration of the Scandinavians when war was averted and two neighboring nations were united, to the equally gay celebration of the centenary of Garibaldi's birth; from the Chinese dragon cleverly trailing its way through the streets, to the Greek banners flung out in honor of immortal heroes, there is an infinite variety of suggestions and possibilities for public recreation and for the corporate expression of stirring emotions. After all, what is the function of art but to preserve in permanent and beautiful form those emotions and solaces which cheer life and make it kindlier, more heroic and easier to comprehend; which lift the mind of the worker from the harshness and loneliness of his task, and, by connecting him with what has gone before, free him from a sense of isolation and hardship?

Were American cities really eager for municipal art, they would cherish as genuine beginnings the tarentella danced so interminably at Italian weddings; the primitive Greek pipe played throughout the long summer nights; the Bohemian theaters crowded with eager Slavophiles; the Hungarian musicians strolling from street to street; the fervid oratory of the young Russian preaching social righteousness in the open square. . . .

Let us cherish these experiments as the most precious beginnings of an attempt to supply the recreational needs of our in-industrial cities. . . . To insist that young people shall forecast their rose-colored future only in a house of dreams, is to deprive the real world of that warmth and reassurance which it so sorely needs and to which it is justly entitled; furthermore, we are left outside with a sense of dreariness, in company with that shadow which already lurks only around the corner for most of us—a skepticism of life's value.

[1930]   The early School of Education at the University of Chicago, founded by Dr. John Dewey, demonstrated that a child, after an historic period had made itself at home in his imagination, would wholeheartedly live in it for weeks at a time. . . . But because this fresh imaginative life with its instinct for play is in a sense the mission of art itself we have found at Hull-House that our educational efforts tend constantly toward a training for artistic expression; in a music school, a school of dramatics, classes in rhythm and dancing and the school of the plastic and graphic arts. In the last which we call the Hull-House Art School the children are given great freedom in the use of color and clay and other media through which they may express those images which arc perpetually welling up from some inner fountain, and which suggest not only their secret aspirations, but, curiously enough, something of their historic background. . . .

Norah Hamilton, the head of our little art school, says . . .

The children seem to find in their inner lives a world of color and beauty in which they are perfectly at home. They work with freedom and endless facility, with faith in their own way of seeing, and with faith in hands and material to carry out their vision. They give their best, and take it for granted that what they give is good. They are free from our inhibitions, use their full selves and make use also, perhaps, of an instinctive self. They give the reality as it comes to them but the reality is living and filled with the spirit of play, that "other seeing" that finds the playworld as real as the material world "peopled with psychic beings kin to them," as were the hills and streams to the Greeks, the kings of all artists. To sum up the charm of the children's work, they give us a new world seen with new eyes. Perhaps, with the great primitives, they follow nature's very ways, are close to her rhythm; perhaps obey some law inherent in things as they are. . . .

. . . It is both travel and adventure for the children to visit a museum and they refer to these trips years afterwards as to great events. . . . Sketching classes are held every summer . . . the children vie with each other as to which season was found to be the most beautiful and defend certain aspects of light and color with genuine enthusiasm. . . .

Social life and art have always seemed to go best together at Hull-House . . . in . . . the Big Studio, . . . where young people come year after year, . . . led by Enella Benedict, a teacher at the Art Institute. . . . Between them all, there seems to be created an atmosphere in which each can find his own way in art. . . .

. . . It is rather interesting that out of ten of these artists who may be said to have "arrived," at least half of them are Jewish. This may be partly because the Jewish youth seems more persistent in the pursuit of his object and partly because the family are willing to free the time of a gifted young man, as Jewish families, however meager their resources, have for ages supported the Talmud scholar.

The people who seize upon the plastic arts with the most enthusiasm are the Mexicans. A few weeks spent in Mexico one gorgeous spring convinced me that the Mexicans took their art seriously. We saw the enthusiasm on the part of Saens, assistant secretary of Education, of Vasconcelos who was previously secretary, of the school of gifted artists who decorated the vast halls of the educational buildings with scenes from the history of Mexico. The artists always bear in mind the progressive educational theory as they conceive it. . . .

It is to be hoped that such experiments as are carried on in the art school at Hull-House and in many other places in America, including the advanced public schools, will at last influence the entire system of public education. To give every child in our schools the ability to use his hands with ease and pleasure, not upon the narrow basis of fitting him for factory life as educated clerks have been formerly prepared for the merchants, but in order to retain that power of unfolding human life which is implicit in the play instinct. . . .

SOCIAL ACTION

[1909]   Even as we pass by the joy and beauty of youth on the streets without dreaming it is there, . . . we may easily fail to sense those spiritual realities, which, in every age, have haunted youth and called to him without ceasing. . . .

. . . We [may be] dogged by a sense of lost opportunity, of needless waste and perplexity, when we, . . . as adults, see . . . the dreams of youth in conflict with the efforts of our own contemporaries. . . . For youth is so vivid an element in life that unless it is cherished, all the rest is spoiled. The most praiseworthy journey grows dull and leaden unless companioned by youth's iridescent dreams. Not only that, but the mature of each generation run a grave risk of putting their efforts in a futile direction, in a blind alley as it were, unless they can keep in touch with the youth of their own day and know at least the trend in which eager dreams are driving them. . . .

At times every one possessed with a concern for social progress is discouraged by the formless and unsubdued modern city, as he looks upon that complicated life which drives men almost without their own volition, that life of ingenuous enterprises, great ambitions, political jealousies, where men tend to become mere "slaves of possessions." . . . A serious attempt to ennoble and enrich the content of city life that it may really fill the ample space their ruthless wills have provided, means that we must call upon energies other than theirs. . . . We find ourselves appealing to the confident spirit of youth. We know that it is crude and filled with conflicting hopes, some of them unworthy and most of them doomed to disappointment, yet these young people have the advantage of "morning in their hearts"; they have such power of direct action, such ability to stand free from fear, to break through life's trammelings, that in spite of ourselves we become convinced that

> "They to the disappointed earth shall give
> The lives we meant to live." . . .

. . . The form of the dreams for beauty and righteousness change with each generation and . . . while it is always difficult for the fathers to understand the sons, at those periods when the demand of the young is one of social reconstruction, the misunderstanding easily grows into bitterness. . . .

All of us forget how very early we are in the experiment of founding self-government in this trying climate of America, and that we are making the experiment in the most materialistic period of all history, having as our court of last appeal against that materialism only the wonderful and inexplicable instinct for justice which resides in the hearts of men,—which is never so irresistible as when the heart is young. . . . We may listen to the young voices rising clear above the roar of industrialism and the prudent councils of commerce, or we may become hypnotized by the sudden new emphasis placed upon wealth and power, and forget the supremacy of spiritual forces in men's affairs. . . .

We may either smother the divine fire of youth or we may feed it. We may either stand stupidly staring as it sinks into a murky fire of crime and flares into the intermittent blaze of folly or we may tend it into a lambent flame with power to make clean and bright our dingy city streets.

The Arts

Introduction by ALINE B. SAARINEN

Author of
The Proud Possessors; *writer on art for* The New York Times

Extracts selected and arranged by

Lydia Lewis Rickman

Jane Addams looked at the arts without the myopia of either the sociologist or the esthete. She saw the arts—painting, sculpture, and crafts, music, drama, and dance—as part of the wholeness of human life. The release of imagination and the creative impulse, on the one hand, and the understanding and appreciation of the arts, on the other, seemed to her essential activities which enriched, not only the life of the individual, but also the community—and, ultimately, our entire civilization.

From the beginning, the arts had an important place in Hull-House. With astonishing farsightedness, Jane Addams recognized that because of the universality of their language, the arts could communicate to many different groups. Thus, they could be used to bridge the many gaps that divided society. The loan exhibition of paintings from Chicago collections in 1891, for example, made a link between Chicagoans of upper-income brackets and the workers in the industrial quarter. The concerts at Hull-House bridged the barriers of different languages and backgrounds.

Jane Addams realized the role of the arts in orientation and integration of immigrant groups. Especially for older immigrants who came from culture-oriented lands, the arts at Hull-House were comforting reassurances that America offered more than bleak materialism. The programs which preserved the folk songs and folk dances, the craft skills and the literature of their homelands gave the older immigrants a heartening sense of continuity. Perhaps even more strategically, these programs worked as catalysts toward dispelling the tragic lack of understanding and respect shown by Americanized children to their old-country parents.

Jane Addams saw the arts as necessary sources of delight and stimulating enrichments in the dreary lives of the people of her neighborhood. But she understood also their value as education. The classes in the plastic and graphic arts, in drama, music and dance, and crafts at Hull-House served their psychological "occupational therapy" role, so to speak, in affording emotional release and the freeing of creative impulse, but they also served to develop skills and techniques. (And, indeed, Jane

Addams' insistence on the importance of skills and quality is refreshing today when "outlet" seems to be more important than excellence.)

Long before our language included such clichés as "togetherness," Jane Addams understood the strategic significance of dramatic, musical, and dance productions. For the audience, they furnished emotional catharsis and a deep sense of companionship. For the participants, they offered the simultaneous experiences of self-expression and cooperative effort. For both, they could project, through the magic of a larger-than-life presentation, horizon-expanding ideas, situations, and experiences.

Many of Jane Addams' far-reaching ideas have yet to be fully appreciated and realized. Few city-planners really comprehend her belief that the justification of the city was as a place that would offer "the opportunity for varied and humanizing social relationships." Comparatively little of her wide vision of the potentials of the festival and orchestral music in public parks, of the vast neglected resources in foreign heritages which could be used in public recreational entertainments, of the importance of the plastic arts in educational systems, has been realized.

Jane Addams' remarks on the arts are still fertile and provocative. None more so than this: "The patriotism of the modern state must be based not upon a consciousness of homogeneity but upon a respect for variation, not upon inherited memory but upon refined imagination. . . . It is always easy for a democracy which insists upon writing its own programs to shut out imagination, to distrust sentiment and to make short work of recreation. It takes something like a united faith and a collective energy to insist that the great human gifts shall be given the sort of expression which will develop into the arts."

ALINE B. SAARINEN

THE ARTS AT HULL-HOUSE*

[1910]   The first building erected for Hull-House contained an art gallery well lighted for day and evening use and our first exhibit of loaned pictures was opened in June, 1891, by Mr. and Mrs. Barnett of London. It is always pleasant to associate their hearty sympathy with that first exhibit, and thus to connect it with their pioneer efforts at Toynbee Hall to secure for working people the opportunity to know the best art, and with their establishment of the first permanent art gallery in an industrial quarter.

We took pride in the fact that our first exhibit contained some of the best pictures Chicago afforded, and we conscientiously insured them against fire and carefully guarded them by night and day.

We had five of these exhibits during two years, after the gallery was completed: two of oil paintings, one of old engravings and etchings, one of water colors, and one of pictures especially selected for use in the public schools. These exhibits were surprisingly well attended and thousands of votes were cast for the most popular pictures. Their value to the neighborhood of course had to be determined by each one of us according to the value he attached to beauty and the escape it offers from dreary reality into the realm of the imagination. . . .

The exhibits afforded pathetic evidence that the older immigrants do not expect the solace of art in this country; an Italian expressed great surprise when he found that we, although Americans, still liked pictures, and said quite naïvely that he didn't know that Amer-

* Further consideration of the arts will be found in the section on Child Welfare, pages 164–168.

icans cared for anything but dollars—that looking at pictures was something people only did in Italy.

The extreme isolation of the Italian colony was demonstrated by the fact that he did not know that there was a public art gallery in the city nor any houses in which pictures were regarded as treasures.

A Greek was much surprised to see a photograph of the Acropolis at Hull-House because he had lived in Chicago for thirteen years and had never before met any Americans who knew about this foremost glory of the world. Before he left Greece he had imagined that Americans would be most eager to see pictures of Athens, and as he was a graduate of a school of technology, he had prepared a book of colored drawings and had made a collection of photographs which he was sure Americans would enjoy. But although from his fruit stand near one of the large railroad stations he had conversed with many Americans and had often tried to lead the conversation back to ancient Greece, no one had responded, and he had at last concluded that "the people of Chicago knew nothing of ancient times." . . .

. . . Buildings on the Hull-House quadrangle furnish studios for artists who find something of the same spirit in the contiguous Italian colony that the French artist is traditionally supposed to discover in his beloved Latin Quarter. These artists uncover something of the picturesque in the foreign colonies, which they have reproduced in painting, etching, and lithography. They find their classes filled not only by young people possessing facility and sometimes talent, but also by older people to whom the studio affords the one opportunity of escape from dreariness; a widow with four children who supplemented a very inadequate income by teaching the piano, for six years never missed her weekly painting lesson because it was "her one pleasure"; another woman whose youth and strength had gone into the care of an invalid father, poured into her afternoon in the studio once a week, all of the longing for self-expression which she had habitually suppressed.

Perhaps the most satisfactory results of the studio have been obtained through the classes of young men who are engaged in the commercial arts, and who are glad to have an opportunity to work out their own ideas. This is true of young engravers and lithographers; of the men who have to do with posters and illustrations in various ways. The little pile of stones and the lithographer's hand-press in a corner of the studio have been used in many an experiment, as has a set of beautiful type loaned to Hull-House by a bibliophile.

The work of the studio almost imperceptibly merged into the crafts and well within the first decade a shop was opened at Hull-House under the direction of several residents who were also members of the Chicago Arts and Crafts Society. This shop is not merely a school where people are taught and then sent forth to use their teaching in art according to their individual initiative and opportunity, but where those who have already been carefully trained, may express the best they can in wood or metal. . . . The Hull-House shop affords many examples of the restorative power in the exercise of a genuine craft; a young Russian who, like too many of his countrymen, had made a desperate effort to fit himself for a learned profession, and who had almost finished his course in a night law school, used to watch constantly the work being done in the metal shop at Hull-House. One evening in a moment of sudden resolve, he took off his coat, sat down at one of the benches, and began to work, obviously a very clever silversmith. He had long concealed his craft because he thought it would hurt his efforts as a lawyer and because he imagined an office more honorable and "more American" than a shop. As he worked on during his two leisure evenings each week, his entire bearing and conversation registered the relief of one who abandons the effort he is not fitted for and becomes a man on his own feet, expressing himself through a familiar and delicate technique. . . .

From the very first winter, concerts which are still continued were given every Sunday afternoon in the Hull-House drawing-room and later, as the audiences increased, in the larger halls. For these we are indebted to musicians from every part of the city. Mr. William Tomlins early trained large choruses of adults as his assistants did of children, and the response to all of these showed that while the number of people in our vicinity caring for the best music was not large, they constituted a steady and appreciative group. . . . In addition to sharing with our neighborhood the best music we could procure, we have conscientiously provided careful musical instruction that at least a few young people might understand those old usages of art; that they might master its trade secrets, for after all it is only through a careful technique that artistic ability can express itself and be preserved.

From the beginning we had classes in music, and the Hull-House Music School, which is housed in quarters of its own in our quieter court, was opened in 1893. The school is designed to give a thorough musical instruction to a limited number of children. From the first lessons they are taught to compose and to reduce to order the musical suggestions which may come to them, and in this wise the school has sometimes been able to recover the songs of the immigrants through their children. Some of these folk songs have never been committed to paper, but have survived through the centuries because of a touch of undying poetry which the world has always cherished; as in the song of a Russian who is digging a post hole and finds his task dull and difficult until he strikes a stratum of red sand, which, in addition to making digging easy, reminds him of the red hair of his sweetheart, and all goes merrily as the song lifts into a joyous melody. I recall again the almost hilarious enjoyment of the adult audience to whom it was sung by the children who revived it, as well as the more sober appreciation of the hymns taken from the lips of the cantor, whose father before him had officiated in the synagogue.

The recitals and concerts given by the school are attended by large and appreciative audiences. On the Sunday before Christmas the program of Christmas songs draws together people of the most diverging faiths. In the deep tones of the memorial organ erected at Hull-House, we realize that music is perhaps the most potent agent for making the universal appeal and inducing men to forget their differences.

Some of the pupils in the music school have developed during the years into trained musicians and are supporting themselves in their chosen profession. On the other hand, we constantly see the most promising musical ability extinguished when the young people enter industries which so sap their vitality that they cannot carry on serious study in the scanty hours outside of factory work. . . . [A] young girl whom Hull-House had sent to the high school so long as her parents consented, because we realized that a beautiful voice is often unavailable through lack of the informing mind, later extinguished her promise in a tobacco factory; . . . a young man whose music-loving family gave him every possible opportunity, and who produced some charming and even joyous songs during the long struggle with tuberculosis which preceded his death, had made a brave beginning, not only as a teacher of music but as a composer. In the little service held at Hull-House in his memory, when the children sang his composition, "How Sweet is the Shepherd's Sweet Lot," it was hard to realize that such an interpretive pastoral could have been produced by one whose childhood had been passed in a crowded city quarter. . . .

. . . We would have been dull indeed if we had not availed ourselves of the use of the play at Hull-House, not only as an agent of recreation and education, but as a vehicle of self-expression for the teeming young life all about us.

Long before the Hull-House theater was built we had many plays, first in the drawing-room and later in the gymnasium. The young people's clubs never tired of rehearsing and preparing for these dramatic occasions, and we also discovered that older people were almost equally ready and talented. We quickly learned that no celebration at Thanksgiving was so popular as a graphic portrayal on the stage of the Pilgrim Fathers, and we were often put to it to reduce to dramatic effects the great days of patriotism and religion.

At one of our early Christmas celebrations Longfellow's "Golden Legend" was given, the actors portraying it with the touch of the miracle play spirit which it reflects. I remember an old blind man, who took the part of a shepherd, said, at the end of the last performance, "Kind Heart," a name by which he always addressed me, "it seems to me that I have been waiting all my life to hear some of these things said. I am glad we had so many performances, for I think I can remember them to the end. It is getting hard for me to listen to reading, but the different voices and all made this very plain." Had he not perhaps made a legitimate demand upon the drama, that it shall express for us that which we have not been able to formulate for ourselves, that it shall warm us with a sense of companionship with the experiences of others; does not every genuine drama present our relations to each other and to the world in which we find ourselves in such wise as may fortify us to the end of the journey?

The immigrants in the neighborhood of Hull-House have utilized our little stage in an endeavor to reproduce the past of their own nations through those immortal dramas which have escaped from the restraining bond of one country into the land of the universal.

A large colony of Greeks near Hull-House, who often feel that their history and classic background are completely ignored by Americans, and that they are easily confused with the more ignorant immigrants from other parts of southeastern Europe, welcome an occasion to present Greek plays in the ancient text. With expert help in the difficulties of staging and rehearsing a classic play, they reproduced the Ajax of Sophocles upon the Hull-House stage. It was a genuine triumph to the actors who felt that they were "show-ing forth the glory of Greece" to "ignorant Americans." The scholar who came with a copy of Sophocles in hand and followed the play with real enjoyment, did not in the least realize that the revelation of the love of Greek poets was mutual between the audience and the actors. The Greeks have quite recently assisted an enthusiast in producing "Electra," while the Lithuanians, the Poles, and other Russian subjects often use the Hull-House stage to present plays in their own tongue, which shall at one and the same time keep alive their sense of participation in the great Russian revolution and relieve their feelings in regard to it. There is something still more appealing in the yearning efforts the immigrants sometimes make to formulate their situation in America. I recall a play written by an Italian playwright of our neighborhood, which depicted the in-solent break between Americanized sons and old country parents, so touchingly that it moved to tears all the older Italians in the audience. Did the tears of each express relief in finding that others had had the same experience as himself, and did the knowledge free each one from a sense of isolation and an injured belief that his children were the worst of all? . . .

. . . The development of the little theater at Hull-House has . . . depended upon . . . the genuine enthusiasm and sustained effort of a group of residents, several of them artists who have ungrudgingly given their time to it year after year. This group has long fostered junior dramatic associations, through which it seems possible to give a training in manners and morals more directly than through any other medium. . . .

Sometimes all the artistic resources of the House unite in a Wagnerian combination; thus the text of the "Troll's Holiday" was written by one resident, set to music by another; sung by the Music School, and placed upon the stage under the careful direction and training of the dramatic committee; and the little brown trolls could never have tumbled about so gracefully in their gleaming caves unless they had been taught in the gymnasium.

Some such synthesis takes place every year at the Hull-House annual exhibition, when an effort is made to bring together in a spirit of holiday the nine thousand people who come to the House every week during the duller times. Curiously enough the central feature at the annual exhibition seems to be the brass band of the boys' club which apparently dominates the situation by sheer size and noise, but perhaps their fresh boyish enthusiasm expresses that which the older people take more soberly.

THE LABOR MUSEUM

[1910]   An overmastering desire to reveal the humbler immigrant parents to their own children lay at the base of what has come to be called the Hull-House Labor Museum. This was first suggested to my mind one early spring day when I saw an old Italian woman, her distaff against her homesick face, patiently spinning a thread by the simple stick spindle so reminiscent of all southern Europe. I was walking down Polk Street, perturbed in spirit, because it seemed so difficult to come into genuine relations with the Italian women and because they themselves so often lost their hold upon their Americanized children. It seemed to me that Hull-House ought to be able to devise some educational enterprise which should build a bridge between European and American experiences in such wise as to give them both more meaning and a sense of relation. I meditated that perhaps the power to see life as a whole, is more needed in the immigrant quarter of a large city than anywhere else, and that the lack of this power is the most fruitful source of misunderstanding between European immigrants and their children, as it is between them and their American neighbors; and why

should that chasm between fathers and sons, yawning at the feet of
each generation, be made so unnecessarily cruel and impassable to
these bewildered immigrants? Suddenly I looked up and saw the
old woman with her distaff, sitting in the sun on the steps of a tenement house. She might have served as a model for one of Michael
Angelo's Fates, but her face brightened as I passed and holding up
her spindle for me to see, she called out that when she had spun a
little more yarn, she would knit a pair of stockings for her god-
daughter. The occupation of the old woman gave me the clew that
was needed. Could we not interest the young people working in
the neighboring factories, in these older forms of industry, so that,
through their own parents and grandparents, they would find a
dramatic representation of the inherited resources of their daily
occupation. . . .

. . . Within a month a room was fitted up to which we might in-
vite those of our neighbors who were possessed of old crafts and
who were eager to use them.

We found in the immediate neighborhood, at least four varieties
of these most primitive methods of spinning and three distinct variations of the same spindle in connection with wheels. It was possible
to put these seven into historic sequence and order and to connect
the whole with the present method of factory spinning. The same
thing was done for weaving, and on every Saturday evening a little
exhibit was made of these various forms of labor in the textile industry. Within one room a Syrian woman, a Greek, an Italian, a
Russian, and an Irish-woman enabled even the most casual observer
to see that there is no break in orderly evolution if we look at history
from the industrial standpoint; that industry develops similarly and
peacefully year by year among the workers of each nation, heedless
of differences in language, religion, and political experiences. . . .

. . . The textile museum is connected directly with the basket
weaving, sewing, millinery, embroidery, and dressmaking constantly being taught at Hull-House, and so far as possible with the
other educational departments; we have also been able to make a
collection of products, of early implements, and of photographs
which are full of suggestion. Yet far beyond its direct educational
value, we prize it because it so often puts the immigrants into the
position of teachers, and we imagine that it affords them a pleasant

change from the tutelage in which all Americans, including their own children, are so apt to hold them. I recall a number of Russian women working in a sewing-room near Hull-House, who heard one Christmas week that the House was going to give a party to which they might come. They arrived one afternoon when, unfortunately, there was no party on hand and, although the residents did their best to entertain them with impromptu music and refreshments, it was quite evident that they were greatly disappointed. Finally it was suggested that they be shown the Labor Museum— where gradually the thirty sodden, tired women were transformed. They knew how to use the spindles and were delighted to find the Russian spinning frame. Many of them had never seen the spinning wheel, which has not penetrated to certain parts of Russia, and they regarded it as a new and wonderful invention. They turned up their dresses to show their homespun petticoats; they tried the looms; they explained the difficulty of the old patterns; in short, from having been stupidly entertained, they themselves did the entertaining. Because of a direct appeal to former experiences, the immigrant visitors were able for the moment to instruct their American hostesses in an old and honored craft, as was indeed becoming to their age and experience.

In some such ways as these have the Labor Museum and the shops pointed out the possibilities which Hull-House has scarcely begun to develop, of demonstrating that culture is an understanding of the long-established occupations and thoughts of men, of the arts with which they have solaced their toil. . . .

. . . I recall a certain Italian girl who came every Saturday evening to a cooking class in the same building in which her mother spun in the Labor Museum exhibit; and yet Angelina always left her mother at the front door while she herself went around to a side door because she did not wish to be too closely identified in the eyes of the rest of the cooking class with an Italian woman who wore a kerchief over her head, uncouth boots, and short petticoats. One evening, however, Angelina saw her mother surrounded by a group of visitors from the School of Education, who much admired the spinning, and she concluded from their conversation that her mother was "the best stick-spindle spinner in America." When she inquired from me as to the truth of this deduction, I took occasion to describe the Italian village in which her mother had lived, something of her free life, and how, because of the opportunity she and the other women of the village had to drop their spindles over the edge of a precipice, they had developed a skill in spinning beyond that of the neighboring towns. I dilated somewhat on the freedom and beauty of that life—how hard it must be to exchange it all for a two-room tenement, and to give up a beautiful homespun kerchief for an ugly department store hat. I intimated it was most unfair to judge her by these things alone, and that while she must depend on her daughter to learn the new ways, she also had a right to expect her daughter to know something of the old ways.

That which I could not convey to the child but upon which my own mind persistently dwelt, was that her mother's whole life had been spent in a secluded spot under the rule of traditional and narrowly localized observances, until her very religion clung to local sanctities,—to the shrine before which she had always prayed, to the pavement and walls of the low vaulted church,—and then suddenly she was torn from it all and literally put out to sea, straight away from the solid habits of her religious and domestic life, and she now walked timidly but with poignant sensibility upon a new and strange shore.

It was easy to see that the thought of her mother with any other background than that of the tenement was new to Angelina and at least two things resulted; she allowed her mother to pull out of the big box under the bed the beautiful homespun garments which had been previously hidden away as uncouth; and she openly came into the Labor Museum by the same door as did her mother, proud at least of the mastery of the craft which had been so much admired.

A club of necktie workers formerly meeting at Hull-House, persistently resented any attempt on the part of their director to improve their minds. The president once said that she "wouldn't be caught dead at a lecture," that she came to the club "to get some fun out of it," and indeed it was most natural that she should crave recreation after a hard day's work. One evening I saw the entire club listening to quite a stiff lecture in the Labor Museum and to my rather wicked remark to the president that I was surprised to see her enjoying a lecture, she replied, that she did not call this a lecture, she called this "getting next to the stuff you work with all the time." It was perhaps the sincerest tribute we have ever received as to the success of the undertaking. . . .

These women and a few men, who come to the museum to utilize their European skill in pottery, metal, and wood, demonstrate that immigrant colonies might yield to our American life something very valuable, if their resources were intelligently studied and developed. I recall an Italian, who had decorated the doorposts of his tenement with a beautiful pattern he had previously used in carving the reredos of a Neapolitan church, who was "fired" by his landlord on the ground of destroying property. His feelings were hurt, not so much that he had been put out of his house, as that his work had been so disregarded; and he said that when people traveled in Italy they liked to look at wood carvings but that in America "they only made money out of you." . . .

The celebration of national events has always been a source of new understanding and companionship with the members of the contiguous foreign colonies not only between them and their American neighbors but between them and their own children. . . .

To me personally the celebration of the hundredth anniversary of Mazzini's birth was a matter of great interest . . . and as the Chicago branch of the Society of Young Italy marched into our largest hall and presented to Hull-House an heroic bust of Mazzini, I found myself devoutly hoping that the Italian youth, who have committed their future to America, might indeed become "the Apostles of the fraternity of nations" and that our American citizenship might be built without disturbing these foundations which were laid of old time.

THE PLAY INSTINCT AND THE ARTS

[1930]   . . . In America . . . the state is composed of people brought together from all the nations of the earth. The patriotism of the modern state must be based not upon a consciousness of homogeneity but upon a respect for variation, not upon inherited memory but upon refined imagination. We are told that the imaginative powers are realized most easily in an atmosphere of joy and release, that which we have come to call recreation. This must be held in mind if the city would preserve for its inhabitants the greatest gift in its possession—that which alone justifies the existence of the city —the opportunity for varied and humanizing social relationships. It must avoid those limited loyalties and that sense of restricted obligation which may prove so disastrous to the common good. It is always easy for a democracy which insists upon writing its own programs to shut out imagination, to distrust sentiment and to make short work of recreation. It takes something like a united faith and a collective energy to insist that the great human gifts shall be given the sort of expression which will develop into the arts.

Perhaps one of the most notable expressions of the play instinct in these later times has been connected with the amateur drama. Many years ago a little theater was built for Hull-House which has sheltered many interesting plays in many tongues. Perhaps nothing better illustrates the connection between the play instinct and the arts than the history of six dramatic clubs which were all started with very young children and have preserved their continuity through the years, their membership at the present moment numbering almost three hundred persons. Some of the individual members of these clubs have become successful actors and have long had their headquarters in New York. One of them is the leading male dancer at La Scala Theater in Milan. He gave a recital in Chicago one Sunday afternoon recently to an audience which held many of his proud countrymen but no one there had a greater sense of participation than the Marionette Club, of which he had been a member for many years. One young woman who began her training at Hull-House as a little child is now a member of the faculty in the Department of Dramatics at Yale University. These achievements as professionals have been in a sense secondary to the fact that the young people as a whole have been able to refine the play instinct into dramatic expression, to realize the pleasure which a devotion to an art entails. . . .

The National Federation of Settlements which has been so great a factor in unifying settlement activities throughout the country, has sustained committees on dramatics, on music—the latter has been able to report an astonishing growth in music schools in Philadelphia, New York and in other cities—and one on poetry. The last both encourages children to care for poetry and to write it if they choose. One of the best methods of obtaining the first object is to have the children recite in chorus somewhat in the spirit of the speaking choruses, which John Masefield has so skillfully encouraged in England that hundreds of people, the timbre of whose voices has been carefully selected, can recite with great beauty. We find the children at Hull-House will fit their rhythm to music or easily chant to a distinct meter. We have had one or two rather heartbreaking experiences with regard to composition. The following verse was written by a little girl whose uncle had been executed for murder. There was no possible way of knowing that the child would select such a theme of which these are the last lines:

> He was doomed to die that night
> Oh, it was a dreadful sight
> They brought him coffee to make it right
> But a shock came and he was dead. . . .

The arts have, I think, always been embodied in the ultimate aims of Hull-House. From time to time in moments of depression or of exhilaration over some public undertaking to which the residents were committed, we have urged Miss Smith to phrase in music the social compunction which at the moment it seemed impossible to express in any other way. This might be considered a demonstration that the function of art was germane to the group and that the teaching of music was not akin to the motive of the Vermont farmer who "only raised wheat for seed." When we came to the twenty-fifth anniversary of the opening of Hull-House in September, 1914, only a few weeks after the beginning of the World War, it seemed impossible to arrange for an occasion of rejoicing at such a moment. We decided, however, to record the ending of our first quarter of a century by publishing five Hull-House songs composed by the head of the Music School. . . . Because old-fashioned songs, with the exception of those of religion and patriotism, chiefly expressed the essentially individualistic emotions of love, hope or melancholy, it is perhaps all the more imperative that socialized emotions should also find musical expression, if the manifold movements of our contemporaries are to have the inspiration and solace they so obviously need. We believed that all the songs in this collection fulfilled the highest mission in music, first in giving expression to the type of emotional experience which quickly tends to get beyond words, and second in affording an escape from the unnecessary disorder of actual life, into the wider region of the spirit which, under the laws of a great art, may be filled with an austere beauty and peace.

The release function of art, the offering of an escape from the monotony of daily living is doubtless provided most widely by the movie and its new child the talkie. Whether the audience in a movie house is composed of adults or children, there is no doubt that they all come with a simple desire to be amused or a willingness to be instructed if done entertainingly. . . .

. . . There is no doubt that the function of release in neighborhoods such as ours, is marvelously performed by the movies. It is no small achievement that millions of men, women and children with no hope for an opportunity for travel, are still easily familiar with ships on wide seas, with a moon shining on snow-capped mountains, with the rice fields of China, and the temples in India and Egypt. To have made thousands of immigrants familiar with the life of the wild west is to give them the background for at least one aspect of our national development. One may safely assume that certain standard pictures will arise in the minds of the simplest audience when given subjects are discussed.

From my own experience I should say that one of the most beneficent features of the movie is the recreation and release it offers to old people. I recall an old Scotchwoman whose declining years were quite made over by the movies. She lived in an apartment house on Halsted Street, whose lower floor of two stores had been turned into a moving picture house. By using the back stairs she did not need to go out of doors and the kind proprietor saved her a seat night after night so near to her point of entrance that she could reach it unobserved and, therefore, she "never had to dress for the show." As she sat there in the dark her poverty, her deafness and all her other disabilities slipped from her and she was transported to one absorbing scene after another. At first she saved out Wednesday evenings for prayer meeting, but as she had the genuine excuse of the difficulty of walking three blocks with a lame knee, she gradually gave that up, and for a modest lump sum was entitled to the first performance during six nights a week, for her Presbyterianism held out against Sunday night until the very end. Her old eyes would shine with the light of youth as she told us of yet another wonderful experience in this world of ours which she had never had a chance to explore until she was about to leave it.

It is impossible to attend international meetings of any sort without encountering discussion upon motion pictures, their influence upon international opinion, and upon the estimate accorded by one nation to another. . . . Certainly we all recall seeing cinemas in foreign countries which had little to do with the higher values of life. "Chicago, oh, yes; that is where they pursue the thief over the tops of the roofs," was said to me in Tokio. At the moment, the Japanese newspapers were full of what they termed a new stage in the "westernization" of Japan. The criminal element in Japan was, according to their news reports, copying the West in its methodology and the police were greatly worried over the change in tactics of the lawless element with which they had to deal. They credited these marked changes in violence to the criminal procedure of Chicago and other Western metropolitan centers, as presented by the "cultural medium" of the movies. . . .

. . . So-called recreation has been allowed to get too far away from art expression which while universal in its interests still imposes long-established restraints upon a portrayal of the individual experience, connecting it in some subtle fashion with those permanent experiences forming the basis of our human heritage. . . .

. . . Doubtless our scientific advance depends more upon disinterested intellectual curiosity than upon any other human trait but we may be faced at this moment with an opportunity to so revitalize our own experiences that we may score as never before in the very Art of Living itself. We may drink from a fountain into which are flowing fresh waters from remote mountain ranges which only the artists could have discovered and made part of our familiar world.

Trade Unions and Labor

Introduction by HILDA W. SMITH

Specialist in labor education

Extracts selected and arranged by

Eleanor Fowler

In rereading *Twenty Years at Hull-House* and Jane Addams' own account of her long and close association with organized labor, one realizes again her essentially modern approach to the problems of the unions in their wide relationships to the community, to government, and to world affairs.

That the unions in those earlier days (1890 on)—a period of tumult and anxiety—called on Jane Addams for help and welcomed her cooperation was daily evidence of her clear thinking and integrity of purpose. Then, as now, union members were not too ready to accept help from outside their own ranks, often being suspicious of friendly gestures from "the other side." But the Chicago unions, invited by Miss Addams, met constantly at Hull-House.

The chaotic sewing trades were all around her, Russians, Poles, and English-speaking workers, men and women, competing to undercut the miserable wages of the sweat shop. She rejoiced when six hundred Italian women were organized by the union and discovered that by standing together they could improve their wages and hours. Women shirt- and cloakmakers also organized at Hull-House. Scrubwomen found a new sense of fellowship and protection under its hospitable roof. "A Settlement has to understand and alleviate," commented Miss Addams, when enemies of the tempestuous labor movement leveled sharp attacks at her and at Hull-House for encouraging these troublesome pioneer groups.

At a time when statistics on industrial conditions were seldom compiled, Jane Addams realized the need to establish facts as the basis for legislation. Daily in her work at Hull-House she was sadly aware of the needs of individuals whom she met: the children who refused Christmas candy because they worked in a candy factory and "couldn't bear the sight of it"; the worn mother sewing half the night to earn a few cents in a home little better than an annex of the sweat shop; the unemployed immigrant, at the mercy of the *padrone* and unscrupulous employment bureaus, struggling to learn a little English in the hope of finding a job. A generous store of personal sympathy from her own warm heart was never merely an emotional response with Jane Addams but a springboard to social action, based on a study of all the facts; organized action which was still a novelty in the field of civic responsibility she had chosen for her own.

This led her straight into the road of labor legislation and to a natural alliance with the unions which had long been concerned with the need for it. Faced with the utter lack of statistical information in Chicago on the evils of child labor and the sweatshop, she encouraged an investigation by Florence Kelley, then a resident at Hull-House, and for three months put on a lively campaign of evening meetings to inform the public. With a joint committee of the unions, a report of the survey and its distressing findings was sent to the Illinois Legislature. The first Illinois state factory legislation, passed in spite of strong opposition, was the final result of this campaign. Later, a state Board of Conciliation and Arbitration and a law establishing free employment bureaus and regulating private ones were among the achievements of such civic action.

In her association with the unions, Miss Addams appreciated the long-range ethical purposes of the labor movement, even while she recognized its shortcomings and occasional cases of corruption. In a period when, as in our own, it was popular to condemn the entire labor movement for the malpractices of a few leaders, she defended labor's moral purposes. She pointed out, however, a fact still true in our day—that the unions had had to assume responsibility which rightfully should rest on the community as a whole. She never ceased to emphasize this wider community responsibility and to work toward it.

In her paper "Trades Union and Public Duty" she gives a detailed and masterly analysis of the purposes and methods of organized labor, in an effort to create wider understanding of these turbulent groups. She deals with strike techniques—familiar to her from many episodes in her neighborhood—with the apprentice system, the boycott, the employer's attitude, and other phases of union problems. In line with her educational purpose, she often mentions the variety of discussion groups at Hull-House, with trade unionists and many others. These informal discussions, one of the earlier signs of the labor education movement, would have given Jane Addams a fine understanding of this movement in a later day, now involving many unions, universities, settlements, and government departments. She would have been among the first to encourage them in their long-range purposes and to point out their mistakes and limitations. And as a pioneer for world peace, she would have been an active leader in labor's international programs, in the exchange of workers with other countries, and in labor's other consistent efforts toward a just and peaceful world.

HILDA W. SMITH

PIONEER LABOR LEGISLATION IN ILLINOIS

[1910]   Our very first Christmas at Hull-House, when we as yet knew nothing of child labor, a number of little girls refused the candy which was offered them as part of the Christmas good cheer, saying simply that they "worked in a candy factory and could not bear the sight of it." We discovered that for six weeks they had worked from seven in the morning until nine at night, and they were exhausted as well as satiated. The sharp consciousness of stern economic conditions was thus thrust upon us in the midst of the season of good will.

During the same winter three boys from a Hull-House club were injured at one machine in a neighboring factory for lack of a guard which would have cost but a few dollars. When the injury of one of these boys resulted in his death, we felt quite sure that the owners of the factory would share our horror and remorse, and that they would do everything possible to prevent the recurrence of such a tragedy. To our surprise they did nothing whatever, and I made my first acquaintance then with those pathetic documents signed by the parents of working children, that they will make no claim for damages resulting from "carelessness."

The visits we made in the neighborhood constantly discovered women sewing upon sweatshop work, and often they were assisted by incredibly small children. I remember a little girl of four who pulled out basting threads hour after hour, sitting on a stool at the feet of her Bohemian mother, a little bunch of human misery. But even for that there was no legal redress, for the only child labor law in Illinois, with any provision for enforcement, had been secured by the coal miners' union, and was confined to children employed in mines. . . .

While we found many pathetic cases of child labor and hard-driven victims of the sweating system who could not possibly earn enough in the short busy season to support themselves during the rest of the year, it became evident that we must add carefully collected information to our general impression of neighborhood conditions if we would make it of any genuine value.

There was at that time no statistical information on Chicago industrial conditions, and Mrs. Florence Kelley, an early resident of Hull-House, suggested to the Illinois State Bureau of Labor that they investigate the sweating system in Chicago with its attendant child labor. The head of the Bureau adopted this suggestion and engaged Mrs. Kelley to make the investigation. When the report was presented to the Illinois Legislature, a special committee was appointed to look into the Chicago conditions. I well recall that on the Sunday the members of this commission came to dine at Hull-House, our hopes ran high, and we believed that at last some of the worst ills under which our neighbors were suffering would be brought to an end.

As a result of its investigations, this committee recommended to the Legislature the provisions which afterwards became those of the first factory law of Illinois, regulating the sanitary conditions of the sweatshop and fixing fourteen as the age at which a child might be employed. Before the passage of the law could be secured, it was necessary to appeal to all elements of the community, and a little group of us addressed the open meetings of trades-unions and of benefit societies, church organizations, and social clubs literally every evening for three months. Of course the most energetic help as well as intelligent understanding came from the trades-unions. The central labor body of Chicago, then called the Trades and Labor Assembly, had previously appointed a committee of investigation to inquire into the sweating system. This committee consisted of five delegates from the unions and five outside their membership. Two of the latter were residents of Hull-House, and continued with the unions in their well-conducted campaign until the passage of Illinois's first Factory Legislation was secured, a statute which has gradually been built upon by many public-spirited citizens until Illinois stands well among the States, at least in the matter of protecting her children. . . .

The bitterest opposition to the law came from the large glass companies who were so accustomed to use the labor of children, that they were convinced the manufacturing of glass could not be carried on without it. . . .

Chicago had for years been notoriously lax in the administration of law, and the enforcement of an unpopular measure was resented equally by the president of a large manufacturing concern and by the former victim of a sweatshop who had started a place of his own. Whatever the sentiments towards the new law on the part of the employers, there was no doubt of its enthusiastic reception by the trades-unions, as the securing of the law had already come through them, and through the years which have elapsed since, the experience of the Hull-House residents would coincide with that of an English statesman who said that "a common rule for the standard of life and the condition of labor may be secured by legislation, but it must be maintained by trades unionism."

This special value of the trades-unions first became clear to the residents of Hull-House in connection with the sweating system. We early found that the women in the sewing trades were sorely in need of help. The trade was thoroughly disorganized, Russian and Polish tailors competing against English-speaking tailors, unskilled Bohemian and Italian women competing against both. These women seem to have been best helped through the use of the label when unions of specialized workers in the trade are strong enough to insist that the manufacturers shall "give out work" only to those holding union cards. It was certainly impressive when the garment makers themselves in this way finally succeeded in organizing six hundred of the Italian women in our immediate vicinity, who had finished garments at home for the most wretched and precarious wages. To be sure, the most ignorant women only knew that "you couldn't get clothes to sew" from the places where they paid the best, unless "you had a card," but through the veins of most of them there pulsed the quickened blood of a new fellowship, a sense of comfort and aid which had been held out to them by their fellow-workers.

During the fourth year of our residence at Hull-House we found ourselves in a large mass meeting ardently advocating the passage of a Federal measure called the Sulzer Bill. Even in our short struggle with the evils of the sweating system it did not seem strange that the center of the effort had shifted to Washington, for by that time we had realized that the sanitary regulation of sweatshops by city officials, and a careful enforcement of factory legislation by state factory inspectors will not avail, unless each city and State shall be able to pass and enforce a code of comparatively uniform legislation. Although the Sulzer Act failed to utilize the Interstate Commerce legislation for its purpose, many of the national representatives realized for the first time that only by federal legislation could their constituents in remote country places be protected from contagious diseases raging in New York or Chicago, for many country doctors testify as to the outbreak of scarlet fever in rural neighborhoods after the children have begun to wear the winter overcoats and cloaks which have been sent from infected city sweatshops. . . .

In the first years of Hull-House we came across no trades-unions among the women workers, and I think, perhaps, that only one union composed solely of women was to be found in Chicago then, —that of the bookbinders. I easily recall the evening when the president of this pioneer organization accepted an invitation to take dinner at Hull-House. She came in rather a recalcitrant mood, expecting to be patronized and so suspicious of our motives, that it was only after she had been persuaded to become a guest of the house for several weeks in order to find out about us for herself, that she was convinced of our sincerity and of the ability of "outsiders" to be of any service to working women. She afterward became closely identified with Hull-House, and her hearty coöperation was assured until she moved to Boston and became a general organizer for the American Federation of Labor.

The women shirt makers and the women cloak makers were both organized at Hull-House as was also the Dorcas Federal Labor Union, which had been founded through the efforts of a working woman, then one of the residents. The latter union met once a month in our drawing-room. It was composed of representatives from all the unions in the city which included women in their membership and also received other women in sympathy with unionism. It was accorded representation in the central labor body of the city, and later it joined with those of others to found the Woman's Union Label League. In what we considered a praiseworthy effort to unite it with other organizations, the president of a leading Woman's Club applied for membership. We were so sure of her election that she stood just outside of the drawing-room door, or, in trade-union language, "the wicket gate," while her name was voted upon. To our chagrin she did not receive enough votes to secure her admission, not because the working girls, as they were careful to state, did not admire her, but because she "seemed to belong to the other side." Fortunately, the big-minded woman so thoroughly understood the vote and her interest in working women was so genuine, that it was less than a decade afterward when she was elected to the presidency of the National Woman's Trade Union League. The incident and the sequel registers, perhaps, the change in Chicago towards the labor movement, the recognition of the fact that it is a general social movement concerning all members of society and not merely a class struggle.

Some such public estimate of the labor movement was brought home to Chicago during several conspicuous strikes; at least labor legislation has twice been inaugurated because its need was thus made clear. After the Pullman strike various elements in the community were unexpectedly brought together that they might soberly consider and rectify the weaknesses in the legal structure which the strike had revealed. These citizens arranged for a large and representative convention to be held in Chicago on Industrial Conciliation and Arbitration. I served as secretary of the committee from the new Civic Federation having the matter in charge, and our hopes ran high when, as a result of the agitation, the Illinois legislature passed a law creating a State Board of Conciliation and Arbitration. But even a state board cannot accomplish more than public sentiment authorizes and sustains, and we might easily have been discouraged in those early days could we have foreseen some of the industrial disturbances which have since disgraced Chicago. . . .

. . . The cruelty and waste of the strike as an implement for securing the most reasonable demands, came to me at another time, during the long strike of the clothing cutters. They had protested, not only against various wrongs of their own, but against the fact that the tailors employed by the custom merchants were obliged to furnish their own workshops and thus bore a burden of rent which belonged to the employer. One of the leaders in this strike, whom I had known for several years as a sober, industrious and unusually intelligent man, I saw gradually break down during the many trying weeks and at last suffer a complete moral collapse. . . .

. . . One of his stories was indeed pathetic. His employer, during the busy season, had met him one Sunday afternoon in Lincoln Park whither he had taken his three youngest children, one of whom had been ill. The employer scolded him for thus wasting his time and roughly asked why he had not taken home enough work to keep himself busy through the day. The story was quite credible because the residents at Hull-House have had many opportunities to see the worker driven ruthlessly during the season and left in idleness for long weeks afterward. We have slowly come to realize that periodical idleness as well as the payment of wages insufficient for maintenance of the manual worker in full industrial and domestic efficiency, stand economically on the same footing with the "sweated" industries, the overwork of women, and employment of children.

But of all the aspects of social misery nothing is so heart-breaking as unemployment, and it was inevitable that we should see much of it in a neighborhood where low rents attracted the poorly paid worker and many newly arrived immigrants who were first employed in gangs upon railroad extensions and similar undertakings. The sturdy peasants eager for work were either the victims of the padrone who fleeced them unmercifully, both in securing a place to work and then in supplying them with food, or they became the mere sport of unscrupulous employment agencies. Hull-House made an investigation both of the padrone and of the agencies in our immediate vicinity, and the outcome confirming what we already suspected, we eagerly threw ourselves into a movement to procure free employment bureaus under State control until a law authorizing such bureaus and giving the officials intrusted with their management power to regulate private employment agencies, passed the Illinois Legislature in 1899. The history of these bureaus demonstrates the tendency we all have, to consider a legal enactment in itself an achievement and to grow careless in regard to its administration and actual results; for an investigation into the situation ten years later discovered that immigrants were still shamefully imposed upon. . . .

The stormy teamsters' strike, ostensibly undertaken in defense of the garment workers, but really arising from causes so obscure and dishonorable that they have never yet been made public, was the culmination of a type of trades-union which had developed in Chicago during the preceding decade in which corruption had flourished almost as openly as it had previously done in the City Hall. . . . At various times during these years the better type of trades-unionists had made a firm stand against this corruption and a determined effort to eradicate it. . . . And yet even in the midst of these things were found touching examples of fidelity to the earlier principles of brotherhood totally untouched by the corruption. At one time the scrub women in the downtown office buildings had a union of their own affiliated with the elevator men and the janitors. Although the union was used merely as a weapon in the fight of the coal teamsters against the use of natural gas in downtown buildings, it did not prevent the women from getting their first glimpse into the fellowship and the sense of protection which is the great gift of trades-unionism to the unskilled, unbefriended worker. I remember in a meeting held at Hull-House one Sunday afternoon, that the president of a "local" of scrub women stood up to relate her experience. She told first of the long years in which the fear of losing her job and the fluctuating pay were harder to bear than the hard work itself, when she had regarded all the other women who scrubbed in the same building merely as rivals and was most afraid of the most miserable, because they offered to work for less and less as they were pressed harder and harder by debt. Then she told of the change that had come when the elevator men and even the lordly janitors had talked to her about an organization and had said that they must all stand together. She told how gradually she came to feel sure of her job and of her regular pay, and she was even starting to buy a house now that she could "calculate" how much she "could have for sure." Neither she nor any of the other members knew that the same combination which had organized the scrub women into a union, later destroyed it during a strike inaugurated for their own purposes.

That a Settlement is drawn into the labor issues of its city can seem remote to its purpose only to those who fail to realize that so far as the present industrial system thwarts our ethical demands, not only for social righteousness but for social order, a Settlement is

committed to an effort to understand and, as far as possible, to alleviate it. That in this effort it should be drawn into fellowship with
the local efforts of trades-unions is most obvious. This identity of
aim apparently commits the Settlement in the public mind to all
the faiths and works of actual trades-unions. Fellowship has so long
implied similarity of creed that the fact that the Settlement often
differs widely from the policy pursued by trades-unionists and
clearly expresses that difference, does not in the least change public
opinion in regard to its identification. This is especially true in
periods of industrial disturbance, although it is exactly at such
moments that the trades-unionists themselves are suspicious of all
but their "own kind." It is during the much longer periods between
strikes that the Settlement's fellowship with trades-unions is most
satisfactory in the agitation for labor legislation and similar undertakings. The first officers of the Chicago Women's Trades Union
League were residents of Settlements, although they can claim little
share in the later record the League made in securing the passage
of the Illinois Ten-Hour Law for Women and in its other fine undertakings.

Nevertheless the reaction of strikes upon Chicago Settlements
affords an interesting study in social psychology. For whether Hull-
House is in any wise identified with the strike or not, makes no difference. When "Labor" is in disgrace we are always regarded as
belonging to it and share the opprobrium. In the public excitement
following the Pullman strike Hull-House lost many friends; later
the teamsters' strike caused another such defection, although my
office in both cases had been solely that of a duly appointed
arbitrator. . . .

There has gradually developed between the various Settlements
of Chicago a warm fellowship founded upon a like-mindedness resulting from similar experiences. . . . This sense of comradeship is
never stronger than during the hardships and perplexities of a strike
of unskilled workers revolting against the conditions which drag
them even below the level of their European life. At such times the
residents in various Settlements are driven to a standard of life argument running somewhat in this wise,—that as the very existence of
the State depends upon the character of its citizens, therefore if
certain industrial conditions are forcing the workers below the

standard of decency, it becomes possible to deduce the right of State regulation. Even as late as the stockyard strike this line of argument was denounced as "socialism" although it has since been confirmed as wise statesmanship by a decision of the Supreme Court of the United States which was apparently secured through the masterly argument of the Brandeis brief in the Oregon ten-hour case.

In such wise the residents of an industrial neighborhood gradually comprehend the close connection of their own difficulties with national and even international movements. The residents in the Chicago Settlements became pioneer members in the American branch of the International League for Labor Legislation, because their neighborhood experiences had made them only too conscious of the dire need for protective legislation. In such a league, with its ardent members in every industrial nation of Europe, with its encouraging reports of the abolition of all night work for women in six European nations, with its careful observations on the results of employer's liability legislation and protection of machinery, one becomes identified with a movement of world-wide significance and manifold manifestation.

THE SETTLEMENT AS A FACTOR IN THE LABOR MOVEMENT

[1895]   Hull-House is situated in the midst of the sweaters' district of Chicago. The residents came to the district with the general belief that organization for working-people was a necessity. They would doubtless have said that the discovery of the power to combine was the distinguishing discovery of our time; . . . and that working-people likewise cannot be successful until they too, learn, skilfully to avail themselves of this power. . . .

. . . The residents have lived for five years in a neighborhood largely given over to the sewing-trades, which is an industry totally disorganized. Having observed the workers in this trade as compared to those in organized trades, they have gradually discovered that lack of organization in a trade tends to the industrial helplessness of the workers in that trade. If in all departments of social, political, and commercial life, isolation is a blunder, and results in dreariness and apathy, then in industrial affairs isolation is a social crime; for it there tends to extermination.

This process of extermination entails starvation and suffering, and the desperate moral disintegration which inevitably follows in their train, until the need of organization in industry gradually assumes a moral aspect. The conviction arrived at entails a social obligation.

No trades are so overcrowded as the sewing-trades; for the needle has ever been the refuge of the unskilled woman. The wages paid throughout the manufacture of clothing are less than those in any other trade. . . . The residents of Hull-House have carefully investigated many cases, and are ready to assert that the Italian widow who finishes the cheapest goods, although she sews from six in the morning until eleven at night, can only get enough to keep her children clothed and fed; while for her rent and fuel she must always depend upon charity or the hospitality of her countrymen. If the American sewing-woman, supporting herself alone, lives on bread and butter and tea, she finds a Bohemian woman next door whose diet of black bread and coffee enables her to undercut. She competes with a wife who is eager to have home finishing that she may add something to the family comfort; or with a daughter who takes it that she may buy a wedding outfit.

The Hebrew tailor, the man with a family to support, who, but for this competition of unskilled women and girls, might earn a wage upon which a family could subsist, is obliged, in order to support them at all, to put his little children at work as soon as they can sew on buttons. . . .

. . . The mother who sews on a gross of buttons for seven cents, in order to buy a blue ribbon with which to tie up her little daughter's hair, or the mother who finishes a dozen vests for five cents, with which to buy her children a loaf of bread, commits unwittingly a crime against her fellow-workers, although our hearts may thrill with admiration for her heroism, and ache with pity over her misery.

The maternal instinct and family affection is woman's most holy attribute; but if she enters industrial life, that is not enough. She must supplement her family conscience by a social and an industrial conscience. She must widen her family affection to embrace the children of the community. She is working havoc in the sewing-trades, because with the meagre equipment sufficient for family life she has entered industrial life.

Have we any right to place before untrained women the alternative of seeing their little children suffer, or of complicating the industrial condition until all the children of the community are suffering? We know of course what their decision would be. But the residents of a settlement are not put to this hard choice, although it is often difficult to urge organization when they are flying to the immediate relief of the underfed children in the neighborhood.

If the settlement, then, is convinced that in industrial affairs lack of organization tends to the helplessness of the isolated worker, and is a menace to the entire community, then it is bound to pledge itself to industrial organization, and to look about it for the lines upon which to work. And at this point the settlement enters into what is more technically known as the labor movement.

The labor movement may be called a concerted effort among the workers in all trades to obtain a more equitable distribution of the product, and to secure a more orderly existence for the laborers. How may the settlement be of value to this effort?

If the design of the settlement is not so much the initiation of new measures, but fraternal co-operation with all good which it finds in its neighborhood, then the most obvious line of action will be organization through the trades-unions, a movement already well established.

The trades-unions say to each workingman, "Associate yourself with the fellow-workers in your trade. Let your trade organization federate with the allied trades, and they in turn, with the National and International Federation, until working-people become a solid body, ready for concerted action. It is the only possible way to prevent cuts in the rate of wages, and to regulate the hours of work. Capital is organized, and has influence with which to secure legislation in its behalf. We are scattered and feeble because we do not work together."

Trades-unionism, in spite of the many pits into which it has fallen, has the ring of altruism about it. It is clearly the duty of the settlement to keep it to its best ideal, and to bring into it something of the spirit which has of late characterized the unions in England. This keeping to the ideal is not so easy as the more practical work of increasing unions, although that is difficult enough. Of the two women's unions organized at Hull-House, and of the four which have regularly held their meetings there, as well as those that come to us during strikes at various times, I should venture to say of only one of them that it is filled with the new spirit, although they all have glimpses of it, and even during times of stress and disturbance strive for it.

It was perhaps natural, from the situation, that the unions organized at Hull-House should have been those in the sewing-trades. The shirtmakers were organized in the spring of 1891. The immediate cause was a cut in a large factory from twenty-five cents a dozen for the making of collars and cuffs to twelve cents. The factory was a model in regard to its sanitary arrangements, and the sole complaint of the girls was of the long hours and low rate of wages. The strike which followed the formation of the union was wholly unsuccessful; but the union formed then has thriven ever since, and has lately grown so strong that it has recently succeeded in securing the adoption of the national labels.

The cloakmakers were organized at Hull-House in the spring of 1892. Wages had been steadily falling, and there was great depression among the workers of the trade. The number of employees in the inside shops was being rapidly reduced, and the work of the entire trade handed over to the sweaters. The union among the men numbered two hundred; but the skilled workers were being rapidly supplanted by untrained women, who had no conscience in regard to the wages they accepted. The men had urged organization for several years, but were unable to secure it among the women. One apparently insurmountable obstacle had been the impossibility of securing any room, save one over a saloon, that was large enough and cheap enough for a general meeting. To a saloon hall the women had steadfastly refused to go. . . . The first meeting at Hull-House was composed of men and girls, and two or three of the residents. The meeting was a revelation to all present. The men, perhaps forty in number, were Russian-Jewish tailors, many of whom could command not even broken English. They were ill-dressed and grimy, suspicious that Hull-House was a spy in the service of the capitalists. They were skilled workers, easily superior to the girls when sewing on a cloak, but shamefaced and constrained in meeting with them. The American-Irish girls were well-dressed, and comparatively at ease. They felt chaperoned by the presence of the residents, and talked volubly among themselves. These two sets of people were held together only by the pressure upon their trade. . . .

There was much less difference of any sort between the residents and the working-girls than between the men and girls of the same trade. It was a spectacle only to be found in an American city, under the latest conditions of trade-life. Working-people among themselves are being forced into a social democracy from the pressure of the economic situation. It presents an educating and broadening aspect of no small value.

The Woman's Cloakmakers' Union has never been large, but it always has been characterized by the spirit of generosity which marked its organization. It feels a strong sense of obligation toward the most ill-paid and ignorant of the sweaters' victims, and no working-people of Chicago have done more for abolition of the sweating-system than this handful of women.

TRADE UNIONS AND PUBLIC DUTY

[1899]   In this paper I have assumed that the general organization of trades unions and their ultimate purposes are understood, and also, that we recognize that the public has a duty toward the weak and defenseless members of the community. With these assumptions granted, two propositions are really amazing: First, that we have turned over to those men who work with their hands the fulfillment of certain obligations which we must acknowledge belong to all of us, such as protecting little children from premature labor, and obtaining shorter hours for the overworked; and, second, that while the trades unions, more than any other body, have secured orderly legislation for the defense of the feeblest, they are persistently misunderstood and harshly criticised by many people who are themselves working for the same ends.

The first proposition may be illustrated by various instances in which measures introduced by trades unions have first been opposed by the public, and later have been considered praiseworthy and valuable, when the public as a whole has undertaken to establish and enforce them.

For years trades unions have endeavored to secure laws regulating the occupations in which children may be allowed to work, the hours of labor permitted in those occupations, and the minimum age below which children may not be employed. Workingmen have accepted women into their trades unions, as an inevitable development of industrial conditions, but they resent the entrance of children into their trades, not only because children bring down wages, for women do that as well, but because children are injured by premature labor. The regulation of child labor is one of the few points in which society as a whole has made common cause with the voluntary efforts of trades unions, but the movement was initiated and is still largely carried forward by them. . . .

. . . Workingmen, in their feebleness in all but numbers, have been forced to the state to secure protection for themselves and for their children. They cannot all rise out of their class, as the occasionally successful man has done; some of them must be left to do the work in the factories and mines, and they have no money to spend in ameliorating philanthropy.

In order to secure help from the state they have been obliged to agitate, and to make a moral appeal to the community as a whole —that most successful appeal which has ever distinguished great popular movements, but which we seem to distrust, and do not ordinarily use so often as the appeals to self-interest, national tradition, or class prejudice. Almost all the labor legislation which has been secured in this country to protect the workman against the harshest conditions of industry has been secured through the efforts of trades unions, the training in which naturally leads men to appeal to the state, and to use those tools which democracy affords.

Child-labor laws once enacted and enforced are a matter of pride to the entire community, and they even come to be regarded as a register of the community's humanity and enlightenment.

To consider the second proposition: For many years I have been impressed with the noble purposes of trades unions, and the desirability of the ends which they seek; and at the same time I have been amazed at the harshness with which their failures are judged by the public, and the undue stress which is laid upon the violence and disorder which sometimes accompany their efforts.

How far is this violence and the consequent condemnation of the public the result of ignoble purposes on the part of the trades unions, and how far is it the result of the partial effort and failure which we thrust upon them, when the trades unions alone are obliged to do what the community as a whole should undertake? Scenes of disorder and violence are enacted because trades unions are not equipped to accomplish what they are undertaking. The state alone could accomplish it without disorder. The public shirks its duty, and then holds a grievance toward the men who undertake the performance of that duty. It blames the union men for the disaster which arises from the fact that the movement is a partial one.

The public is forced to one of two alternatives: that the state should not attempt to ameliorate the lot of workingmen by regulating hours, etc.—and this in spite of the recent decision of the United States Supreme Court in sustaining the eight-hour law— or that the trades unions, unassisted, are doing that for which we are all responsible, and which we all ought to undertake.

What, then, is this labor movement, which, when it incorporates its doctrine into legal measures, becomes orderly and smooth-working, and, when it undertakes to enforce them, itself becomes violent and difficult? . . .

It is easy to misjudge from the outside act. The man who reads the newspapers, and has no other acquaintance with labor organizations than the record of their outside and often unofficial acts, is almost sure to be confused in regard to their ultimate objects. It is also difficult for the victorious side to see fairly. There is no doubt that the employer, the man who represents vested interest, often routs and defeats labor organizations, drives them from the field with an honest misunderstanding of what they are trying to do, and of the principles which they represent. He is flushed with triumph and imagines a victory which he has never achieved.

We may consider half a dozen measures which trades unions have urged, and concerning which the community has often been stirred by indignation, and find that, when the public undertakes to enforce identical, or similar, measures, they are regarded with great complacency. The disapproval may be merely the result of the fact that the trades unions alone are doing that which belongs to the entire public.

The following six measures may be thus considered: *first*, the harsh treatment of a non-union laborer during a strike; *second*, the dictatorship of the walking delegate; *third*, the use of the boycott; *fourth*, the insistence upon shorter hours of labor; *fifth*, the limitation of apprentices; *sixth*, the sympathetic strike. It is quite possible to compare all of these to national measures of which we approve and concerning which we are a part, but which the community as a whole undertakes to enforce. Reasoning by analogy is always dangerous, and its conclusions may well be questioned, but to find that we can parallel these six efforts of trades unions with six others undertaken by the government is certainly suggestive.

1. We hear from time to time of a strike in which men are prevented from taking the places of the strikers, and in the ensuing struggle are beaten and injured. We call the whole affair brutal and unjustifiable, and our sympathies are aroused for the men whom the strikers drive away from the chance to work. . . .

Let us put ourselves in the position of the striking men who have fallen upon workmen who have taken their places. The strikers have for years belonged to an organization devoted to securing better wages and a higher standard of living, not only for themselves, but for all the men in that trade. To this end they have steadily contributed from their wages. They have given their time to the study of trade conditions, and enthusiastic and unceasing service to bettering those conditions in the only way that seems to them possible. They have thus worked, not only for themselves and their children, but for all their class. Every gain they have made, every advance they have secured, has been shared with the very men who now, when these gains are at stake, range themselves on the other side. They honestly believe, whether they are right or wrong, that their position is exactly the same which a nation, in time of war, takes toward a traitor who has deserted his country's camp for that of the enemy. . . .

2. We hear contemptuous references to the walking delegate and agitator, without stopping to ask ourselves why the workingman is not entitled to his advocate, paid to represent his legal and in-

dustrial rights, quite as much as the manager of the corporation is entitled to his lawyer. We ignorantly allow ourselves to believe that a walking delegate may declare a strike at his own pleasure, without taking the pains to discover that the organization of a trades union is so democratic that no one man, even in exceptional crises, can set aside the constitution of his union. . . .

In spite of all these facts, the community continues to dogmatize concerning the dictatorial action of the walking delegate, whose every executive act has been authorized by his constituency. An ignorant person might easily consider a peace commissioner sent by the United States to Paris as a raging dictator. That is quite possible if one looks at his outside acts alone, but we are accustomed to consider a minister plenipotentiary in relation to government, and do not misunderstand his power, but we are slower to realize that it is only as a commissioner that the business agent of the union orders strikes and arranges terms of settlement.

3. We condemn the boycott, and say that the trades unions are bigoted in their allegiance to each other, and harsh to those outside their membership. . . .

. . . Who cannot recall the political speech urging high tariff for the protection of the American workingmen, in their wages and standard of living? It is singularly like the argument used by the workingman when he urges the boycott, or the more peaceful method of purchasing labeled goods made by union workmen who have been paid union wages. Here, again, as in the case of industrial warfare, I do not wish to commit myself to the ethics involved, but merely to point the analogy, and call attention to the fact that the public is apt to consider the government righteous and the trades unions unjustifiable.

4. For years trades unions in every country have steadily bent their efforts towards securing a shorter working day. In many unions these persistent efforts have been crowned with success, but many others are still making the attempt to secure the eight-hour day, and have before them a long and troublous undertaking. Here, again, trades unions are trying to do for themselves what the government should secure for all its citizens; has, in fact, secured in many instances. Almost all the large cities of the United States employ men upon municipal works for only eight hours a day and the

federal government has established eight hours as the normal working day in several departments. . . . A law passed in Illinois in
1893, regulating the working hours of women who were employed
in manufacture to eight hours a day, or forty-eight hours a week,
was successfully resisted by the manufacturers, and declared un-
constitutional by the Illinois Supreme Court. The argument urged
by the manufacturers against its enforcement was that the Illinois
employers could not sustain the competition of their rivals in other
states, who were not restricted by the same law. The difficulty of
limiting the hours of labor in some states and leaving them unlimited
in others shows most clearly the magnitude of the undertaking assumed by the trades unions, and the unfairness of leaving the task
to them.

5. The limitation of the number of apprentices is a position which
the skilled trades-unionists have long held, but which is gradually
being given up as indefensible. Still there have been reasons in
the minds of trades-unionists, ethical concepts which did once induce them to undertake this line of action. . . . The limitation of
number of apprentices was instituted in those trades which required
a long apprenticeship before a man became a journeyman or a
master workman. The man who had submitted to this long course
of training, from one to eight years, during which time he earned
but little, held that he had a right to secure to himself reasonable
expectation that this trade would be valuable to him after it was
once acquired; he demanded a guarantee that he should not be
obliged to throw away all those years of training, simply because
too many men were allowed to enter the trade and reduce its wages.

All this was nearly analogous to the plea of the inventor when
he applies to the government to protect his invention, which has
cost him years of work and study, from the unlimited competition of
others; and possibly even more analogous to the position of the
author who wishes to be secured by a copyright.

6. We see a great sympathetic strike ramifying throughout the
entire union of a trade and its allied trades; we suddenly hear of
men all over the country leaving their work, places which they may
have held for years, which they know that it may be difficult, and
perhaps impossible, again to secure. They certainly do this under
some dictate of conscience, and under some ethical concept that

stands to them as a duty. Later many of them see their wives and children suffer, and yet they hold out, for the sake of securing better wages for workmen whom they have never seen, for men who are living in another part of the country, and who are often of another race and religion. We see this manifestation, and read about it, and do not make a really intelligent effort to discover its ethical significance. We say the men are foolish and doomed to fail; we allow our minds to become confused between the motives of the strike, and the riots and militia which often become associated with it. We are lost in its manifestation, and do not even comprehend that at such a time a great accumulation of moral force has overmastered hundreds of our fellow-citizens. They are, for the time being, in the grasp of a great social passion, which is making for the emancipation of the wage-earner, as, in another time, a great social passion insisted upon the emancipation of the slave. . . .

. . . If the objects of trades unions could find quiet and orderly expression in legislative enactment, and if their measures could be submitted to the examination and judgment of the whole without a sense of division or of warfare, we should have the ideal development of the democratic state.

Probably the labor organizations come nearer to expressing moral striving in political action than any other portion of the community, for their political efforts in most instances have been stimulated by a desire to secure some degree of improvement in the material condition of working people. . . . They are still endeavoring to secure each advance in ethics by a step taken in politics, and this endeavor is the one safeguard of democracy. . . .

The body of trade-unionists in America are becoming discouraged from the fact that moral appeal and open agitation do not have fair play, because the "interests of capital" are not confined to these, but have methods of securing legislation which are perforce denied to workingmen. . . . The confidence of workingmen in the courts has been shaken by the fact that judges have so often been trained as corporation attorneys, and it is a common assertion which may often be heard in workingmen's meetings that the militia and United States troops are almost invariably used to protect the interests of the employer in time of strike. . . .

That all its citizens may be responsible is, then, perhaps the final reason why it should be the mission of the state to regulate the conditions of industry. The only danger in the movement, as at present conducted, lies in the fact that it is a partial movement, and antagonizes those whom it does not include. It may certainly be regarded as the duty of the whole to readjust the social machinery in such a way that the issue shall be a higher type of character, and that there shall be a moral continuity to society answering to its industrial development. This is the attempt of factory legislation. It is concerned in the maintenance of a certain standard of life, and would exercise such social control over the conditions of industry as to prevent the lowering of that standard. After all, society as society is interested in this, and there is no more obligation upon workingmen to maintain a standard of living than there is upon the rest of us. It is well, sometimes, to remind ourselves that, after all, the mass of mankind work with their hands. . . .

MILITARISM AND INDUSTRIAL LEGISLATION

[1907]   American cities have been slow to consider industrial questions as germane to government, and the Federal authorities have persistently treated the millions of immigrants who arrive every year upon a political theory and method adopted a century ago, because both of them ignore the fact that the organization of industry has completed a revolution during that period. The gigantic task of standardizing the successive nations of immigrants throughout the country has fallen upon workmen because they alone cannot ignore the actual industrial situation. To thousands of workmen the immigration problem is a question of holding a job against a constantly lowering standard of living, and to withstand this stream of "raw labor" means to them the maintenance of industrial efficiency and of life itself. Workingmen are engaged in a desperate struggle to maintain a standard of wages against the constant arrival of unskilled immigrants at the rate of three-quarters of a million a year, at the very period when the elaboration of machinery permits the largest use of unskilled men.

It may be owing to the fact that the workingman is brought into direct contact with the situation as a desperate problem of a living wage against starvation; it may be that wisdom is at her old trick of residing in the hearts of the simple, or that this new idealism, which is that of a reasonable life and labor, must, from the very nature of things, proceed from those who labor; . . . but certainly it is true, that, while the rest of the country talks of assimilation as if it were a huge digestive apparatus, the man with whom the immigrant has come most sharply into competition, has been forced into fraternal relations with him. . . .

The first real lesson in self-government to many immigrants has come through the organization of labor unions, and it could come in no other way, for the union alone has appealed to their necessities. One sees the first indication of an idealism arising out of these primal necessities, and at moments one dares to hope that it may be sturdy enough and sufficiently founded upon experience to make some impression upon the tremendous immigration situation.

The movements embodying a new idealism have traditionally sought refuge with those who are near to starvation. Although the spiritual struggle is associated with the solitary garret of the impassioned dreamer, it may be that the idealism fitted to our industrial democracy will be evolved in crowded sewer ditches and in noisy factories. It may be contended that this remarkable coming together of the workingman and the immigrant has been the result of an economic pressure, and is without merit or idealism, and that the trades union record on Chinese exclusion and Negro discrimination has been damaging. Be that as it may, this assimilation between the immigrant and the workingman has exhibited amazing strength which may be illustrated from two careful studies made in two different parts of the country.

To quote first from a study made from the University of Wisconsin of the stock yards strike which took place in Chicago in 1904 [*Trade Unionism and Labor Problems,* by John R. Commons, page 248]: "Perhaps the fact of the greatest social significance is that this was not merely a strike of skilled labor for the unskilled, but was a strike of Americanized Irish, Germans, and Bohemians, in behalf of Slovaks, Poles and Lithuanians. . . ." The visitors who attended the crowded meetings of the strikers during the summer of 1904 and heard the same address successively translated by interpreters into six or eight languages, who saw the respect shown to the most uncouth of the speakers by the skilled American men representing a distinctly superior standard of life and thought, could never doubt the power of the labor organizations for amalgamation, whatever opinion they might hold concerning their other values. . . .

The other study was made in the anthracite coal fields, and was undertaken from the University of Pennsylvania [*The Slav Invasion,* by F. J. Warne, pages 118, 119]: "The United Mine Workers of America is taking men of a score of nationalities, English-speaking and Slav, men of widely different creeds, languages, and customs, and of varying powers of industrial competition, and is welding them into an industrial brotherhood, each part of which can at least understand of the others that they are working for one great and common end. . . ."

It was during a remarkable struggle on the part of this amalgamation of men from all countries, that the United States government, in spite of itself, was driven to take a hand in an industrial situation, owing to the long strain and the intolerable suffering entailed upon the whole country. Even then, however, the Government endeavored to confine its investigation to the mere commercial questions of tonnage and freight rates with their political implications, and it was only when an aroused and moralized public opinion insisted upon it that the national commission was driven to consider the human aspects of the case. . . . Did the union encourage violence against non-union men, or did it really do everything to suppress violence? Did it live up to its creed which was to maintain a standard of living that families might be properly housed and protected from debilitating toil and disease, and that children might be nurtured into American citizenship? Did the operators protect their men as far as possible from mine damp, from length of hours proven by experience to be exhausting? Did they pay a wage to a mine laborer sufficient to allow him to send his children to school? Questions such as these, a study of the human problem, invaded the commission day after day during the sitting. One felt for the moment the first wave of a rising tide of humanitarianism, until the normal ideals of the laborer to secure food and shelter for his family, a security for his own old age, and a larger opportunity for his children became the ideals of democratic government. . . .

Workingmen dream of an industrialism which shall be the hand-maid of a commerce ministering to an increased power of consumption among the producers of the world, binding them together in a genuine internationalism. Existing commerce has long ago reached its international stage, but it has been the result of business aggression and constantly appeals for military defense and for the forcing of new markets. In so far as commerce has rested upon the successful capture of the resources of the workers, it has been a relic of the mediaeval baron issuing forth to seize the merchants' boats as they passed his castle on the Rhine. . . . As its prototype rested upon slavery and vassalage, so this commerce is founded upon a contempt for the worker and believes that he can live on low wages. It assumes that his legitimate wants are the animal ones comprising merely food and shelter and the cost of replacement. The industrialism of which this commerce is a part, exhibits this same contemptuous attitude, but it is more easily extended to immigrants than to any other sort of workmen because they seem further away from a common standard of life. This attitude toward the immigrant simply illustrates once more that it is around the deeply significant idea of the standard of life that our industrial problems of to-day centre. The desire for a higher standard of living in reality forms the base of all the forward movements of the working class. . . .

. . . All that devotion of the trades union for the real issues and trials of life could, of course, easily be turned into a passion for self-government and for the development of the national life if we were really democratic from the modern evolutionary standpoint, and held our town-meetings upon the topics of vital concern.

So long, however, as the Government declines to concern itself with these deeper issues involved in the standard of life and the industrial status of thousands of its citizens, we must lose it. . . .

. . . Unless we subordinate class interests and class feeling to a broader conception of social progress, unless we take pains to come in contact with the surging and diverse peoples who make up the nation, we cannot hope to attain a sane social development. We need rigid enforcement of the existing laws, while at the same time, we frankly admit the inadequacy of these laws, and work without stint for progressive regulations better fitted to the newer issues among which our lot is cast; for, unless the growing conscience is successfully embodied in legal enactment, men lose the habit of turning to the law for guidance and redress.

GROUP MORALITY IN THE LABOR MOVEMENT

[1907]   . . . The earlier struggle of democracy was for its recognition as a possible form of government and the struggle is now on to prove democracy an efficient form of government. So the earlier struggles of trades unions were for mere existence, and the struggle has now passed into one for a recognition of contractual relations and collective bargaining which will make trades unions an effective industrial instrument. It is much less justifiable of course in the later effort than it was in the earlier to carry on the methods of primitive warfare.

This new effort, however, from the very nature of things, is bringing another type of union man into office and is modifying the entire situation. The old-time agitator is no longer useful and a cooler man is needed for collective bargaining. At the same time the employers must put forth a more democratic and a more reasonable type of man if they would bear their side of this new bargaining, so that it has come about quite recently that the first attempts have been made in Chicago towards controlling in the interests of business itself this natural tendency of group morality.

It may offer another example of business and commerce, affording us a larger morality than that which the moralists themselves teach. Certain it is that the industrial problems engendered by the industrial revolutions of the last century, and flung upon this century for solution, can never be solved by class warfare nor yet by ignoring their existence in the optimism of ignorance.

America is only beginning to realize, and has not yet formulated, all the implications of the factory system and of the conditions of living which this well-established system imposes upon the workers. . . . In their attempt to formulate and correct various industrial ills, trades unions are often blamed for what is inherent in the factory system itself and for those evils which can be cured only through a modification of that system. For instance, factory workers in general have for years exhibited a tendency to regulate the output of each worker to a certain amount which they consider a fair day's work. . . . The real trouble, which this "limitation" is an awkward attempt to correct, is involved in the fact that the intricate subdivision of factory work, and the lack of understanding on the part of employees of the finished product, has made an unnatural situation, in which the worker has no normal interest in his work and no direct relation to it. In the various makeshifts on the part of the manufacturer to supply motives which shall take the place of the natural ones so obviously missing, many devices have been resorted to, such as "speeding up" machinery, "setting the pace," and substituting "piece work" for day work. . . . Reaction from such a course is inevitably an uncompromising attempt on the part of the workers to protect themselves from overexertion and to regulate the output. The worst cases I have ever known have occurred in unorganized shops and have been unregulated and unaided by any trades union. The "pace setter" in such a shop is often driven out and treated with the same animosity which the "scab" receives in a union shop.

In the same spirit we blame trades unionists for that disgraceful attitude which they have from time to time taken against the introduction of improved machinery—a small group blindly attempting to defend what they consider their only chance to work. . . .

A society which made some effort to secure an equitable distribution of the leisure and increased ease which new inventions imply would remove the temptations as well as the odium of such action from the men who are blinded by what they consider an infringement of their rights.

If the wonderful inventions of machinery, as they came along during the last century, could have been regarded as in some sense social possessions, the worst evils attending the factory system of production—starvation wages, exhausting hours, unnecessary monotony, child labor, and all the rest of the wretched list—might have been avoided in the interest of society itself. All this would have come about had human welfare been earlier regarded as a legitimate object of social interest.

But no such ethics had been developed in the beginning of this century. Society regarded machinery as the absolute possession of the man who owned it at the moment it became a finished product, quite irrespective of the long line of inventors and workmen who represented its gradual growth and development. Society was, therefore, destined to all the maladjustment which this century has encountered. . . . The possessor of the machine, like the possessor of arms who preceded him, regards it as a legitimate weapon for exploitation. . . .

One of the exhibits in the Paris Exposition of 1900 presented a contrast between a medieval drawing of a castle towering above the hamlets of its protected serfs, and a modern photograph of the same hill covered with a huge factory which overlooked the villages of its dependent workmen. The two pictures of the same hill and of the same plain bore more than a geographic resemblance. This suggestion of modern exploitation would be impossible had we learned the first lessons which an enlarged industrialism might teach us.

Civil Liberties

Introduction by ROGER N. BALDWIN

Director, American Civil Liberties Union, 1917–1950,
National Chairman, 1950–1955

Extracts selected and arranged by

Freda Kirchwey

Years before any organized movement to defend civil liberties existed, indeed before the phrase came into common use, Jane Addams had testified through bitter and dramatic experience to her unfailing devotion to these basic American principles. I doubt if any other American of her time could duplicate even remotely the courageous service she rendered both to public understanding and to the victims of prejudice and hysteria. Her restrained account in these pages does only half-justice to the efforts she exerted against the fury and passions directed against foreign, mainly (then as now) Russian, revolutionists.

Hull-House gave a home to its neighbors without distinction of politics. Among them were anarchists and socialists fresh from their struggles against European tyrants. Chicago in the 1890's and early 1900's was particularly sensitive to foreign radicals; it had not recovered from the shock of the Haymarket bomb explosion of 1887, for which anarchists were executed and for which a governor who had pardoned others was pilloried.

Yet despite violent press misrepresentation, Jane Addams stood stoutly by principle in defense of detested and feared radicals, not out of sympathy but out of compassion. What she exhibited then of courage and humanity, because she could do no other, persisted through all her years. She had no legal formulation of civil liberties, but she obviously accepted the Bill of Rights and the philosophy of free speech and association as basic to democracy. She would not qualify moral principles by distinctions between liberty and license. "Freedom for the thought we hate" was as natural to her as it was to the author of that phrase, Justice Holmes.

When in 1906 as a young man just out of Harvard, running a neighborhood house in St. Louis, I first met Jane Addams, she was a national figure with a reputation for municipal reform in Chicago coupled with an air of controversy over her defense of the rights of aliens and radicals to be fairly heard and justly treated. The incidents she relates in this chapter had been front-page stories, often garbled, calculated to arouse both intense loyalty and passionate opposition.

Civil liberties as such were unknown then, but the struggles of minorities for free speech, press, association, and justice in the courts were daily news items. Yet only a few centers of influence such as Hull-House in Chicago aided the most persecuted among them. Not until the World War did an organized civil liberties movement appear, and then under the auspices of an organization opposed to the war—the American Union Against Militarism, in which I served. Jane Addams was among its earliest supporters as a pacifist, although not formally on its board. Her account of her experiences as a pacifist in the war, related in *Peace and Bread*, is not to be distinguished from civil liberties in principle, for pacifists were denied their rights of speech and expression and suffered ostracism and, in many cases, prosecution and prison.

Miss Addams became thus the defender not only of other people's rights but of her own. Although she describes herself as a middle-of-the-roader striving only for the "best possible," she was forced, as she writes, to the left of the road on the issue of war and peace. I was closely associated with her during the war. She never flinched under the pressures; she aided all of us who sought her counsel. When after the war, in 1920, the American Civil Liberties Union grew out of the wartime Union Against Militarism, Miss Addams was one of the founders as a member of the national committee. Conspicuous at the top of the alphabetical listing, she attracted the attention of that fringe of superpatriots defending the nation from subversives. Her name shortly appeared on a Senate black-list, the first of many to follow. It was taken less seriously in those days; Secretary of War Newton Baker disposed of it by remarking that "the name of Jane Addams lends dignity to any list on which it appears."

Miss Addams served for a decade on the Union's committee, actively sponsoring meetings in Chicago, conferring with colleagues in New York, giving her counsel without caution or criticism, even when some was merited. She was as faithful and active a supporter as the Union had.

But it was in the Women's International League for Peace and Freedom that Jane Addams had the greater opportunity to exert her influence for civil liberties as well as peace, for the League has always coupled civil liberties with its concept of freedom. The League and the Civil Liberties Union have long fought on the same side, and they have had the same opponents—the professional patriots and guardians of the status quo. Miss Addams by moral power rose above her adversaries; if she did not precisely love her enemies, she surrounded them with that tolerance and compassion which are the spiritual foundations of civil liberty.

The struggle for freedom for minorities, for the underdogs, for the unpopular causes and ideas, goes ceaselessly on in democratic societies. What Jane Addams so valiantly fought for is never finally won. Each new generation fights its own battles on the same ground of principle. For the visible future, our country and indeed the world have need of the tolerance, the instant response to injustice, and the unflinching conviction which Jane Addams brought to the conflicts of her times.

ROGER N. BALDWIN

A DECADE OF ECONOMIC DISCUSSION*

[1910]   When Hull-House was established in 1889, the events of the Haymarket riot were already two years old, but during that time Chicago had apparently gone through the first period of repressive measures, and in the winter of 1889-1890, by the advice and with the active participation of its leading citizens, the city had reached the conclusion that the only cure for the acts of anarchy was free speech and an open discussion of the ills of which the opponents of government complained. Great open meetings were held every Sunday evening in the recital hall of the then new auditorium, presided over by such representative citizens as Lyman Gage, and every possible shade of opinion was freely expressed. A man who spoke constantly at these meetings used to be pointed out to the visiting stranger as one who had been involved with the group of convicted anarchists, and who doubtless would have been arrested and tried, but for the accident of his having been in Milwaukee when the explosion occurred. One cannot imagine such meetings being held in Chicago today [1909, when the book was written], nor that such a man should be encouraged to raise his voice in a public assemblage presided over by a leading banker. It is hard to tell just what change has come over our philosophy or over the minds of those citizens who were then convinced that if these conferences had been established earlier, the Haymarket riot and all its sensational results might have been avoided. . . .

A Settlement is above all a place for enthusiasms, a spot to which those who have a passion for the equalization of human joys and

* Further consideration of civil liberties will be found in the section on International Peace, pages 289–310.

opportunities are early attracted. It is this type of mind which is in itself so often obnoxious to the man of conquering business faculty, to whom the practical world of affairs seems so supremely rational that he would never vote to change the type of it even if he could. The man of social enthusiasm is to him an annoyance and an affront. He does not like to hear him talk and considers him *per se* "unsafe." Such a business man would admit, as an abstract proposition, that society is susceptible of modification and would even agree that all human institutions imply progressive development, but at the same time he deeply distrusts those who seek to reform existing conditions. There is a certain common-sense foundation for this distrust, for too often the reformer is the rebel who defies things as they are, because of the restraints which they impose upon his individual desires rather than because of the general defects of the system. When such a rebel poses for a reformer, his shortcomings are heralded to the world, and his downfall is cherished as an awful warning to those who refuse to worship "the god of things as they are."

And yet as I recall the members of this early club [Working People's Social Science Club], even those who talked the most and the least rationally, seem to me to have been particularly kindly and "safe." The most pronounced anarchist among them has long since become a convert to a religious sect, holding Buddhistic tenets which imply little food and a distrust of all action; he has become a wraith of his former self but he still retains his kindly smile.

In the discussion of these themes, Hull-House was of course quite as much under the suspicion of one side as the other. I remember one night when I addressed a club of secularists, which met at the corner of South Halsted and Madison streets, a rough looking man called out: "You are all right now, but, mark my words, when you are subsidized by the millionaires, you will be afraid to talk like this." The defense of free speech was a sensitive point with me, and I quickly replied that while I did not intend to be subsidized by millionaires, neither did I propose to be bullied by working-men, and that I should state my honest opinion without consulting either of them. To my surprise, the audience of radicals broke into applause, and the discussion turned upon the need of resisting tyranny wherever found, if democratic institutions were to endure.

ECHOES OF THE RUSSIAN REVOLUTION

[1910]   The residents of Hull-House have always seen many evidences of the Russian [1905] Revolution; a forlorn family of little children whose parents have been massacred at Kishinev are received and supported by their relatives in our Chicago neighborhood; or a Russian woman, her face streaming with tears of indignation and pity, asks you to look at the scarred back of her sister, a young girl, who has escaped with her life from the whips of the Cossack soldiers; or a studious young woman suddenly disappears from the Hull-House classes because she has returned to Kiev to be near her brother while he is in prison, that she may earn money for the nourishing food which alone will keep him from contracting tuberculosis; or we attend a protest meeting against the newest outrages of the Russian government in which the speeches are interrupted by the groans of those whose sons have been sacrificed and by the hisses of others who cannot repress their indignation. At such moments an American is acutely conscious of our ignorance of this greatest tragedy of modern times, and our indifference to the waste of perhaps the noblest human material among our contemporaries. Certain it is, as the distinguished Russian revolutionists have come to Chicago, they have impressed me, as no one else ever has done, as belonging to that noble company of martyrs who have ever and again poured forth blood that human progress might be advanced. Sometimes these men and women have addressed audiences gathered quite outside the Russian colony and have filled to overflowing Chicago's largest halls with American citizens deeply touched by this message of martyrdom. One significant meeting was addressed by a member of the Russian Duma and by one of Russia's oldest and sanest revolutionists; another by Madame Breshkovsky, who later languished a prisoner in the fortress of St. Peter and St. Paul.

In this wonderful procession of revolutionists, Prince Kropotkin, or, as he prefers to be called, Peter Kropotkin, was doubtless the most distinguished. When he came to America to lecture, he was heard throughout the country with great interest and respect; that he was a guest of Hull-House during his stay in Chicago attracted little attention at the time, but two years later, when the assassination of President McKinley occurred, the visit of this kindly scholar, who had always called himself an "anarchist" and had certainly written fiery tracts in his younger manhood, was made the basis of an attack upon Hull-House by a daily newspaper, which ignored the fact that while Prince Kropotkin had addressed the Chicago Arts and Crafts Society at Hull-House, giving a digest of his remarkable book on "Fields, Factories, and Workshops," he had also spoken at the State Universities of Illinois and Wisconsin and before the leading literary and scientific societies of Chicago. These institutions and societies were not, therefore, called anarchistic. Hull-House had doubtless laid itself open to this attack through an incident connected with the imprisonment of the editor of an anarchistic paper, who was arrested in Chicago immediately after the assassination of President McKinley. In the excitement following the national calamity and the avowal by the assassin of the influence of the anarchistic lecture to which he had listened, arrests were made in Chicago of every one suspected of anarchy, in the belief that a widespread plot would be uncovered. The editor's house was searched for incriminating literature, his wife and daughter taken to a police station, and his son and himself, with several other suspected anarchists, were placed in the disused cells in the basement of the city hall.

It is impossible to overstate the public excitement of the moment and the unfathomable sense of horror with which the community regarded an attack upon the chief executive of the nation, as a crime against government itself which compels an instinctive recoil from all law-abiding citizens. Doubtless both the horror and recoil have their roots deep down in human experience; the earliest forms of government implied a group which offered competent resistance to outsiders, but assuming no protection was necessary between any two of its own members, promptly punished with death the traitor who had assaulted any one within. An anarchistic attack against an official thus furnishes an accredited basis both for unreasoning hatred and for prompt punishment. Both the hatred and the determination to punish reached the highest pitch in Chicago after the assassination of President McKinley, and the group of wretched men detained in the old-fashioned, scarcely habitable cells, had not the least idea of their ultimate fate. They were not allowed to see an attorney and were kept "incommunicado" as their excited friends called it. I had seen the editor and his family only during Prince Kropotkin's stay at Hull-House, when they had come to visit him several times. The editor had impressed me as a quiet, scholarly man, challenging the social order by the philosophic touchstone of Bakunin and of Herbert Spencer, somewhat startled by the radicalism of his fiery young son and much comforted by the German domesticity of his wife and daughter. Perhaps it was but my hysterical symptom of the universal excitement, but it certainly seemed to me more than I could bear when a group of his individualistic friends, who had come to ask for help, said: "You see what becomes of your boasted law; the authorities won't even allow an attorney, nor will they accept bail for these men, against whom nothing can be proved, although the veriest criminals are not denied such a right." Challenged by an anarchist, one is always sensitive for the honor of legally constituted society, and I replied that of course the men could have an attorney, that the assassin himself would eventually be furnished with one, that the fact that a man was an anarchist had nothing to do with his rights before the law! I was met with the retort that that might do for a theory, but that the fact still remained that these men had been absolutely isolated, seeing no one but policemen, who constantly frightened them with tales of public clamor and threatened lynching.

This conversation took place on Saturday night and, as the final police authority rests in the mayor, with a friend who was equally disturbed over the situation, I repaired to his house on Sunday morning to appeal to him in the interest of a law and order that should not yield to panic. We contended that to the anarchist above all men it must be demonstrated that law is impartial and stands the test of every strain. The mayor heard us through with the ready sympathy of the successful politician. He insisted, however, that the men thus far had merely been properly protected against lynching, but that it might now be safe to allow them to see some one;

he would not yet, however, take the responsibility of permitting an attorney, but if I myself chose to see them on the humanitarian errand of an assurance of fair play, he would write me a permit at once. I promptly fell into the trap, if trap it was, and within half an hour was in a corridor in the city hall basement, talking to the distracted editor and surrounded by a cordon of police, who assured me that it was not safe to permit him out of his cell. The editor, who had grown thin and haggard under his suspense, asked immediately as to the whereabouts of his wife and daughter, concerning whom he had heard not a word since he had seen them arrested. Gradually he became composed as he learned, not that his testimony had been believed to the effect that he had never seen the assassin but once, and had then considered him a foolish half-witted creature, but that the most thoroughgoing "dragnet" investigations on the part of the united police of the country had failed to discover a plot and that the public was gradually becoming convinced that the dastardly act was that of a solitary man with no political or social affiliations.

The entire conversation was simple and did not seem to me unlike, in motive or character, interviews I had had with many another forlorn man who had fallen into prison. I had scarce returned to Hull-House, however, before it was filled with reporters, and I at once discovered that whether or not I had helped a brother out of a pit, I had fallen into a deep one myself. A period of sharp public opprobrium followed, traces of which, I suppose, will always remain. And yet in the midst of the letters of protest and accusation which made my mail a horror every morning came a few letters of another sort, one from a federal judge whom I had never seen and another from a distinguished professor in constitutional law, who congratulated me on what they termed a sane attempt to uphold the law in time of panic.

Although one or two ardent young people rushed into print to defend me from the charge of "abetting anarchy," it seemed to me at the time that mere words would not avail. I had felt that the protection of the law itself, extended to the most unpopular citizen, was the only reply to the anarchistic argument, to the effect that this moment of panic revealed the truth of their theory of government, that the custodians of law and order have become the government itself quite as the armed men hired by the medieval guilds to protect them in the peaceful pursuit of their avocations, through sheer possession of arms finally made themselves rulers of the city. At that moment I was firmly convinced that the public could only be convicted of the blindness of its course, when a body of people with a hundred-fold of the moral energy possessed by a Settlement group, should make clear that there is no method by which any community can be guarded against sporadic efforts on the part of half-crazed, discouraged men, save by a sense of mutual rights and securities which will include the veriest outcast. . . .

It seemed to me then that in the millions of words uttered and written at that time, no one adequately urged that public-spirited citizens set themselves the task of patiently discovering how these sporadic acts of violence against government may be understood and averted. We do not know whether they occur among the discouraged and unassimilated immigrants who might be cared for in such a way as enormously to lessen the probability of these acts, or whether they are the result of anarchistic teaching. By hastily concluding that the latter is the sole explanation for them, we make no attempt to heal and cure the situation. Failure to make a proper diagnosis may mean treatment of a disease which does not exist, or it may furthermore mean that the dire malady from which the patient is suffering is permitted to develop unchecked. And yet as the details of the meager life of the President's assassin were disclosed, they were a challenge to the forces for social betterment in American cities. Was it not an indictment to all those whose business it is to interpret and solace the wretched, that a boy should have grown up in an American city so uncared for, so untouched by higher issues, his wounds of life so unhealed by religion that the first talk he ever heard dealing with life's wrongs, although anarchistic and violent, should yet appear to point a way of relief? . . .

The attempt a Settlement makes to interpret American institutions to those who are bewildered concerning them either because of their personal experiences, or because of preconceived theories, would seem to lie in the direct path of its public obligation, and yet it is apparently impossible for the overwrought community to distinguish between the excitement the Settlements are endeavoring to understand and to allay and the attitude of the Settlement itself. At times of public panic, fervid denunciation is held to be the duty of every good citizen, and if a Settlement is convinced that the incident should be used to vindicate the law and does not at the moment give its strength to denunciation, its attitude is at once taken to imply a championship of anarchy itself.

The public mind at such a moment falls into the old medieval confusion—he who feeds or shelters a heretic is upon *prima facie* evidence a heretic himself—he who knows intimately people among whom anarchists arise, is therefore an anarchist. I personally am convinced that anarchy as a philosophy is dying down, not only in Chicago, but everywhere; that their leading organs have discontinued publication, and that their most eminent men in America have deserted them. Even those groups which have continued to meet are dividing, and the major half in almost every instance calls itself socialist-anarchists, an apparent contradiction of terms, whose members insist that the socialistic organization of society must be the next stage of social development and must be gone through with, so to speak, before the ideal state of society can be reached, so nearly begging the question that some orthodox socialists are willing to recognize them. It is certainly true that just because anarchy questions the very foundations of society, the most elemental sense of protection demands that the method of meeting the challenge should be intelligently considered.

Whether or not Hull-House has accomplished anything by its method of meeting such a situation, or at least attempting to treat it in a way which will not destroy confidence in the American institutions so adored by refugees from foreign governmental oppression, it is of course impossible for me to say.

And yet it was in connection with an effort to pursue an intelligent policy in regard to a so-called "foreign anarchist" that Hull-House again became associated with that creed six years later. This again was an echo of the Russian revolution, but in connection with one of its humblest representatives. A young Russian Jew named Averbuch appeared in the early morning at the house of the Chicago chief of police upon an obscure errand. It was a moment of panic everywhere in regard to anarchists because of a recent murder in Denver which had been charged to an Italian anarchist, and the chief of police, assuming that the dark young man standing in his hallway was an anarchist bent upon his assassination, hastily called for help. In a panic born of fear and self-defense, young Averbuch was shot to death. The members of the Russian-Jewish colony on the west side of Chicago were thrown into a state of intense excitement as soon as the nationality of the young man became known. They were filled with dark forebodings from a swift prescience of what it would mean to them were the odium of anarchy rightly or wrongly attached to one of their members. It seemed to the residents of Hull-House most important that every effort should be made to ascertain just what did happen, that every means of securing information should be exhausted before a final opinion should be formed, and this odium fastened upon a colony of law-abiding citizens. The police might be right or wrong in their assertion that the man was an anarchist. It was, to our minds, also most unfortunate that the Chicago police in the determination to uncover an anarchistic plot should have utilized the most drastic methods of search within the Russian-Jewish colony composed of families only too familiar with the methods of the Russian police. Therefore, when the Chicago police ransacked all the printing offices they could locate in the colony, when they raided a restaurant which they regarded as suspicious because it had been supplying food at cost to the unemployed, when they searched through private houses for papers and photographs of revolutionaries, when they seized the library of the Edelstadt group and carried the books, including Shakespeare and Herbert Spencer, to the city hall, when they arrested two friends of young Averbuch and kept them in the police station forty-eight hours, when they mercilessly "sweated" the sister, Olga, that she might be startled into a confession—all these things so poignantly reminded them of Russian methods that indignation, fed both by old memory and bitter disappointment in America, swept over the entire colony. The older men asked whether constitutional rights gave no guarantee against such violent aggression of police power, and the hot-headed younger ones cried out at once that the only way to deal with the police was to defy them, which was true of police the world over. It was said many times that those who are without influence and protection in a strange country fare exactly as hard as do the poor in Europe; that all the talk of guaranteed protection through political institutions is nonsense.

Every Settlement has classes in citizenship in which the principles of American institutions are expounded and of these the community, as a whole, approves. But the Settlements know better than any one else that while these classes and lectures are useful, nothing can possibly give lessons in citizenship so effectively and make so clear the constitutional basis of a self-governing community as the current event itself. The treatment at a given moment of that foreign colony which feels itself outraged and misunderstood, either makes its constitutional rights clear to it, or forever confuses it on the subject.

The only method by which a reasonable and loyal conception of government may be substituted for the one formed upon Russian experiences, is that the actual experience of refugees with government in America shall gradually demonstrate what a very different thing government means here. Such an event as the Averbuch affair affords an unprecedented opportunity to make clear this difference and to demonstrate beyond the possibility of misunderstanding that the guarantee of constitutional rights implies that officialism shall be restrained and guarded at every point, that the official represents, not the will of a small, administrative body, but the will of the entire people, and that methods therefore have been constituted by which official aggression may be restrained. The Averbuch incident gave an opportunity to demonstrate this to that very body of people who need it most; to those who have lived in Russia where autocratic officers represent autocratic power and where government is officialism. It seemed to the residents in the Settlements nearest the Russian-Jewish colony that it was an obvious piece of public spirit to try out all the legal value involved, to insist that American institutions were stout enough not to break down in times of stress and public panic.

The belief of many Russians that the Averbuch incident would be made a prelude to the constant use of the extradition treaty for the sake of terrorizing revolutionists both at home and abroad, received a certain corroboration when an attempt was made in 1908 to extradite a Russian revolutionist named Rudovitz who was living in Chicago. The first hearing before a United States Commissioner gave a verdict favorable to the Russian Government although this was afterwards reversed by the Department of State in Washington. Partly to educate American sentiment, partly to express sympathy with the Russian refugees in their dire need, a series of public meetings was arranged in which the operations of the extradition treaty were discussed by many of us who had spoken at a meeting held in protest against its ratification fifteen years before. It is impossible for any one unacquainted with the Russian colony to realize the consternation produced by this attempted extradition. I acted as treasurer of the fund collected to defray the expenses of halls and printing in the campaign against the policy of extradition and had many opportunities to talk with members of the colony. One old man, tearing his hair and beard as he spoke, declared that all his sons and grandsons might thus be sent back to Russia; in fact, all of the younger men in the colony might be extradited, for every high-spirited young Russian was, in a sense, a revolutionist.

Would it not provoke to ironic laughter that very nemesis which presides over the destinies of nations, if the most autocratic government yet remaining in civilization should succeed in utilizing for its own autocratic methods the youngest and most daring experiment in democratic government which the world has ever seen? Stranger results have followed a course of stupidity and injustice resulting from blindness and panic!

It is certainly true that if the decision of the federal office in Chicago had not been reversed by the Department of State in Washington, the United States government would have been committed to return thousands of spirited young refugees to the punishments of Russian autocracy. . . .

The Settlement has also suffered through its effort to secure open discussion of the methods of the Russian government. During the excitement connected with the visit of Gorki to this country, three different committees of Russians came to Hull-House begging that I would secure a statement in at least one of the Chicago dailies of their own view, that the agents of the Czar had cleverly centered public attention upon Gorki's private life and had fomented a scandal so successfully that the object of Gorki's visit to America had been foiled; he who had known intimately the most wretched of the Czar's subjects, who was best able to sympathetically portray their wretchedness, not only failed to get a hearing before an American audience, but could scarcely find the shelter of a roof. I told two of the Russian committees that it was hopeless to undertake any explanation of the bitter attack until public excitement had somewhat subsided; but one Sunday afternoon when a third committee arrived, I said that I would endeavor to have reprinted in a Chicago daily the few scattered articles written for the magazines which tried to explain the situation, one by the head professor in political economy of a leading university, and others by publicists well informed as to Russian affairs.

I hoped that a cosmopolitan newspaper might feel an obligation to recognize the desire for fair play on the part of thousands of its readers among the Russians, Poles, and Finns, at least to the extent of reproducing these magazine articles under a noncommittal caption. That same Sunday evening in company with one of the residents, I visited a newspaper office only to hear its representative say that my plan was quite out of the question, as the whole subject was what newspaper men called "a sacred cow." He said, however, that he would willingly print an article which I myself should write and sign. I declined this offer with the statement that one who had my opportunities to see the struggles of poor women in securing support for their children, found it impossible to write anything which would however remotely justify the loosening of marriage bonds, even if the defense of Gorki made by the Russian committees was sound. We left the newspaper office somewhat discouraged with what we thought one more unsuccessful effort to procure a hearing for the immigrants.

I had considered the incident closed, when to my horror and surprise several months afterwards it was made the basis of a story with every possible vicious interpretation. One of the Chicago newspapers had been indicted by Mayor Dunne for what he considered an actionable attack upon his appointees to the Chicago School Board of whom I was one, and the incident enlarged and coarsened was submitted as evidence to the Grand Jury in regard to my views and influence. Although the evidence was thrown out, an attempt was again made to revive this story by the managers of Mayor Dunne's second campaign, this time to show how "the protector of the oppressed" was traduced. The incident is related here as an example of the clever use of that old device which throws upon the radical in religion, in education, and in social reform, the odium of encouraging "harlots and sinners" and of defending their doctrines.

DURING AND AFTER THE WORLD WAR

[1930]   Chicago with its diversified population, inevitably displayed many symptoms of an inflamed nationalism, perhaps the most conspicuous [of which] were the deportations and trials of "Reds." Throughout the period of the war we were very anxious that Hull-House should afford such refuge as was legitimate to harassed immigrants. Organizations whose headquarters were constantly being raided brought us their libraries—pitiful little collections of battered books—to keep for them until the war was over. I always said that we would not hide them, but if they wanted to put the books in our open reading room we would be glad to lend them the use of our shelves. There would be an occasional copy of Karl Marx or Bakunin, more often Herbert Spencer, but almost always there were Shakespeare's complete works and a library of American Literature. One Sunday afternoon I received a call from a man from the Secret Service Department, who asked me if I knew that Bulgarian communists were holding a meeting in our largest public hall. I told him that I knew some Bulgarians were having a concert in Bowen Hall—what better could "the alien enemy" do, I queried, than to spend a Sunday afternoon in a decent place listening to good music. He replied that his orders were to arrest the leaders, and he went back to the hall for that purpose. He returned in an hour to say that he couldn't find the leading communists for no one had said a word, and because he was young and perplexed, he asked me what I would do in his place. I replied that I was afraid that I should return to headquarters and resign because I happened to feel very strongly in regard to arresting people without warrants. He answered that it wouldn't be necessary to resign because he "would be fired fast enough." I never heard of his fate but I was thankful that we got through the entire period of the

war and post-war without a single arrest at Hull-House, if only because it gave a certain refuge to those who were surrounded by the
suspicions and animosities inevitably engendered by the war toward
all aliens. . . .

Social progress during the decade from 1919 to 1929 was condi-
tioned at every turn by the fact that we were living in the midst of
post-war psychology and that, which complicated the situation
much more, these years were concurrent with the development of
a revolution in Russia which filled the entire civilized world with a
paralyzing fear. Men were in a panic not only lest orderly methods
of government be broken up by violence but even more lest the
rights of private property be abrogated in other parts of the world
as they had been in Russia.

The situation was analogous to the cold fear which held Europe in
its grip during the three decades following the French Revolution,
from 1789 to 1815. Free-born Englishmen, members of Parliament,
abandoned their advocacy of the abolition of slavery and even the
regulation of the slave trade because any attempt to modify existing
conditions was looked upon as revolutionary and held up as an attack upon religion and upon the family. A brilliant study has been
made of this social psychology by an Oxford man who lost his life
in the World War, in a book entitled, *The French Revolution in
English History*. It remains for an American student to make a
similar study of the Russian revolution in American history. If such
a student turn philosopher he might well point out that as both
religion and the family survived the French revolution—which was
indeed the merest episode in the long history of both—so the institution of private property may survive the Russian revolution.

It was, however, undoubtedly a great detriment to our national
development in the . . . [third] decade of the twentieth century that
our policies were directed so largely by the panic-stricken and by
those who were skeptical of the essential integrity of human nature
itself. Any proposed change was suspect, even those efforts that had
been considered praiseworthy before the war. To advance new
ideas was to be a radical, or even a bolshevik. The nation forgot
that nothing is so dangerous as to prohibit social changes, nothing
so unnatural to the very structure and function of society as to for-
bid its growth and development.

Throughout the decade this fear of change, this tendency to play safe, was registered most conspicuously in the field of politics, but it spread over into other fields as well. There is little doubt that social workers exhibited many symptoms of this panic and with a kind of protective instinct carefully avoided any identification with the phraseology of social reform. . . .

Certainly the courage and conviction of American social workers was put to the test in the effort to secure an amendment to the Constitution, which came to be known as the Child Labor Amendment. . . .

A public discussion of all the issues involved would have been most valuable, but that was impossible because a much easier way was at hand for defeating the Amendment, the very simple expedient of calling it Bolshevistic. The entire subject of child labor was described as

a Trojan horse concealing Bolshevists, Communists, Socialists and all that traitorous and destructive brood. . . . That the pacifist and seditious crew train with them and fraternize with them goes far to support the assertion.

I recall a talk in the course of that campaign to a group of professional men, most of them with a college background, who asked me to state categorically the author of the Child Labor Amendment and the city in which it was written. To my reply that the bill had been drawn by a professor in the University of Pennsylvania, and that he had probably been in Philadelphia when he wrote it although he may have been in Washington in conference with the Child Labor Committee, they asked me whether I could make an affidavit to those statements, otherwise they would have to believe what they had been authoritatively told that the amendment had been written by Trotsky in Moscow. There was no discussion and the arguments for such a constitutional amendment could not be entered into, because all the time was taken talking about this preposterous statement which seemed to them so important. Had the public overlearned its lesson of "being good" during the war because of the severe punishments meted out to him who dared to differ?

A liberal journal has recently stated:

Within a year after the war began the old causes were gone, and we were steadily forced back from our advanced positions—public ownership and enfranchisement of labor, economic freedom, industrial co-operation, and political equality for the black man with the white man, for the alien with the citizen—these were all abandoned like war trenches on the Western Front, and we found ourselves fighting in the last ditch for the primary bases of democratic society, the civil liberties proclaimed in the Declaration of Independence and guaranteed in the Constitution.

Certainly the elementary bases of American liberties were universally challenged by 1920, and in January of that year there was formed a new organization known as the American Civil Liberties Union, "to champion in the highest courts the civil liberty rights of persons and organizations." It was organized to contest in the courts all attempts "to violate the right of free speech, free press and free assembly," adding that it was proposed to "keep the industrial struggles in conformity with the Constitution of the United States and of the several States in the Union." I was a member of its national committee throughout the first decade of its existence. Perhaps of all the wartime organizations, it was most open to attack, partly because it became identified with the people and the associations whose constitutional rights it defended, and partly because it was easy to take definite statements out of their literature which, isolated from their context, had a dangerous sound. The Military Intelligence Association in Chicago, which had no official standing with the Government, but whose name gave the public the impression that it had, never ceased to use membership on the board of the Civil Liberties Union as a grave charge of disloyalty. Year after year they supplied material drawn from the publications of the Union, to whomsoever wished to attack the pacifists. I find a copy of a letter, written by a friend of mine to the *Chicago Tribune*, which explains the situation. It read as follows:

Gentlemen: Relative to the article on Miss Jane Addams which appeared in the issue of January 14th, may I draw attention to the extraordinary method the military gentlemen took to discover her views on world peace; despite the fact that Miss Addams is constantly speaking on international affairs, that she has written several books on the subject and various signed articles in magazines, they proceeded as follows:

They find her a member of the general committee of an organization with headquarters in New York known as the Civil Liberties Union. The president, Rev. Harry Ward, professor in the Union Theological Seminary in that city, has written a pamphlet on free speech in which he discusses the Anglo-Saxon contention that the "overt act" deserves punishment.

The military gentlemen select a paragraph from this pamphlet, take it out of its context, construe it as Miss Addams' sentiments, and upon that basis they denounce her as a red. In order to give this statement color—no pun intended—they refer to the defense fund raised by the Civil Liberties Union some years ago for Wm. Z. Foster and others involved in a raid in Michigan, but say nothing of the later activities of the Union, such as the defense of Mr. Scopes at Dayton, Tennessee, or the still more recent defense of the young colored physician in Detroit, Michigan.

The whole proceeding is so unconvincing, and so like an amateur detective story, that I am quite sure no one of your readers will be able to take it seriously.

Perhaps the crowning absurdity was the offer by Captain Hopkins to Miss Addams that if she would repudiate these statements made by Mr. Harry Ward in New York as to the historic basis of the Anglo-Saxon theory of free speech, that he, Captain Hopkins, "would never mention her again." Whether this was meant as a bribe or a threat, or was an effort to dictate the organizations which Miss Addams is at liberty to join, it is hard to say.

We found the most curious and widespread misunderstanding of the word "internationalism," which was doubtless traceable directly to the connection of the Third Internationale with the Russian regime, although during the summer school of the Women's International League held in Salzburg in 1921 we found that internationalism was considered friendship for the Jews and an attack on Anti-Semitism. In the United States it took me some time to discover why "pacifism" should so often connote bolshevism, until it was gradually made clear that some people believed that the pacifist advocated reducing the armed forces of the country so that when the Bolshevists arrived in America, they should find no resistance. We were slow to understand this elaborate charge and it would have been hard to anticipate an interpretation so complicated and remote.

What I found very difficult in the post-war decade was the habit of the press who divided all the public activities which they reported and any sort of speech which they considered worthy of notice, into the broad divisions of one hundred per cent patriotism or such lack of it that it bordered upon treason. We used to remind ourselves that when the first biological discoveries were published, they were regarded as indecencies, to be put out of sight as much as possible and never discussed in polite society; when the first anthropological discoveries were made the statements were regarded as blasphemy, and it is not impossible to find contemporary minds by which they are still so regarded; when the first efforts were made to open better international relationships between widely separated people, it was perhaps quite natural that such efforts should be regarded as treason.

It is always easy to discredit those who are working out a new line of action, by applying to them opprobious epithets. The situation in regard to the press made everything more difficult. Left over from the war period was the habit of refusal to discuss those subjects which might imperil the morale of the reading public and censorship was accepted as a part of patriotic obligation. England after the war made a vigorous effort to restore freedom of discussion, but in this country no such concerted movement took place.

There is no doubt that the enlightened press might have agreed, even then, with the abstract proposition that it is difficult to give balance to our public opinion or to get the emphasis which each new generation demands unless both sides in a given situation are allowed to express themselves. The press might also have conceded that the only safe way either to maintain or to modify social institutions is by free discussion, yet any attempt at modification of existing institutions or even a restatement of well established beliefs was, throughout this decade, denounced as dangerous and Bolshevistic.

We felt the censorship of the newspaper most sharply when we tried to talk of the League of Nations or the entrance of the United States into the World Court. The attitude toward the League of Nations doubtless arose from the fact that when the plan of the League was brought to the United States the nation was already so inclined to prejudge it, that its practical usefulness to the world was never discussed. Americans are said to be pragmatic in philosophy and inclined to proceed on the theory that a thing is good if it works well. When we discussed the League of Nations, however, we were met with talk about the supreme sovereignty of a nation, the ideals in our early history and other abstractions easily turned into slogans which were not subject to change. The country missed the opportunity of a prolonged public discussion on foreign affairs and our possible relations to them.

In lectures advocating the entrance of the United States into the World Court we encountered everywhere the isolation theory, which seemed the result of a national timidity—a nostalgia for the national nursery—rather than consideration of virile standards of conduct based on the merits of an adult situation. I recall an evening of spirited discussion when a leading citizen said that he would give his last drop of blood to prevent his beloved country from joining any Court to which Russia finally would also adhere. During a series of lectures given at the state universities of the Middle West I could discover in the heat of the opposition and by the very phrases used in the discussion, those towns which habitually read a leading Mid-West newspaper. The opposition was almost always confined to the faculty, the students over and over again coming to my rescue—perhaps they had less time for newspaper reading. It was hard sometimes not to retaliate to quotations taken from our national documents by quoting from the very writers of those documents—Thomas Jefferson's position so often used by Lincoln, "Let America remember that free speech and respect for the opinions of others are measures of safety," or "Error of opinion may be tolerated where reason is left free to combat it," although such quotations would have been considered unpardonable radicalism. When the shades of the founders of the republic were gravely utilized against our entrance into the World Court it was, of course, possible to reply that they were the very men who had devised and made workable an Interstate Court new in the history of jurisprudence; and that the Supreme Court of the United States was more experimental in its day than the World Court is now. . . .

During this decade, 1919 to 1929, which was so dominated by fear-control that many normal activities were prohibited, the W.I.L. [Women's International League] held four international congresses, one in Vienna in 1921, one in Washington in 1924, one in Dublin in 1926, and one in Prague in 1929. The Washington meeting was so difficult that we very much doubted the wisdom of having extended an invitation to hold it in the United States. We found the newspapers, the patriotic societies and the military, making a charge against us of "internationalism," as if that in itself was altogether damaging. The American members of the organization were almost as surprised as our visitors, for we had long assumed that devotion to international aims does not interfere with love of country any more than good citizenship detracts from family devotion; rather, as Mazzini pointed out, the duties of family, nation, and humanity are but concentric circles of one obligation.

Survival of war psychology is an unaccountable thing; it constitutes a new indictment, if one were needed, of the devastating effects of war upon human character. As American citizens we were mortified that our guests, in the moment of landing, felt certain currents of intolerance never before encountered in our international congresses. In my presidential address I begged them not to take the situation too seriously, and assured them that the American delegation did not, for it knew only too well how easily newspaper attacks are manufactured and how ephemeral are the consequences of such attacks. I was able to illustrate this from a recent experience; when in the interests of our league I was in London in 1915, the business portion of that great town was placarded by huge posters, black on a yellow ground, which fairly shouted to the passer-by "To the Tower with Ramsay MacDonald," "The Pacifist to the Tower," etc. These placards had been put up by one Horatio Bottomley, the editor of *John Bull*, who was, as our English delegates knew, at the time of the Washington Congress in jail himself while at the same moment Ramsay MacDonald was prime minister of England. It seemed to prove once more that this old world of ours, which does not always progress, certainly always turns around and that night and day alternate with fair regularity. We feared most of all that the delegates might be frightened by the clamor into holding a dress parade congress, and we urged them to speak from the depths of their own experience, quite sure that they would meet a response from the churches, colleges, cities, and farms of the United States. In fact an entire nation was demanding that war should cease whatever might be true of a handful of people living in the capital where army and navy men, both those who have retired and those in active service, were so vocal in their opposition to peace that our foreign visitors might easily be deceived.

The opposition in Washington was manifested especially in connection with the current propaganda for chemical warfare, a subject on which the W.I.L. Congress had created a special committee. The Major General in charge of the Chemical Warfare Divisions in Washington was at that moment both very enthusiastic over the possibilities of this type of warfare, and confident that the chemical manufacturers would popularize his department throughout the country. He was naturally very much annoyed by this feature of our congress. It was not difficult for him to combine his cause with that of the ladies representing ancestors who fought in the War of 1812. Although the delegates to the congress were received by the President of the United States and had other governmental courtesies extended to them, the Europeans were perplexed to find so much war hysteria in a country which they had idealized as committed to the utterances of President Wilson. . . .

It is hard to give a chronological account of the opposition of the Daughters of the American Revolution and similar bodies to all of the organizations of every sort who were committed to securing better international relations. This opposition extended over a series of years. I had myself belonged to the Daughters because my sister, who was devoted to them, had made me a member in the late 'nineties. I am afraid that I paid little attention to the membership at the time, but when as a juror in social economics at the Paris Exposition in 1900 I was able to secure a grand prix for the D.A.R. exhibit there, they hastened to make me an honorary member. I supposed at the time that it had been for life, but it was apparently only for good behavior, for I am quite sure that during the war I was considered unfit for membership. The D.A.R. with a beautiful building in Washington, and with a certain prestige in governmental circles, persistently published black lists for the information of their members, and they also made use of the famous "Spiderweb Chart." This was a chart giving the names of about fifty persons which were connected by fine black lines—although in a disorder no spider would tolerate—with organizations described variously as "yellow," "pink," "red," and "part red" and "rose colored"; although they were obliged to add a sixth group, marked Congress, to accommodate the four Senators and twelve Congressmen who were on the list. They claimed that:

The world revolutionary movement . . . encouraged by its advancement in Russia, Mexico and other countries, firm in its belief that it can and will destroy the government of the United States by the slow yet certain "poison of liberalism," is working here through every possible agency. It is "boring from within."

The Women's International League they asserted was:

1. One of two hundred organizations operating in a world revolutionary movement; or its members are
2. Dupes of the world revolutionary movement,
3. A factor in a movement to destroy civilization and Christianity and
4. Aiming to destroy the government of the United States.

They sent out a *dossier* against individuals found on the list, which was a curious mixture of truth and fiction, and of sinister interpretations of simple situations. It was a continuation of the same war hysteria which had produced the Lusk report, issued by a committee of the Legislature of New York State; of the attacks made on the floor of Congress upon those who had fostered the Children's Bureau and the Shepard-Towner Bill for maternity care. Mrs. Carrie Chapman Catt, who was not a member of the W.I.L., made a gallant defense of Florence Kelley, as a defender of the rights of children, of Rose Schneiderman, as a labor leader, and of myself as a pacifist, in an able document, "An Open Letter to the D.A.R.," published in the *Woman Citizen* in July, 1927.

The W.I.L. was persistently attacked by the state chairmen of the American Legion, who were anxious to send a full state quota of young men to the summer military camps, and found that it was not always easy to secure the required number. We knew nothing of their difficulties but because the camps seemed unduly to exalt military service for one's country as over against useful forms of civilian service, the W.I.L. promoted a plan for various forms of civilian training in governmental summer camps. We were more easily able to do this because the War Department under whose auspices the military camps were conducted, did not carry them from their own appropriations but secured special funds from Congress. We felt that the Federal government might be asked to appro-

priate similar sums for civilian camps to be conducted by the Department of Agriculture, by the Bureau of Forestry, by the Reclama-
tion Service or by the Coast and Life Guard Service. Because many
boys on the farms who could not leave home in the summer to join
the military camps, were eager for some such training at other times
in the year, the agricultural papers began to promote the idea and
the scheme suddenly appeared very dangerous. The American
Legion denounced the W.I.L. in no uncertain terms for this base
suggestion, and it was made the subject of prolonged attacks by the
official organ of the R.O.T.C. in the colleges and universities. After
a surprising attack upon me by one of the officers in the Illinois
Legion, my friends arranged a great banquet for me in the huge
Furniture Mart in Chicago, in which quite undeserved panegyrics
were delivered, ranging from the kind telegrams from the President
of the United States to the affectionate tributes of my humblest
neighbors. It was undoubtedly a case of the swinging of the
pendulum.

In addition to existing organizations devoted to the war type of
patriotism others were founded as emergency measures in order to
control what were considered dangerous situations. There was a
surprising number of such organizations and they flourished on the
credulity of those still under the influence of war propaganda. A
new one was attempted in Chicago as late as 1927, the American
Citizenship Foundation, to control and supervise speakers at all
church and public forums, lecture courses, women's club meetings,
and so forth. They began by establishing a black list, both of persons
and organizations. The latter in their enthusiasm included the
League of Women Voters and the American Association of University Women. They planned a two million dollar fund to keep the
heretics silent. This hope, however, was never realized in spite of the
heroic efforts of a professional promoter, who began perhaps a
year too late.

Our generation has evolved many new words as occasion demanded them; for scientific discoveries words like electrons, for
new inventions words like radio, and dozens more for new gro-
ceries and automobile parts. We evidently need new words for this
new panic which then seized the public mind. To apply the word
patriotism to it is certainly a misuse of the word which has long

connoted courage and candid loyalty to the highest achievement of which one's country is capable. . . .

The established attitude of the public which having made up its mind for war regarded any symptom of international good will as treason, reappeared in 1929. Rosika Schwimmer, a Hungarian pacifist, closely identified with the W.I.L. in its organization at The Hague in 1915, who was living in the United States, was denied final citizenship papers on the general ground of her reply to the following hypothetical situation: Would she, as a citizen of the United States, nursing a soldier in time of war who might be lying in an unprotected tent, defend him from an enemy training his gun upon him from the tent door, if she had a revolver close at hand? Her reply that she hoped in such a situation that she might have the courage to defend her patient with her own life if necessary, but that she would not shoot the man at the tent door, was deemed unsatisfactory and citizenship was denied. The opinion was reversed by the unanimous decision of the three Appellate Court judges, but was sustained by the Supreme Court of the United States, although with the dissenting opinion by three of the Supreme Court Justices, whose stirring dissent, written by Mr. Justice Holmes, bids fair to become one of the treasured documents in our history.

In that same month a Canadian professor, Doctor MacIntosh, in Yale University, was denied American citizenship because of his unsatisfactory reply to the question, "If necessary, are you willing to take up arms in the defense of this country?" He was a veteran of the World War, but said he would not go to war again unless he approved of the objects for which the war was carried on. The decision of a New Haven judge quite deliberately stated that the religious scruples of the individual must make way for the demands of the State. Another decision by a Federal judge in Richmond, Ind., concerning a Canadian Quaker made this point even clearer. At the moment it would seem that nationalism, growing over bold, was legally claiming the place of religion as Tomlinson's London vicar had predicted in the following words:

My church is done, my God has been dropped again. There is another god now, the State, the State Almighty. I tell you that god will be worse than Moloch. You had better keep that in mind. It has no vision, it has only expediency. It has no morality, only power, and it will have no arts, for it will punish the free spirit with death. It will allow no freedom, only uniformity. . . . You will have to face the truth, you will have to face it. It is nothing but our worst, nothing but the worst of us lifted up.

Was ego-compensation, formerly placed in another world, now being achieved through the identification of the individual with the State? During the months of 1919 which I had spent in war-stricken Europe I had often felt as if the minds of Europeans had been so submerged under a great emotionalism, as if the love of country had for so long a time inhibited family affection and daily interest that people had not yet returned to normal life and perhaps would not be able to return for many years. The spirit of nationalism in 1919 was very unlike what I had seen in Europe during the latter decades of the nineteenth century when it was greatly enriching the literature of the Romantic Period and feeding Wagner's mighty genius with folk-tales and ballads and also reviving dying languages like Gaelic and Czech.

Had the war forced the growth of this beneficent nationalism and given it an exaggerated place in human affairs, fulfilling the prediction of the psychologist that when a single trait is unduly developed, a form of exclusion results? Are the widespread evidences of inhibited conduct and of intimidated opinion due to such exaggerations which only kindly Time in its amplitude will be able to modify?

International Peace

Introduction by **JOHN HAYNES HOLMES**

Minister Emeritus, Community Church, New York City

Extracts selected and arranged by

Emily Cooper Johnson

There was no surprise in Jane Addams. She did precisely what she was expected to do by those who knew and loved her. There was a logic in her life which was as rigorous as it was sublime, a rare consistency that made her career a perfect round.

She lived at one with the slum dwellers of Chicago and the poor everywhere. From her neighbors, who were her friends, she knew the struggles of the disadvantaged. Crusaders for great reforms regarded their ranks as empty without Jane Addams, who, when challenged to join them, never failed to answer "Here!" Her impulse was always to trudge along humbly, quietly, gallantly, eager to do her part, with whatever loss of standing, in a heroic and perhaps desperate battle for the right. We saw this singleness of purpose in her face—anguish and serenity fused to an inward grace of spirit that led outwardly to triumph.

The same was true of her attitude toward the problems of war and peace. People were surprised, many of them shocked, by her refusal to support the Great War, and accused her of abandoning patriotism for pacifism. But Jane Addams was always a pacifist. In the prewar days when arbitration and conciliation represented the furthest extension of the pacifist principle, she joined the conventional peace societies, an act representing her opposition to war as the most monstrous evil of the time. When the war came (1914), she took her place in the ranks of those who supported the Wilson neutrality policy as the one way of restoring peace to a shattered world. But when the President declared war, she stood with the pacifists who initiated active steps to stop the conflict. She had worked for a Conference of Neutrals with Henry Ford, Mme. Schwimmer, and others. She had earlier presided over a great Congress of Women at The Hague, as a result of which she visited heads of government in a number of the capitals of Europe. She was one of the pacifist statesmen who moved in the van of the only effective work for peace in all that dark period, which ended with the unstable truce of 1919.

Meanwhile, as the war dragged on, the dire consequences of poverty, famine, disease, and uprooted peoples began to appear and to challenge the pacifist forces of the world to new and more immediate endeavors. The people of the stricken countries stood in desperate need of food, shelter, healing, compassion. Jane Addams was among the first to see and understand the nature of this problem, and later told the epic tale of what she did in this crisis in her book, *Peace and Bread in Time of War.* She ran the whole gamut of humanity in need. No mass of want so near as to tempt to indifference, no throng of misery so far away as to dim her vision of discernment. The cry, near or far, was enough.

It was interesting to see how Jane Addams, most undramatic of personages, was always getting into the most dramatic situations. One thinks with excitement of her presence in 1912 on the platform of the Progressive Party Convention, when it seemed to many that the millennium had come at last. She appeared before Woodrow Wilson, President of the United States, pleading with him to make peace while there was yet time. With grace, integrity, and unfaltering resolution she faced angry audiences and slanderous attacks. She traveled long journeys to head the international congresses of the Women's International League for Peace and Freedom. The undeflected efforts of a lifetime were at last given worldwide recognition in the award of the Nobel Peace Prize in 1931, shared with Dr. Nicholas Murray Butler.

Thus did Jane Addams bring the age-long dream of peace into the forefront and climax of her career. The logic of her life was as truly the abolition of war as it was the abolition of poverty. "In my long advocacy of peace," she said in 1930, "I had consistently used one line of appeal, contending that peace is no longer an abstract dogma; that a dynamic peace is found in that new internationalism promoted by the men of all nations who are determined upon the abolition of degrading poverty, disease, and ignorance, with their resulting inefficiency and tragedy. I believed that peace was not merely an absence of war but the nurture of human life, and that in time this nurture would do away with war as a natural process."

While poverty, disease, and hunger were upon the earth, Jane Addams could not live apart from those who suffered. While war swept in successive storms over the world, she must be in the forefront of the fight for peace. Another "lady with a lamp," she walked the ways of darkness, and brought light where she trod.

JOHN HAYNES HOLMES

MATURING CONCEPTS OF PEACE

[1904]   There is an old story of a London showman who used to exhibit two skulls of Shakespeare—one skull of him when he was a boy and went poaching, and another when he was a man and wrote plays. It seemed more probable to that showman that two acts of creation should have taken place than that the roistering boy who went poaching should ever have peopled the London stage with all the world.

I should like to confide a secret to this audience; that is, that the human family, as old as it is in its national life, in its national relations, is still a very young roistering boy, that it is still using its poacher's head. . . .

During this Conference many times I have wished that we might induce people to use not the poacher's skull, but that we might bid the international man to move into his grown-up skull; that we might tell him that adventure is not only to be found in going forth into new lands and shooting; that youth and spirit can find other outlets; that we might make clear to him the pleasures that lie in the human city. . . .

If we could only stop thinking of mankind as a poacher, if we could believe that he is no longer quite so young as all that, if we could really make out that the gaiety of nations is not altogether horse-play, then I believe the peace movement would get a swing which would simply astonish us all.

. . . It seems to me that the power of soldiery is impotent if it employs the old-fashioned instruments that have been used for thousands of years. It is easy to kill a man. It is not easy to bring him forward in the paths of civilization. It is easy to have one broad road such as the British have laid out, and to say, "Some people are at this milestone, other people are at that milestone." But we know that civilization is no such thing; that it has no metes and bounds, but that it advances along devious paths. A man has not begun to read history aright, he does not know the very first rudiments of human life, if he imagines that we are all going to march down one narrow road. If we could only convert our men and women, and make them see that war is destructive, that peace is creative, that if a man commit himself to warfare he is committing himself to the played-out thing, and not to the new, vigorous and fine thing along the lines of the highest human development, we should have accomplished very much.

[1907]   . . . A social life to be healthy must be consciously and fully adjusted to the march of social needs, and as we may easily make a mistake by forgetting that enlarged opportunities are ever demanding an enlarged morality, so we will fail in the task of substitution if we do not demand social sympathy in a larger measure and of a quality better adapted to the contemporaneous situation.

Perhaps the one point at which this undertaking is most needed is in regard to our conception of patriotism, which, although as genuine as ever before, is too much dressed in the trappings of the past and continually carries us back to its beginnings in military prowess and defence. To have been able to trace the origin and development of patriotism and then to rest content with that, and to fail to insist that it shall respond to the stimulus of a larger and more varied environment with which we are now confronted, is a confession of weakness; it exhibits lack of moral enterprise and of national vigor. . . .

To seek our patriotism in some age other than our own is to accept a code that is totally inadequate to help us through the problems which current life develops. We continue to found our patriotism upon war and to contrast conquest with nurture, militarism with industrialism, calling the latter passive and inert and the former active and aggressive, without really facing the situation as it exists. We tremble before our own convictions, and are afraid to find newer manifestations of courage and daring lest we thereby lose the virtues bequeathed to us by war. It is a pitiful acknowledgment that we have lost them already and that we shall have to give up the ways of war, if for no other reason than to preserve the finer spirit of courage and detachment which it has engendered and developed.

[1930]   . . . These days of platform building and ratifying [for the Progressive Party, 1912] were not all halcyon. We were, first and foremost, faced with the necessity of selecting from our many righteous principles those that might be advocated at the moment, and deciding which must still wait for a more propitious season. To illustrate from my own experience: For many years I had advocated the cause of international peace and had been a member, sometimes an official, of various international, national, and local peace societies, committed to international arbitration. But, when I sat as a delegate in the convention of the Progressive Party, I voted to adopt a platform, as a whole, which advocated the building of two battleships a year, "pending an international agreement for the limitation of naval forces"—so much we did secure. I confess that I found it very difficult to swallow those two battleships. I knew only too well the outrageous cost of building and maintaining them —that fatal seventy cents out of every dollar of federal taxes which is spent indirectly for war; and I would have liked to see the Progressive Party declare itself against the preposterous unnecessary burden and courageously commit the future to arbitration. It was a serious matter even to appear to desert the cause and the comrades with which I had been for so many years identified. In my long advocacy of peace I had consistently used one line of appeal; contending that peace is no longer an abstract dogma; that a dynamic peace is found in that new internationalism promoted by the men of all nations who are determined upon the abolition of degrading poverty, disease and ignorance, with their resulting inefficiency and tragedy. I believed that peace was not merely an absence of war but the nurture of human life, and that in time this nurture would do away with war as a natural process. . . .

On the whole the plank upon fortifying the Panama Canal was really harder for me to accept than any other one. It seemed as if the wonderful sanitary system and daily regimen which preserved the life and health of the workers who dug the Panama Canal, ought to make it very difficult for the same government to build upon the same spot huge fortifications to threaten with destruction that same sort of human stuff which it had so painstakingly kept alive. In my unavailing arguments against this policy was I perhaps vaguely anticipating the "point" made so short a time later by President Wilson against the fortification of strategic waterways, or was it evident even then that to fortify the canal would make it less "a life artery for the world" than an axis of our naval power. Madariaga wrote in the *Forum* last March after the canal had long been fortified: "the canal has led the United States from intervention to intervention, and from naval base to naval base. It is evident that the Caribbean is fast becoming another Mediterranean."

[1916]   [The] efforts at spiritual adjustment necessitated by the war [1914-1918] are attempted by many people, from the simple souls whose hard-won conceptions of a friendly universe have been brought tumbling about their ears, to the thinking men who are openly disappointed to find civilized nations so irrational. Such efforts are encountered in all the belligerent nations as well as in the neutral ones, although in the former they are often inhibited and overlaid by an overwhelming patriotism. Nevertheless, as I met those women who were bearing their hardships and sorrows so courageously, I often caught a glimpse of an inner struggle, as if two of the most fundamental instincts, the two responsible for our very development as human beings, were at strife with each other. The first is tribal loyalty, such unquestioning acceptance of the tribe's morals and standards that the individual automatically fights when the word comes; the second is woman's deepest instinct, that the child of her body must be made to live.

We are told that the peasants in Flanders, whose fields border upon the very trenches, disconsolately came back to them last Spring and continued to plough the familiar soil, regardless of the rain of shrapnel falling into the fresh furrows; that the wine growers of Champagne last Autumn insistently gathered their ripened grapes, though the bombs of rival armies were exploding in their vineyards; why should it then be surprising that certain women in every country have remained steadfast to their old occupation of nurturing life, that they have tenaciously held to their anxious concern that men should live, through all the contagion and madness of the war fever which is infecting the nations of the earth.

In its various manifestations the struggle in women's souls suggests one of those movements through which, at long historic intervals, the human spirit has apparently led a revolt against itself, as it were, exhibiting a moral abhorrence for certain cherished customs which, up to that time, had been its finest expression. A moral rebellion of this sort was inaugurated three thousand years ago both in Greece and Judea against the old custom of human sacrifice. That a man should slay his own child and stand unmoved as the burning flesh arose to his gods was an act of piety, of courage, and of devotion to ideals, so long as he performed the rite wholeheartedly. But after there had gradually grown up in the minds of men first the suspicion, and then the conviction, that it was unnecessary and impious to offer human flesh as a living sacrifice, courage and piety shifted to the men who refused to conform to this long-established custom. At last both the Greeks and the Jews guarded themselves against the practice of human sacrifice with every possible device. It gradually became utterly abhorrent to all civilized peoples, an outrage against the elemental decencies, a profound disturber of basic human relations. Poets and prophets were moved to call it an abomination; statesmen and teachers denounced it as a hideous barbarism, until now it is so nearly abolished by the entire race that it is no longer found within the borders of civilization and exists to-day only in jungles and hidden savage places.

There are indications that the human consciousness is reaching the same stage of sensitiveness in regard to war as that which has been attained in regard to human sacrifice. In this moment of almost universal warfare there is evinced a widespread moral abhorrence against war, as if its very existence were more than human nature could endure. Citizens of every nation are expressing this moral compunction, which they find in sharp conflict with current conceptions of patriotic duty. It is perhaps inevitable that women should be challenged in regard to it, should be called upon to give it expression in such stirring words as those addressed to them by Romain Rolland, "Cease to be the shadow of man and of his passion of pride and destruction. Have a clear vision of the duty of pity!

Be a living peace in the midst of war—the eternal Antigone refusing to give herself up to hatred and knowing no distinction between her suffering brothers who make war on each other."

This may be a call to women to defend those at the bottom of society who, irrespective of the victory or defeat of any army, are ever oppressed and overburdened. The suffering mothers of the disinherited feel the stirring of the old impulse to protect and cherish their unfortunate children, and women's haunting memories instinctively challenge war as the implacable enemy of their age-long undertaking.

FIRST REACTIONS TO WAR, 1914

[1930]   At Christmas of 1913, less than eight months before the opening of the great war, the peace advocates made a careful summary of what was actually being done to realize the golden prophecy of peace on earth. Such matters were being widely considered that year because a great palace had been opened at The Hague to stand to all the world as a tangible pledge of a well-planned and continuous effort to substitute arbitration for militarism; an effort which was claiming the ever-increasing allegiance of free men.

At a huge meeting in New York, at which Andrew Carnegie's effort was recognized, not only by his fellow countrymen but by peace advocates from many other nations as well, I tried to set forth a new internationalism which I believed was arising from the experiences of humble people—the hewers of wood and the drawers of water, who for the first time in the history of the world had been able to undertake peaceful travel and to live quietly side by side with people of many nationalities. I believed that there was rising in the cosmopolitan centers of America, a sturdy and unprecedented international understanding which in time would be too profound to lend itself to war. . . .

The advocates of peace in those pre-war days were not so foolish as to believe that war had been abolished because a World Court of Conciliation and Arbitration had been established at The Hague in 1899, but we were proud of the fact that the United States was the first of all the nations to use the court; that Colonel Roosevelt as President, had submitted a difference of long standing between the United States and Mexico which was satisfactorily arbitrated; that between the date of its founding and the World War the Hague Court had arbitrated many such cases and had taken care of even more, through conciliation. We believed that war would become less and less frequent, as all the nations in the world formed the habit of taking their difficulties to an international court. . . .

For many reasons, therefore, it was hard to believe in August, 1914, that war had broken out between Germany and France and later to receive the incredible news that England had also declared war. . . .

It is impossible now to reproduce that basic sense of desolation, of suicide, of anachronism, which that first news of the war brought to thousands of men and women who had come to consider war as a throwback in the scientific sense. A finer conception of patriotism had been gradually built up during thousands of years. Europe had had one revolution after another in the struggle for a patriotism in which full loyalty to the state might be compatible with liberty for the individual to obtain fullness of life. In the genuine democracies war and armed revolution were growing obsolete and inadequate, and because these democracies were developing a system of life which could only be carried forward through times of uninterrupted peace, they had become impatient with war. Whenever war is declared, however, patriotism is reduced to the basic appeal of self-defense. Thousands of men march to death because they have been convinced that they must thus serve their country. It is one of the finest instincts of the human spirit but it is unworthy of modern civilization to utilize it at so fearful a cost.

In our first horror against war we made an indictment comparing warfare to human sacrifice. It is most astonishing that the comparison at the moment was received by our audiences as befitting the situation. I recall a woman's club in Boston in September, 1914, which applauded it heartily. . . . It took the human race thousands of years to rid itself of human sacrifice; during many centuries it relapsed again and again in periods of national despair. So have we fallen back into warfare, and perhaps will fall back again and again, until in self-pity, in self-defense, in self-assertion of the right of life,

not as hitherto, a few, but the whole people of the world, will brook
this thing no longer.

[1922]   When the news came to America of the opening hostilities which were the beginning of the European Conflict, the reaction against war, as such, was almost instantaneous throughout
the country. This was most strikingly registered in the newspaper
cartoons and comments which expressed astonishment that such an
archaic institution should be revived in modern Europe. A procession of women led by the daughter of William Lloyd Garrison
walked the streets of New York City in protest against war and the
sentiment thus expressed, if not the march itself, was universally
approved by the press. . . .

The Carnegie Endowment sent several people lecturing through
the country upon the history of the Peace movement and the various
instrumentalities designed to be used in a war crisis such as this.
I lectured in twelve of the leading colleges, where I found the
audiences of young people both large and eager. The questions
which they put were often penetrating, sometimes touching or
wistful, but almost never bellicose or antagonistic. . . .

It was in the early fall of 1914 that a small group of social workers
held the first of a series of meetings at the Henry Street Settlement
in New York, trying to formulate the reaction to war on the part of
those who for many years had devoted their energies to the reduction of devastating poverty. We believed that the endeavor to
nurture human life even in its most humble and least promising
forms had crossed national boundaries; that those who had given
years to its service had become convinced that nothing of social
value can be obtained save through wide-spread public opinion and
the cooperation of all civilized nations. Many members of this group
meeting in the Henry Street Settlement had lived in the cosmopolitan districts of American cities. All of us, through long experience among the immigrants from many nations, were convinced
that a friendly and cooperative relationship was constantly becoming more possible between all peoples. We believed that war, seeking its end through coercion, not only interrupted but fatally
reversed this process of cooperating good will which, if it had a
chance, would eventually include the human family itself. . . .

The heartening effects of these meetings were long felt by many of the social workers as they proceeded in their different ways to do what they could against the rising tide of praise for the use of war technique in the world's affairs. One type of person present at this original conference felt that he must make his protest against war even at the risk of going to jail—in fact two of the men did so testify and took the consequences; another type performed all non-combatant service open to them through the Red Cross and other agencies throughout the years of the war although privately holding to their convictions as best they might; a third, although condemning war in the abstract were convinced of the righteousness of this particular war and that it would end all wars; still others felt, after war was declared in the United States, that they must surrender all private judgment, and abide by the decision of the majority.

I venture to believe, however, that none of the social workers present at that gathering who had been long identified with the poor and the disinherited, actually accepted participation in the war without a great struggle, if only because of the reversal in the whole theory and practice of their daily living.

Several organizations were formed during the next few months, with which we became identified; Miss Wald was the first president of the Union Against Militarism, and I became chairman of what was called the Woman's Peace Party. . . .

The Woman's Peace Party itself was the outcome of a two days' convention held in Washington concluding a series of meetings in different cities addressed by Mrs. Lawrence and Madame Schwimmer. The "call" to the convention was issued by Mrs. Carrie Chapman Catt and myself, and on January 10, 1915, the new organization was launched at a mass meeting of 3000 people. . . .

All of the officers had long been identified with existing Peace organizations, but felt the need of something more active than the older societies promised to afford. The first plank of our platform, the Conference of Neutrals, seemed so important and withal so reasonable, that our officers in the month following the founding of the organization, with Louis Lochner, secretary of the Chicago Peace Society, issued a call to every public organization in the United States whose constitution, so far as we could discover, contained a plank setting forth the obligations of internationalism. . . .

In March, 1915, we received an invitation signed by Dutch, British and Belgian women to an International Congress of Women to be held at The Hague, April 28 to May 1, at which I was asked to preside. The Congress was designed as a protest against war, in which it was hoped women from all nations would join. I had previously met several of the signers at the International Suffrage Conference and elsewhere. I knew them to be women of great courage and ability, and I had long warmly admired Dr. Alletta Jacobs of Amsterdam, whose name led the list.

A delegation of forty-seven women from the United States accepted the invitation, most of them members of the new Woman's Peace Party. All of the delegates were obliged to pay their own expenses, and to trust somewhat confidingly to the usefulness of the venture.

THE WOMEN'S CONGRESS AT THE HAGUE

[1930]   It was in the early spring of . . . 1915, that a group of European women—Dutch, British, German and Belgian—disappointed that the International Suffrage Alliance had felt obliged to abandon its international congress, which was to have been held in 1915, set about arranging an International Congress of Women at The Hague. Women came from twelve countries: Austria, Belgium, Canada, Denmark, Germany, Great Britain, Hungary, Italy, The Netherlands, Norway, Sweden, and the United States. . . .

[1915]   The women who attended the Congress from the warring countries came from home at a moment when the individual, through his own overwhelming patriotism, fairly merges his personal welfare, his convictions, almost his sense of identity, into the national consciousness. It is a precious moment in human experience, almost worth the price of war, but it made the journey of the women leaving home to attend the Congress little short of an act of heroism. Even to appear to differ from those she loves in the hour of their affliction has ever been the supreme test of a woman's conscience.

For the women who came from neutral nations there were also

great difficulties. In the Scandinavian countries women are enfranchised and for long months had been sensitive to the unusual international conditions which might so easily jeopardize the peace of a neutral nation and because in a large Congress an exaggerated word spoken, or reported as spoken, might easily make new complications, they too took risks and made a moral venture.

The fifteen hundred women who came to the Congress in the face of such difficulties must have been impelled by some profound and spiritual forces. During a year when the spirit of internationalism had apparently broken down, they came together to declare the validity of the internationalism which surrounds and completes national life, even as national life itself surrounds and completes family life; to insist that internationalism does not conflict with patriotism on one side any more than family devotion conflicts with it upon the other.

In the shadow of the intolerable knowledge of what war means, revealed so minutely during the previous months, these women also made solemn protest against that of which they knew. The protest may have been feeble, but the world progresses, in the slow and halting manner in which it does progress, only in proportion to the moral energy exerted by the men and women living in it; advance in international affairs, as elsewhere, must be secured by the human will and understanding united for conscious ends. . . .

It was also said at the Congress that the appeals for the organization of the world upon peaceful lines may have been made too exclusively to reason and a sense of justice, that reason is only a part of the human endowment; emotion and deep-set racial impulses must be utilized as well—those primitive human urgings to foster life and to protect the helpless, of which women were the earliest custodians, and even the social and gregarious instincts that we share with the animals themselves. These universal desires must be given opportunities to expand and to have a recognized place in the formal organization of international relations which, up to this moment, have rested so exclusively upon purely legal foundations in spite of the fact that international law is comparatively undeveloped. There is an international commerce, a great system of international finance, and many other fields in which relationships are not yet defined in law, quite as many of our most settled national customs have never been embodied in law at all. It would be impossible to adjudicate certain of the underlying economic and social causes of this war according to existing international law and this might therefore make more feasible the proposition urged by the Women's Congress at The Hague, of a conference of neutral nations composed of men who have had international experience so long and so unconsciously that they have come to think not merely in the terms but in the realities of internationalism and would therefore readily deal with the economic and human element involved in the situation. Such a conference would represent not one country or another, but human experience as it has developed during the last decades in Europe. It would stand not for "peace at any price," but would seriously and painstakingly endeavor to discover the price to be paid for peace, which should if possible be permanent as well as immediate. The neutral nations might well say: "Standing outside, as we do, refusing to judge your cause, because that must be left to the verdict of history, we beg of you to remember that as life is being lived at this moment on this planet of ours, difficult and complicated situations must in the end be decided and adjudicated by the best minds and the finest good will that can be brought to bear upon them. We who are outside of this fury of fighting agree that you have all proven your valor, you have demonstrated the splendor of patriotism and of united action, but we beg of you, in the name of the humane values of life, in the name of those spiritual bonds you once venerated, to allow us to bring in some other method for ending the conflict. We believe that only through help from the outside will this curious spell be broken. Great and wonderful as the war has been in certain aspects, it cannot commend itself to the people of neutral nations who are striving to look at life rationally. It is certainly possible to give powers of negotiation to some body of men who, without guile and without personal or nationalistic ambitions, will bend their best energies to the task of adjudication."

A survey of the situation from the humane and social standpoint would consider for instance the necessity of feeding those people in the southeast portion of Europe who are pitifully underfed when there is a shortage of crops, in relation to the possession of warm-water harbors which would enable Russia to send them her great stores of wheat. Such harbors would be considered not in their political significance, as when the blockade of the Bosphorus during the Tripolis War put a stop to the transport of crops from Odessa to the Mediterranean, not from a point of view of the claims of Russia nor the counterclaims of some other nation, but from the point of view of the needs of Europe. If men of such temper, experience, and understanding of life were to make propositions to the various Governments, not in order to placate the claims of one nation and to balance them against the claims of another, but from the human standpoint, there is little doubt but that the international spirit would again reassert itself and might eventually obtain a hearing. . . .

An organized and formal effort on the part of women would add but one more to that long procession of outstanding witnesses who in each generation have urged juster and more vital international relations between Governments. Each exponent in this long effort to place law above force was called a dreamer and a coward, but each did his utmost to express clearly the truth that was in him, and beyond that human effort cannot go.

This tide of endeavor has probably never been so full as at the present moment. Religious, social, and economic associations, many of them organized since the war began, are making their contributions to the same great end. Several of them are planning to meet at "the Conference of the Powers which shall frame the terms of the peace settlement after this war," and such meetings are not without valuable precedent.

A federation or a council of European powers should not be considered impossible from the very experience of the nations now at war. The German Empire, Consolidated Italy, or the United Kingdom have been evolved from separate states which had previously been at war with each other during centuries; the response to the call of imperialistic England, during the last months, for more troops has shown that patriotic emotion can be extended to include the Boers of South Africa and the natives of India; certain of these great federated states and empires have again formed alliances with each other and are fighting together against a common enemy.

Is it too much to hope that the good will and the consciousness of common aims and responsibilities can be extended to include all the European nations and that devices for international government can be provided, able to deal in the interests of the whole with each difficult situation as it arises? The very experience of this war should demonstrate its feasibility and the analogy inevitably suggests itself that as the states of Germany and Italy came together under the pressure of war, possibly this larger federation may be obtained under the same sense of united effort.

Out of the present situation, which certainly "presents the spectacle of the breakdown of the whole philosophy of nationalism, political, racial, and cultural," may conceivably issue a new birth of internationalism, founded not so much upon arbitration treaties, to be used in time of disturbance, as upon governmental devices designed to protect and enhance the fruitful processes of coöperation in the great experiment of living together in a world become conscious of itself.

[1930]   The congress at The Hague drew up resolutions which embodied many of the propositions afterwards included by President Wilson in his Fourteen Points. Above all, it advocated a plan first proposed by a Canadian woman, Julia Grace Wales, who was on the faculty of the University of Wisconsin and an ardent delegate to The Hague congress. This plan was for a conference of neutral countries without diplomatic, but with scientific functions, to offer continuous mediation, inviting suggestions from all the belligerent nations and submitting to them all, simultaneously, such proposals for peace as should appear most reasonable.

Immediately after The Hague congress, delegates were sent to the governments of all the chief belligerents and neutrals to present this program and urge a calling of a conference of neutrals.

The delegations [to quote from our own report] were received by the governments in fourteen capitals, Berlin, Berne, Budapest, Christiania, Copenhagen, Hague, Havre (Belgian Government), London, Paris, Petrograd, Rome, Stockholm, Vienna, and Washington. . . .

Our visits to the war capitals convinced us that the belligerent Governments would not be opposed to a conference of neutral nations; that while the belligerents have rejected offers of mediation by single neutral nations, and while no belligerent could ask for mediation, the creation of a continuous conference of neutral nations might provide the machinery which would lead to peace. . . .

[1915]   . . . The delegations from the Congress at The Hague visited the ministry of each nation, who of course represent the civil aspect of government as it is carried on year after year when there is no war. In every country, we were received by a committee of women connected officially with the Congress at The Hague, who had arranged that we should speak in public to larger or smaller audiences, and in every country we naturally met the friends of these women, the mothers of men who were at the front, nurses in the hospitals, and many others. We saw Socialists, aghast at the violence resulting to their international views from the war but already beginning to recover from the first impact; groups of Christians or Jews whose conceptions of religious solidarity had been outraged. We came in touch with new types of pacifist organizations, thrown up by the war, taking the place of the old pacifists, who with few exceptions were submerged by the flood-tide of militarism.

I came to believe that there must be many more of the same type in every country, quite as eager for the retention and development of their national ideals and quite as patriotic as the militarists, but believing with all their hearts that militarism cannot establish those causes which are most dear to them, that human nature has been forced into unnatural channels by the war and that their children are being sacrificed for a purpose which can never be obtained through warfare. I do not wish to imply that in any country we found open division between the people. On the contrary we found that the war had united men, women, and children in a common cause and had bound them together in an overwhelming national consciousness.

Our first striking experience was to find that the same causes and reasons for the war were heard everywhere. Each belligerent nation solemnly assured us that it was fighting under the impulse of self-defence, to preserve its traditions and ideals from those who would come in to disturb and destroy them. And in every capital we heard the identical phrases describing the good qualities of the citizens within the country, and very much the same derogatory phrases in regard to the enemy whom they were fighting. On one point only they always differed and that was in regard to the responsibility for the war.

We always found some officials ready to indict the entire situation. I have never heard war indicted with more earnestness than by responsible men in the belligerent nations. Of course they all deprecated the loss of the youth upon whom depended the progress of the nation and the tremendous debts fastened upon the backs of the humble people. On the other hand, they were all of the opinion that this war was inevitable, and in the end would make for progress.

The warring nations presented another point of similarity; from many people whom we met in each of them we were forced to infer that a certain type of young man did not want the war and considered the older men responsible for it, that enthusiasm for the war was not as universal among the young men who were doing the fighting as it was among the elderly men established in the high places of church and state; that it was the older men who had convinced themselves that this was a righteous war which must be fought to a finish; that there were to be found in each nation young men in the trenches convinced that war was not a legitimate method of settling international difficulties.

Doubtless this is but a partial view. I am quite sure that the large majority of young men in the trenches are confident that they are performing the highest possible duty; that the spirit of righteousness is in the hearts of most of them, but I am also convinced that there are to be found these other men who are doing violence to the highest teachings which they know.

It seemed to me at moments as if the difference between the older generation and the new is something we apprehend dimly in each country; that the older men believed more in abstractions, that certain theological or nationalistic words, patriotic phrases included, meant more to them than they did to young men who had come to take life as it was revealed through experience, who were more pragmatic in their philosophy, who were more empirical in their point of view.

Certain young men in England contended that the older men, surviving as a product of the Victorian age, responded to slogans which had not the same meaning in the ears of this generation, that an intense narrow patriotism was one of them; that the older men were nearer to the type that had been ready to fight for religious abstraction, nearer to the age when men lined up in opposing forces to fight out a difference in dogma as to the composition of the Trinity; and that the governmentalists have reared new abstractions. It is this feeling that causes the protest among the young men, who are still asking new experiences, new contacts with other nations, new reactions to the intelligence of other hemispheres. These young men at the outbreak of the war were just beginning to make themselves felt, they were responding to the promptings toward a new order which might in the end have done away with standing armies and camps. At the present moment they feel themselves violently thrown back and bidden play a rôle in a drama of life which they were outgrowing. Such young men have no notion of shirking their duty, of not standing up to the war at their country's demand, but they go into the trenches with a divided mind which is tragic. Tragedy after all is not a conflict between good and evil; tragedy from the time of Æschylus has been the conflict between one good and another, between two kinds of good, so that the mind of the victim is torn as to which he ought to follow, which should possess his entire allegiance. That sort of tragedy, I am sure, is in the minds of certain young men who are fighting upon every side of the great conflict.

Even in their conception of internationalism, the two groups of young men and old men differed widely. The Victorian group, for instance, in their moral romanticism, fostered a sentiment for a far-off "Federation of the World," and believed that the world would be federated when wise men from many nations met together and accomplished it. The young men do not talk much about internationalism, but they live in a world where common experience has in fact become largely internationalized. A young Frenchman, employed in the Parisian office of a large business enterprise, told me that the day war was declared he went out of the door with an Englishman and a German with whom he had been associated for four years. The three men shook hands in front of the locked door and each man went to fight for his country, but the two said to the third: "We hope never to be brought up against you in the line of battle." They had no theory about loving each other, but in point of fact a genuine friendship had transcended national bounds. The men of the older generation have not shared so largely in such experiences which the new internationalism implies, nor in their devotion to abstract ideas are they so open to modification through experience.

The young men therefore, when bidden to go to war on a purely national issue, have a tendency to question whether that which they are doing is useful and justifiable and are inclined to more or less test it out. Such testing is indeed in line with their philosophy, for while empirically grounded truths do not inspire such violent loyalty as *a priori* truths, they "are more discussable and have a human and social quality," we are told.

This notion that the old gulf between fathers and sons is once more yawning wide in Europe may be a superficial one, but I am at least recording the impression we received in one country after the other. Doubtless at the beginning of the war, the young men even more enthusiastically than the old were caught up into that consciousness of a strong and united nation which has carried its citizens to heights of self-sacrifice which human nature seldom attains, and they all responded to that primitive ethic founded upon obedience to group sentiment and the need of race safety which so completely asserted its sway over that more highly developed ethic supposed to be the possession of the civilized world. But just as there is a gradual return on the part of the Socialists, for instance, to those doctrines of internationalism and peace which they have preached for half a century, so thousands of other citizens are going back to the moral positions they held before the war. The young are perhaps the most eager to make clear their changing position; they continue to salute the flag, but recognize it as a symbol and realize that it has the danger of all abstractions, that a wrong content may be substituted for the right one, and that men in a nation, an army, a crowd may do things horrible as well as heroic that they could never do alone.

The older men have no conception of the extent to which the purely nationalistic appeal has been weakened. They themselves say that this war with its sturdy nationalistic ideals and ambitions shows what nonsense all the talk of internationalism has been and how absurd were the Hague Conferences, although in the very same speech I heard an Englishman say also that Great Britain went into war to protest against the illegal and unjustifiable invasion of Belgium because solemn international treaties had been broken, admitting that international obligations are so genuine that blood must be spilled to preserve them.

The young men on the contrary speak with no uncertain sound.

We met one young German who said: "I happen to live near the line of Schleswig-Holstein. I am told the men of Schleswig-Holstein are my brothers, but my grandfather before me fought them. I do not know whether they are my brothers or my grandfather's enemies; I only know I have no feeling for them different from that I have for men living farther north in Denmark itself. The truth is that neither to my grandfather nor to me do the people of Schleswig-Holstein mean anything; that he hated them and that I love them are both fictions, invented and fostered for their own purposes by the people who have an interest in war." The man who said this was a fine young fellow who had been wounded and sent home to be cured; in those solemn days he was trying to think the thing out and he asked himself what it was he was doing with this life of his. What impresses one in regard to these young men is that it is so desperately irrevocable, that it is their very lives which are demanded. The older men who have had honor and fulness of life and have been put into high places in the state, who are they to deprive even one of these young men of that which should lie before him? . . .

We met a young man in Switzerland who had been in the trenches for three months and had been wounded there. He did not know that he had developed tuberculosis but he thought he was being cured, and he was speaking his mind before he went back to the trenches. He was, I suppose, what one would call a fine young man, but not an exceptional one. He had been in business with his father and had travelled in South Africa, in France, England, and Holland. He had come to know men as *Mensch,* that *gute Menschen* were to be found in every land. And now here he was, at twenty-eight, facing death because he was quite sure when he went back to the trenches that death awaited him. He said that never during that three months and a half had he once shot his gun in a way that could possibly hit another man and nothing in the world could make him kill another man. He could be ordered into the trenches and "to go through the motions," but the final act was in his own hands and with his own conscience. And he said: "*My* brother is an officer." He gave the name and rank of his brother, for he was quite too near the issues of life and death for any shifting and concealing. "He never shoots in a way that will kill. And I know dozens and dozens of young men who do not."

We talked with nurses in hospitals, with convalescent soldiers, with mothers of those who had been at home on furlough and had gone back into the trenches, and we learned that there are surprising numbers of young men who will not do any fatal shooting because they think that no one has the right to command them to take human life. From one hospital we heard of five soldiers who had been cured and were ready to be sent back to the trenches, when they committed suicide, not because they were afraid to die but they would not be put into a position where they would have to kill others.

I recall a spirited young man who said: "We are told that we are fighting for civilization but I tell you that war destroys civilization. The highest product of the universities, the scholar, the philosopher, the poet, when he is in the trenches, when he spends his days and nights in squalor and brutality and horror, is as low and brutal as the rudest peasant. They say, those newspaper writers, that it is wonderful to see the courage of the men in the trenches, singing, joking, playing cards, while the shells fall around them. Courage there is no room for, just as there is no room for cowardice. One cannot rush to meet the enemy, one cannot even see him. The shells fall here or they fall there. If you are brave, you cannot defy them; if you are a coward, you cannot flee from them; it is all chance. You see the man you were playing cards with a while ago lying on the ground a bloody mass and you look at him and think, 'Well, this time it took him; in a few minutes it may be my turn; let's go back to the cards.' And all the time you loathe the squalor, the brutality, the savages around you, and the savage you are yourself becoming. Why should you kill men who live in other countries, men whom in times of peace you would like and respect? At least I can say that as yet I have escaped the horror of killing any one."

It is such a state of mind which is responsible for the high percentage of insanity among the soldiers. In the trains for the wounded there is often a closed van in which are kept the men who have lost their minds. Sometimes they recover after due care, and sometimes they prove to be hopelessly insane. A young Russian wrote home: "Men have fought from the beginning of history, yet no one has ever recorded that so many soldiers lost their minds, were driven mad by war. Do you suppose it was true always, or is it only true in this generation?"

In every country we heard of the loathing against the use of the bayonet felt by this type of young man to whom primitive warfare was especially abhorrent, although he was a brave soldier and serving his country with all his heart. We heard from interned soldiers in Holland that they had escaped across the border dazed and crazed after a bayonet charge; from hospital nurses who said that delirious soldiers are again and again possessed by the same hallucination—that they are in the act of pulling their bayonets out of the bodies of men they have killed; from the returned soldiers one of whom said to us: "A bayonet charge does not show courage, but madness. Men must be brought to the point by stimulants and once the charge is begun they are like insane men. I have been in it and after it was over I was utterly dazed. I did not know what had happened to me any more than if I had been picked up from the water after an explosion on shipboard." . . .

In addition to the revolt against war on the part of the young men, there was discernible everywhere among the civilian population two bodies of enthusiasm: one, and by far the larger, believes that the war can be settled only upon a military basis after a series of smashing victories; the other, a civil party, very much deprecates the exaltation of militarism and contends that the longer the war is carried on, the longer the military continues censoring the press and exercising other powers not ordinarily accorded to it—thus breaking down safeguards of civil government, many of which have been won at the hardest—the more difficult it will be for normal civil life to reëstablish itself.

Many of the people whom we met were therefore anxious that the war should be speedily terminated—of course always a peace with honor—if only because of its effect upon the internal development of national life. They believed in the war and yet they labored under a certain apprehension that the longer it was continued the more difficult it would be for the civil authorities to win back the liberties they had once possessed. In the warring capitals, citizens are under military law and are subject to fine and imprisonment, or both, for its infraction. The military authorities can, on mere suspicion, arrest a citizen without warrant and also enter his house. Such "defence of the realm" acts are submitted to patiently as a part of war, but the people who represent the civil view of life, even in the midst of their patriotic fervor and devotion to the army, long for some other form of settlement than that obtained by military victory. While they ardently desire a release from the intolerable strain, they realize that to have salvation come through the army would be to desperately entrench militarism and to add dangerously to its prestige and glory.

In Germany we met patriotic citizens who felt that one of the dangers of a peace determined through military successes, especially if those were won on the eastern front, would be the likelihood that terms would be made through Russia, establishing militarism yet more firmly. If peace were made through negotiations, then the western nations under England's lead would have the preponderance of influence; that is, the military authorities would be more sympathetic to the Russian type of settlement and the civil authorities to the western type. The longer the war goes on, however, the more likely it is that the settlement will depend upon the victories of one nation or the other.

We were told in England that this war in essence is a conflict between militarism and democracy, but the situation is obviously not so simple as that. War itself destroys democracy wherever it thrives and tends to entrench militarism. If the object of the war is to down militarism, it must be clear that the very prolongation of the war entrenches the military ideal not only in Russia and Germany, but in the more democratic nations as well. No one would urge that a settlement through negotiations is the only way to preserve democratic institutions, but certainly the present method runs great risk. The immediacy of negotiations is therefore a factor in the situation. They should be begun while the civil authorities still have enough power to hold the military to their own purposes and are not obliged to give them the absolute control of the destinies of the nation. If you point out to an Englishman that democracy will not gain if German militarism is crushed and a new war party sits in every capital of Europe, he will tell you that such a situation, if it arises, must be attended to afterwards, that at present the allies are crushing the Prussian type of militarism. It seems clear however to the neutral observer that in the meantime, while the crushing process goes on, militarism is firmly lodged in men's minds and that no body of men is seriously trying to discover how far militarism is being crushed by this war or how far civil forces are merely becoming exhausted and methods of negotiation discredited.

The belief that the restitution of Belgium can only be obtained through "driving out the invaders" by an opposing army has already become established in the minds of thousands of people. Yet we met, during our weeks in Europe, many exiled Belgians, who told us they could not go back to their own country because of the fear that the Germans would be beaten back over the same territory that had already been devastated and that a retreating army is always the worst. Some of these Belgians hoped that Belgium would be evacuated through negotiations and treaties, and yet so completely has method become confused with aim in this war, militarism with the object to be accomplished, that in the desire to drive the invaders out, the aim of getting the peaceful Belgians back in their own country was for the moment overshadowed, although to accomplish this through negotiation rather than bloodshed would be an enormous gain for all concerned. There are civilians in Germany who are anxious to hold the German generals to their own statement that they marched through Belgium as a matter of military necessity and not for conquest, and early in July a petition, signed by eighty-four leading men of Germany, was presented to the Chancellor, urging that there be no annexation of territory as a result of the war.

If the Germans are to evacuate Belgium without bloodshed, it must be through the coöperation of such groups of civilians as these. It is the civilian who is interested in freeing the channels of trade, in breaking down unnatural tariff walls, and restoring life to a normal basis.

Yet so long as the military process absorbs the attention of all of Europe, it is obvious that groups of civilians in different countries are constantly becoming so enfeebled that their counsels may easily be overborne.

Everywhere we were conscious of a certain revolt, not of nationalistic feeling nor of patriotism, but of human nature itself as of hedged in, harassed peoples, "as if the Atlantic Ocean had been partitioned with great bulkheads into private seas and the Gulf Stream blocked in its course." There had apparently been an accumulation within national borders of those higher human affections which should have had an outlet into the larger life of the world but could not, because no international devices had been provided for such expression. No great central authority had been dealing with this sum of human goodwill, as a scientists deals with the body of knowledge in his subject irrespective of its national origins, and the nations themselves became confused between what was legitimate patriotism and those universal emotions which have nothing to do with national frontiers.

THE FORD SHIP AND THE CONFERENCE OF NEUTRALS

[1922]   In the fall of 1915, after we had written our so-called "Manifesto," a meeting of the Woman's Peace Party was called in New York City, at which we were obliged to make the discouraging report that, in spite of the fact that the accredited officials of the leading belligerent nations, namely, Great Britain, France, Russia, Belgium, Italy, Germany, Austria and Hungary, had expressed a willingness to coöperate in a Neutral Conference, and while the neutral nations, Norway, Sweden, Denmark, and Holland had been eager to participate in the proposed conference if it could be called by the United States, our own country was most reluctant. . . .

We seemed to have come to an impasse therefore, so far as calling a conference of neutrals was concerned unless we could bring to bear a tremendous pressure of public opinion upon the officials in Washington. . . .

At this time an unexpected development gave the conference of neutrals only too much publicity and produced a season of great hilarity for the newspaper men of two continents. Madame Rosika Schwimmer, who still remained in the United States, had lectured in Detroit where she had been introduced to Mr. Henry Ford. For many months Mr. Ford had maintained a personal representative in Washington to keep him informed of possible openings for making peace with the understanding that such efforts "should not be mere talk nor education." During a long interview which Madame Schwimmer held with Mr. Ford and his wife, he expressed his willingness to finance the plan of a neutral conference and promised to meet her in New York in regard to it. He arrived in New York the very day the conference of the Woman's Peace Party adjourned and he met with a small committee the same evening. Up to that moment all our efforts had been bent towards securing a conference supported by neutral governments who should send representatives to the body; but as it gradually became clear that the governments would not act, we hoped that a sum large enough to defray all the general expenses of such a conference might initiate it as a private enterprise. . . .

Our hopes were high that evening in New York as we talked over the possible men and a few women from the Scandinavian countries, from Holland and Switzerland, who possessed the international mind and might lend themselves to the plan of a neutral conference. We were quite worldly enough to see that we should have to begin with some well-known Americans, but we were confident that at least a half dozen of them with whom we had already discussed the plan, would be ready to go. Mr. Ford took a night train to Washington to meet an appointment with President Wilson, perhaps still hoping that the plan might receive some governmental sanction and at least wishing to be assured that, as a private enterprise, it would not embarrass the government.

During the day, as I went about New York in the interest of other affairs and as yet saying nothing of the new plan, it seemed to me that perhaps it was in character that the effort from the United States should be initiated not by the government but by a self-made business man who approached the situation from a purely human point of view, almost as a working man would have done. On the evening after his return from Washington Mr. Ford reported that the President had declared him quite within his rights in financing a neutral conference and had wished all success to the enterprise. . . .

Almost immediately upon my return to Chicago, ten days before the *Oscar II* sailed, the newspaper accounts from New York began to be most disquieting. We had not expected any actual coöperation from the newspapers, but making all allowances for that, the enterprise seemed to be exhibiting unfortunate aspects. The conference itself was seldom mentioned, but the journey and the ship were made all important and mysterious people with whom Madame

Schwimmer was said to be in communication, were constantly featured. The day when Mr. Ford's slogan "Get the Boys out of the trenches by Christmas" was spread all over the front pages of the dailies I spent large sums of money telephoning to the secretary in New York begging him to keep to the enterprise in hand, which I reminded him was the conference of neutrals. Having so recently traveled in Europe under wartime regulations, I knew that such propaganda would be considered treasonable and put the enterprise in a very dangerous position. Mr. Lochner reminded me of Mr. Ford's well-known belief that direct appeal to "the boys" was worth much more than the roundabout educational methods we were advocating. Almost simultaneously with this untoward development the secretary received the resignations of three leading internationalists who had seriously considered going, and of two others who had but recently accepted. They had all been convinced of the possible usefulness of a conference of neutrals, at least to the extent of giving "continuous mediation" a trial, but they had become absolutely disconcerted by the extraneous developments of the enterprise. On the other hand, the people in New York in charge of the enterprise believed that the anti-war movement throughout its history had been too quietistic and much too grey and negative; that the heroic aspect of life had been too completely handed over to war, leaving pacifists under the suspicion that they cared for safety first and cherished survival above all else; that a demonstration was needed, even a spectacular one to show that ardor and comradeship were exhibited by the non-militarists as well; in fact, it was the pacifists who believed that life itself was so glorious an adventure that the youth of one nation had no right to deprive the youth of another nation of their share in it; that living itself, which all youth had in common, was larger and more inclusive than the nationalistic differences so unfairly stressed by their elders. . . .

What my interpretation of the enterprise would have been, had I become part of it, is of course impossible to state, for on the eve of leaving home, a serious malady which had pursued me from childhood reappeared and I was lying in a hospital bed in Chicago not only during the voyage of the *Oscar II,* but during the following weeks when the Neutral Conference was actually established in Stockholm. . . .

Difficulties developed during the journey; Mr. Ford left a few days after the group arrived in Norway, in the midst of journalistic misrepresentations, and Madame Schwimmer resigned from the Conference, during the early months of its existence. But in spite of disasters the Neutral Conference was finally set up at Stockholm, on January 26, 1916, after the Burgomaster of the city had introduced an interpellation in the Rikstag, of which he was a member, asking the Swedish Government to define its attitude on neutral mediation.

Gradually the personnel was completed by five representatives each from Denmark, Holland, Norway, Sweden and Switzerland, with three from the United States. Among the Europeans were Professors of International Law, of Economics, of Philosophy, the legal advisor to the Nobel Institute, men and women who were officers of National Peace Societies, members of Parliament and city officials. They first issued a carefully considered appeal addressed "To the Governments and Parliaments of the Neutral Nations represented at the second Hague Conference" begging them to offer official mediation, and quoting from The Hague Conventions to show that such an offer could not be construed as an unfriendly act.

This appeal was given general publicity by the European Press, even in the belligerent countries, and at least served to draw attention once more to the fact that a continuation of the war was not necessarily inevitable. Resolutions based on the appeal were considered by three National Parliaments, and the appeal itself was discussed at a formal meeting of the Prime Ministers of the three Scandinavian countries.

At Easter, 1916, the Conference issued an appeal to "The Governments, Parliaments and people of Belligerent Nations." This was the result of much study, and was founded upon an intelligent effort to obtain the various nationalistic points of view. An enormous correspondence on the subject had taken place, and representatives of many nationalities had appeared before the Conference; these ranged from the accredited governmental officials to the Esthonian peasant who came on skiis, many miles over the ice and snow, crossing the frontier at the risk of his life, not daring even to tell his name, and wishing the bare fact of his appearance to be suppressed, until he should have had time to return to his own country. He added one more to the tragic petitions, received from all parts of Europe. This official appeal to the belligerent nations, foreshadowing the famous Fourteen Points, was also widely published.

The Conference of Neutrals, reorganized into an International Commission devoted to promoting the public opinion necessary for a lasting peace whenever the governments should be ready to act, had much to do with stimulating general meetings held in all the neutral countries on Hague Day, May 18th, and again on the second anniversary of the war in August. George Brandes of Denmark, wrote a stirring appeal for Peace, as did the poets and writers of various countries, including Ellen Key and Selma Lagerlöf. For the moment a demand for the cessation of the war became vocal, at least in those countries where such demands were not officially suppressed.

Because the beginning of actual mediation, founded upon visits between citizens from the belligerent nations with those from the neutral, must of necessity be conducted quietly, the Conference finally left two of its members in each of the five neutral countries, with its headquarters at The Hague, where the two delegates from the United States were established.

When Louis Lochner came back to the United States in October, 1916, he was able to give an enthusiastic report. He arrived in the midst of the "he kept us out of war" Presidential campaign. The Democratic Party in the very convention which re-nominated President Wilson and drew the Party Platform, had endorsed a League of Nations policy. Mr. Lochner reported that even the Germans were ready for international disarmament, and that the question on everybody's lips was "how soon will Wilson act?" We were sure that Mr. Wilson would act in his own best way, and were most anxious not to take the attitude towards him by which the Abolitionist so constantly embarrassed President Lincoln during the Civil War.

Mr. Ford at that time was guaranteeing to the Conference a steady income of ten thousand dollars a month, the first difficulties had subsided and the movement was constantly gaining prestige, the Norway delegation, for instance, then consisting of Christian Lange, general secretary of the Interparliamentary Union, Dr. Horgenstierne, president of the University of Christiania, and Haakon Loeken, state's attorney for Christiania. This personnel was not unlike that of the other countries.

On December 10, 1916, President Wilson issued his famous Peace Note, and it seemed as if at last the world were breathing another air. For the time being the pacifists were almost popular, or at least felt a momentary lift of the curious strain which inevitably comes to him who finds himself differing with every one about him.

In January of 1917, Mr. Lochner returned again to the United States in company with the man who had been engaged in negotiations with Great Britain, and saw the President twice. I was ill and confined to my room at this time. But in a long conversation which I had with Mr. Lochner in Chicago, as he reported recent interviews with Mr. Ford and his secretaries, it was evident that the benefactor of the Neutral Conference was reflecting the change in public opinion, and like many another pacifist, who does not believe in war as such, was nevertheless making an exception of "this war." In February Mr. Ford's changed position was unmistakable. He announced that he would give no more support to the European undertaking after March first, and he withdrew from the Neutral Conference plan almost as abruptly as he had entered it.

Thus came to an end all our hopes for a Conference of Neutrals devoted to continuous mediation. Our women's organizations as such had had nothing to do with the "Ford Ship," but of course we had assiduously urged the Conference which it was designed to serve, and our members in many countries had promoted the de facto Conference. Certainly no one could justly charge us with "passivity" in our efforts to secure it. . . .

As the Great War incredibly continued year after year, as the entrance of one nation after another increased the number of young combatants, as the war propaganda grew ever more bitter and irrational, there were moments when we were actually grateful for every kind of effort we had made. At such times, the consciousness of social opprobrium, of having become an easy mark for the cheapest comment, even the sense of frustration were, I am certain, easier to bear than would have been the consciousness that in our fear of sensationalism we had left one stone unturned to secure the

Conference of Neutrals which seemed at least to us a possible agency for shortening the conflict.

PRESIDENT WILSON'S EARLY POLICIES

[1922]   Pacifists believed that in the Europe of 1914, certain tendencies were steadily pushing towards large changes which in the end made war, because the system of peace had no way of effecting those changes without war, no adequate international organization which could cope with the situation. The conception of peace founded upon the balance of power or the undisturbed *status quo*, was so negative that frustrated national impulses and suppressed vital forces led to war, because no method of orderly expression had been devised.

The world was bent on a change, for it knew that the real denial and surrender of life is not physical death but acquiescence in hampered conditions and unsolved problems. Agreeing substantially with this analysis of the causes of the war, we pacifists, so far from passively wishing nothing to be done, contended on the contrary that this world crisis should be utilized for the creation of an international government able to make the necessary political and economic changes which were due; we felt that it was unspeakably stupid that the nations should fail to create an international organization through which each one, without danger to itself, might recognize and even encourage the impulse toward growth in other nations.

In spite of many assertions to the contrary, we were not advocating the mid-Victorian idea that good men from every country meet together at The Hague or elsewhere, there to pass a resolution that "wars hereby cease" and that "the world hereby be federated." What we insisted upon was that the world could be organized politically by its statesmen as it had been already organized into an international fiscal system by its bankers. We asked why the problem of building a railroad to Bagdad, of securing corridors to the sea for a land-locked nation, or warm water harbors for Russia, should result in war. Surely the minds of this generation were capable of solving such problems as the minds of other generations had solved their difficult problems. Was it not obvious that such situations transcended national boundaries and must be approached in a spirit of world adjustment, that they could not be peacefully adjusted while men's minds were still held apart by national suspicions and rivalries.

The pacifists hoped that the United States might perform a much needed service in the international field, by demonstrating that the same principles of federation and of an interstate tribunal might be extended among widely separated nations, as they had already been established between our own contiguous states. Founded upon the great historical experiment of the United States, it seemed to us that American patriotism might rise to a supreme effort because her own experience for more than a century had so thoroughly committed her to federation and to peaceful adjudication as matters of every-day government. The President's speech before the Senate embodied such a masterly restatement of early American principles that thousands of his fellow citizens dedicated themselves anew to finding a method for applying them in the wider and more difficult field of international relationships. We were stirred to enthusiasm by certain indications that President Wilson was preparing for this difficult piece of American strategy. . . .

. . . Pacifists in every part of the world were not only enormously reassured but were sent up into the very heaven of internationalism, as it were, when President Wilson delivered his famous speech to the Senate in January, 1917, which forecast his Fourteen Points. Some of these points had, of course, become common property among Liberals since the first year of the war when they had been formulated by The League of Democratic Control in England and later became known as a "union" program. Our Women's International Congress held at The Hague in May, 1915, had incorporated most of the English formula and had added others. The President himself had been kind enough to say when I presented our Hague program to him in August, 1915, that they were the best formulation he had seen up to that time.

President Wilson, however, later not only gathered together the best liberal statements yet made, formulated them in his incomparable English and added others of his own, but he was the first responsible statesman to enunciate them as an actual program for guidance in a troubled world. Among the thousands of congratu-latory telegrams received by the President at that time none could have been more enthusiastic than those sent officially and personally by the members of our little group. We considered that the United States was committed not only to using its vast neutral power to extend democracy throughout the world, but also to the conviction that democratic ends could not be attained through the technique of war. In short, we believed that rational thinking and reasonable human relationships were once more publicly recognized as valid in international affairs.

If, after the declaration of his foreign policy, it seemed to our group that desire and achievement were united in one able pro-tagonist, the philosopher become king, so to speak, this state of mind was destined to be short lived, for almost immediately the persistent tendency of the President to divorce his theory from the actual con-duct of state affairs threw us into a state of absolute bewilderment. During a speaking tour in January, 1917, he called attention to the need of a greater army, and in St. Louis openly declared that the United States should have the biggest navy in the world. . . .

. . . What might have happened if President Wilson could have said in January, 1919, what he had said in January, 1917,—"A victor's terms imposed upon the vanquished . . . would leave a sting, a resentment, a bitter memory upon which terms of peace would rest not permanently but only as upon quicksand," or again, "The right state of mind, the right feeling between nations, is as necessary for a lasting peace as is the just settlement of vexed questions of territory, or of racial and national allegiance." At that very moment the wind of idealism was blowing strongly across Europe, there were exaggerated hopes of a new and better world from which war should be forever banished. Europe distrusted any compromise with a monster which had already devoured her young men and all but destroyed her civilization. A man who had stood firmly against participation in war could have had his way with the common people in every country. The President became the center of the world's hopes because of the things he had said against war, and because people believed that he expressed their own abhorrence. Did the League of Nations fail to win their hearts not because it was too idealistic or too pacifistic but because it permitted war in too many instances, because its very structure and functioning is pervaded by the war spirit, the victorious disciplining the defeated, whereas the people had dreamed of a League of Peace lifting up all those who had been the victims of militarism? . . .

. . . Certainly international affairs have been profoundly modified by President Wilson's magnificent contribution. From one aspect of the situation he did obtain his end; to urge "open covenants, openly arrived at" as a basic necessity for a successful society of nations, cuts at the root of a prolific cause for war by simply turning on the light. But the man who would successfully insist upon such a course of procedure in actual negotiations is not only he who sees the situation but he who is bent upon the attainment of a beloved object, whose cause has become his heart's desire. Nothing can ever destroy the effect of the public utterance of the phrase, and the President may well contend that to have aided in the establishment of a League of Nations Secretariat where all treaties must be registered before they are valid is, in fact, the accomplishment of his dictum, although he must inevitably encounter the disappointment of those who believed it to imply an open discussion of the terms of the Peace Treaty, which to his mind was an impossibility. Such an interpretation may explain the paradox that the author of the Fourteen Points returned from Paris, claiming that he had achieved them.

ACTIVITIES IN 1915-1917

[1930]   In spite of the fact that some of the newspapers had distrusted the Women's Congress at The Hague, our reception when we returned was a cordial one. A huge mass meeting in Carnegie Hall had been arranged for us upon our arrival in New York, and the City Council of Chicago later sent a formal committee of welcome to meet us, upon our arrival in their city. . . .

It was in the first years of the World War that women had their best opportunity to make their distinctive contribution to the situation. All the censorship which ingenious minds later evolved did not then exist and women came to know authoritatively the effects of war upon the civilian population. . . .

The Woman's Peace Party at that time numbered some 25,000 members on a count including affiliated membership. Many women throughout the country in those years before the United States entered the war, were ardent for peace and believed that women had a special obligation to withstand war as a human institution.

During these neutral years it was possible for the women in the United States to keep in communication with the international body of women organized after The Hague meeting, with headquarters in Holland. . . .

In February, 1917, there was held in New York City, a conference of the leading peace societies of America. The meeting was inevitably a difficult one, but a committee of five was sent from the conference to President Wilson. We came away from a prolonged interview quite convinced that the United States was about to enter the war. In the course of the conversation the President reminded us that he had made every effort to keep the peace and he also quoted from his recent Senate speech in which he had promulgated the Fourteen Points we all so greatly admired, and which so many thousands of people all over the world had already received with devout thankfulness. Our committee, of course, believed that as the Fourteen Points could only have been formulated by a great neutral so they could be consummated only in an atmosphere free from the rancors of war. Until that time the peace people had regarded the President as a friendly ally in spite of his St. Louis speech, but from that time on we felt officially outlawed, and the committee of five representing the national peace organizations left the White House in deep dejection.

I have written little of the many societies working for peace during this period, although I had been an officer in several of them for many years. I was continually being introduced as a "founder" of the American Peace Society established in 1826; there were the Organisation Centrale pour une Paix Durable, with headquarters in The Hague, The Society for Securing International Friendship through the Churches with its representatives in all the leading nations of Europe, the League for Democratic Control in England, and the Fellowship of Reconciliation of which the United States section had been organized in 1915. I was grateful for the comradeship which service on its national committee afforded and for the meetings, especially for one which was held at a three-day session in a boarding school on the Hudson. It also offered a clearing house for the opinions of the conscientious objectors, whom we were always ready to serve. The most important of all these societies in my own experience was the Friends Service Committee, whose work among the civilian populations in the devastated war regions had been carried on since the beginning of the war.

I had seen something of its work in France in 1915 and had met there old social service friends whom I had known both in England and America who were grateful for the opportunity the Quakers afforded them. They believed that only the spirit of human fellowship could quench the lust for war, that neither horror nor dread can ever suffice to stay the hand of mankind lifted against itself in murderous folly. Fear is too akin to the motives which are responsible for war itself so that we cannot hope for an ally in fear. Two months later after war had been declared, the Woman's Peace Party adopted a "Program during War Time" at a national conference held in the Friends' meeting house in Philadelphia. In the interests of good will and tolerance it was urged, "Let those of opposed opinions be loyal to the highest that they know, and let each understand that the other may be equally patriotic." . . .

As to the attitude of Hull-House during the war, perhaps I may again be permitted to quote from an outside source:

The Hull-House residents were far from being unanimously pacifist. In fact, most of the residents were for the war. Eight young men who were in residence volunteered, and six of them went overseas. A contingent of the Hull-House Boys Band, with their bandmaster, went to the Front, and were afterwards taken into occupied territory. Soldiers from the district were given their last meal at Hull-House before they left for France, with their families and sweethearts standing outside the door until the meal should be finished and they could give their last farewells in the Hull-House courtyard.

A description of Hull-House in wartime, written for the *World Tomorrow*, states the following:

But the distinguishing characteristic of this settlement, its unshakable tolerance, is the fundamental respect its members have for one another's firm beliefs. The specific thing which sets Hull-House apart from others, which has carried its name around the world as a generic title, is this atmosphere of chivalry, so hard to describe, so much harder to achieve. . . .

My own activities were connected with the Department of Food Administration, and I venture to put them into the chapter on efforts for peace in wartime, because I firmly believe that through an effort to feed hungry people, a new and powerful force might be unloosed in the world and would in the future have to be reckoned with as a factor in international affairs. Some of us had felt that the failure of the many international courts and leagues attempted during the last three hundred years might have been due to the fact that there was nothing upon which to focus scattered moral energies and to make operative a new moral ideal. The enthusiasts, having nothing to work upon, were reduced to the negative proposition of preventing war, they had none of the positive incentive which arises from looking after economic and social needs.

The Food Administrator in Washington constantly conferred with the representatives of the neutral as well as the allied nations, that there might be an equitable distribution of existing supplies. He had announced that the situation was more than war, it was a question of human survival. It appeared at moments as if civilization having failed to make a community of nations along political lines was at last tragically driven to the beginnings of one along the old primitive folkways because in six thousand years no other successful method had been devised. Did women in failing to insist upon their own rôle, deprive a great experiment in international relationships of the fresh human motive power which was so sorely needed, and was the League of Nations, unable to utilize these humanitarian motives, inevitably thrown back upon the old political ones?

So throughout the months that the United States was at war I did what I could, not only to induce my fellow countrymen to produce and conserve food, but so far as possible to point out that only through such an effort could the civilian populations throughout a large portion of the globe survive. I was sent out from the Central Office at Washington and from the Food Administration Departments in various states. Some towns would consider me too pacifistic to appear; others apparently had never heard of my deplorable attitude and still others, bent only upon the saving of food, were indifferent.

AFTER WAR WAS DECLARED

[1922]   The first meeting of our national Board, convened after the declaration of war, was in October, 1917, in a beautiful country house at which the members, arriving from New York, Boston, Philadelphia, St. Louis and Chicago, appeared as the guests at a house party, none of the friends of the hostess ever knowing that we had not been invited upon a purely social basis.

It was a blessed relief to be in communication with likeminded people once more and to lose somewhat the sense of social disapprobation and of alienation of which we had become increasingly conscious. After three days' deliberation the Board issued a special manifesto to the various branches, beginning with the statement:

"All the activities of the Woman's Peace Party have been, of course, modified by the entrance of the United States into the World War. . . .

"We have avoided all criticism of our Government as to the declaration of war, and all activities that could be considered as obstructive in respect to the conduct of the war, and this not as a counsel of prudence, but as a matter of principle."

Because we saw even then that there was element of hope in the international administration of food supplies and of other raw materials and clutched at it with something of the traditional desperation of the drowning man, the manifesto ended as follows:

. . . "We recognize that an alliance between seventeen nations in both hemispheres cannot be confined to military operations. We rejoice in the fact that the United States of America has already taken common action with the Allies in regard to the conservation and distribution of food supplies and other matters, quite outside the military field, which require international coöperation. We venture to hope that conferences of this type may be extended until they develop into an international organization sitting throughout the war.

"An interparliamentary conference thus developed might form the nucleus of a permanent international parliament eventually open to all nations. Such an organization of a World Parliament, arising in response to actual world needs, is in line with the genesis and growth of all permanent political institutions."

We could not then realize how very difficult it would be to make our position clear, and not for a long time did we sense the control of public opinion and of all propaganda, which is considered necessary for the successful inauguration and conduct of war. What we were perhaps totally unprepared for as the war continued was the general unwillingness to admit any defect in the institution of war as such, or to acknowledge that, although exhibiting some of the noblest qualities of the human spirit, it yet affords no solution for vexed international problems; further we believed that after war has been resorted to, its very existence, in spite of its superb heroisms and sacrifices which we also greatly admired, tends to obscure and confuse those faculties which might otherwise find a solution. There was not only a reluctance to discuss the very issues for which the war was being fought, but it was considered unpatriotic to talk about them until the war had been won.

Even in the third month of the war, when asked to give an address before the City Club of Chicago on "Patriotism and Pacifists in War Time," I tried quite guilelessly to show that while the position of the pacifist in time of war is most difficult, nevertheless, the modern peace movement, since it was inaugurated three hundred years ago, had been kept alive throughout many great wars, and that even during the present one some sort of peace organization had been maintained in all of the belligerent nations. Our own Woman's International Committee for Permanent Peace [later the Women's International League for Peace and Freedom] had organized branches since the war began in such fighting nations and colonies as Australia, Austria, Belgium, Canada, Finland, Germany, Great Britain, Ireland, Hungary, British India, Italy, France, Poland and Russia. I ventured to hope the United States would be as tolerant to pacifists in time of war as those countries had been, some of which were fighting for their very existence, and that our fellow-citizens, however divided in opinion, would be able to discuss those aspects of patriotism which endure through all vicissitudes.

It is easy enough now to smile at its naïveté, but even then we were dimly conscious that in the stir of the heroic moment when a nation enters war, when men's minds almost without volition are driven back to the earliest obligations of patriotism, the emotions move along the worn grooves of blind admiration for the soldier and of unspeakable contempt for him who, in the hour of danger, declares that fighting is unnecessary. We were not surprised, therefore, when apparently striking across and reversing this popular conception of patriotism, we should be called traitors and cowards, but it seemed to us all the more necessary to demonstrate that in our former advocacy we were urging a reasonable and vital alternative to war. Only slowly did the pacifist realize that when his fellow countrymen are caught up by a wave of tremendous enthusiasm and are carried out into a high sea of patriotic feeling the very virtues which the pacifist extols are brought into unhappy contrast to those which war, with its keen sense of a separate national existence, places in the foreground.

Yet in spite of this sober reasoning it was a distinct shock to me to learn that it had been difficult to secure a chairman to preside over the City Club meeting at which I spoke, and that even my old friends were afraid that the performance of this simple office would commit them to my pacifist position. I later lectured on the same subject at the University of Chicago, trying to be as "sweetly reasonable" as possible, but only to come out of the hall profoundly discouraged, having learned the lesson that during war it is impossible for the pacifist to obtain an open hearing. Nevertheless, we continued to talk, not from a desire of self-defense or justification, I think, for we had long since abandoned any such hope, but because we longed actually to modify the headlong course of events.

In the general mass of misunderstanding and deliberate misrepresentation some things were harder to bear than others. We were constantly accused of wishing to isolate the United States and to keep our country out of world politics. We were, of course, urging a policy exactly the reverse, that this country should lead the nations of the world into a wider life of co-ordinated political activity; that the United States should boldly recognize the fact that the vital political problems of our time have become as intrinsically international in character as have the commercial and social problems

so closely connected with them. . . . We also hoped to make clear
that it has long been the aim of our own government and of similar
types throughout the world to replace coercion by the full consent
of the governed, to educate and strengthen the free will of the
people through the use of democratic institutions; that this age-
long process of obtaining the inner consent of the citizen to the
outward acts of his government is of necessity violently interrupted
and thrown back in war time. . . .

After war was declared, events moved with surprising rapidity.
We had scarcely returned from Washington where we had been
advocating a referendum on the declaration of war before we were
back there again, this time protesting before the Military Affairs
Committee that the measure of conscription should not be passed
without an appeal to the country, without an expression of opinion
from the simple people who form the rank and file of the soldiery in
every war.

The most poignant moment during the war and the preparations
for it, so far as I personally was concerned, came upon me suddenly
one morning after a wretched night of internal debate. For many
years one of the large rooms at Hull-House had been used for a
polling place of the precinct, one election after another had been
held there for some of which, after the women of Illinois had secured
a large measure of the franchise, I had served as a judge of election.
The room that morning was being used to register the men for the
first draft. In they came somewhat heavily, one man after another,
most of them South Italians. I knew many of them had come to this
country seeking freedom from military service quite as much as
they sought freedom of other sorts, and here they were about to be
securely caught once more. The line of dull workmen seemed to
me to represent the final frontier of the hopes of their kind, the
traditional belief in America as a refuge had come to an end and
there was no spot on the surface of the earth to which they might
flee for security. All that had been told them of the American freedom, which they had hoped to secure for themselves and their
children, had turned to ashes. I said nothing beyond the morning's
greeting, but one of the men stopped to speak to me. He had been
in the Hull-House citizenship classes, and only a few months before
I had delivered a little address to those of the class who had re-

ceived their first papers, combining congratulations with a welcome into the citizenship of the United States. The new citizen turned to me and spoke from the bitterness of his heart: "I really have you to thank if I am sent over to Europe to fight. I went into the citizenship class in the first place because you asked me to. If I hadn't my papers now I would be exempted." I could only reply that none of us knew what was going to happen and added, for what comfort it might give him, that at any rate he would be fighting on the side of Italy. But the incident did not add to my peace of mind. . . .

It is impossible to live for years among immigrants and to fail to catch something of their deep-seated hopes for the country of their adoption, to realize that the thought of America has afforded a moral safety valve to generations of oppressed Europeans. War and its conscriptions were something which belonged to the unhappy Europe they had left behind. It was as if their last throw had been lost. Of the 450,000,000 people in Europe 400,000,000 were already involved in the war. Could the United States do nothing more intelligent than to add its quota of 100,000,000 people more?

When it became evident that the measure for conscription would pass, those of us who had known something of the so-called conscientious objector in England hoped that we might at least obtain similar provisions for him in the United States. Although the English tribunals had power to grant absolute exemption from military service, there were in England at that time approximately six thousand men imprisoned or interned in addition to the number who were performing non-military service on the continent in such organizations as the Friends' Ambulance Units.

A committee of us waited upon the Secretary of War, begging him to recommend like provision in the conscription measure then under consideration. The Secretary was ready to talk to our committee, each member of which could claim either acquaintance or friendship with him in the years before the war. He seemed so sympathetic and understanding that possibly we made too much of his somewhat cryptic utterance that "there would be no conscientious objector problem in the United States," and we left his office more reassured perhaps than we had any right to be.

It became evident in a very few weeks that no provision of any sort was to be made for the conscientious objector as such. Each man who objected to war could choose his own method of making his protest and be punished accordingly. If he failed to report for his assigned camp he was tried as a "deserter," if he refused to put on the uniform, the charge was insubordination; if he declined to drill or to obey an order, he might be court-martialed under the charge of resisting an officer, with a wide range of penalties, including imprisonment at Fort Leavenworth. Thus each camp had opportunity to treat the conscientious objector according to its own standard, but above all he was to be given no opportunity to make a dignified statement of his own case, no chance "to play the martyr or to hang out the white flag."

I saw the Secretary of War twice again on the matter, once with a committee and once alone, but it was evident that he had taken the same stand later formulated by the Administration in regard to other political prisoners, that there could be no such thing as a political offense in a democracy; each man was arrested for breaking a law and tried as a criminal. Any other course might have laid the government open to the charge of suppressing a minority, which was to be avoided. The reformer in politics knew only too well how to deal with the reformer out of politics. The latter was hoist by his own petard.

Only after hundreds of men had been placed in military prisons and separated in military camps under charge of violation of various sections of the military code, was a board appointed to review their cases, beginning work in June, 1919. This federal board endeavored to undo some of the injustices of the camps and to work out a system which, however vulnerable, was removed from the whim of individuals. . . .

In camp and even in prison the conscientious objectors were constantly subjected to tremendous pressure by the chaplains to induce them to change their position, although in a sense they were denied the comforts of religion. Certainly the rest of us were. I recall going to church one beautiful summer's day in 1917 when the family whom I was visiting urged me to hear a well known Bishop preach in the village church. The familiar words of the service could not be changed but the bishop was belligerent from his very first utterance and his peroration ended with the statement that if "Jesus were living to-day he would be fighting in the trenches of France."

Not a word of the anxious, pitying, all-embracing love for lack of which the world was perishing!

It was inevitable under these circumstances that new religious organizations should develop. The Fellowship of Reconciliation had, during 1915, attracted to its membership in Chicago a score of people, a few clergymen, one or two publicists and others who felt the need of meeting with like-minded people, and at least comparing their scruples and religious difficulties. We usually met in private houses on a social basis, as it were, not so much because we felt that a meeting discussing the teachings of Jesus could be considered "seditious," but from a desire to protect from publicity and unfriendly discussion the last refuge that was left us. We did not succeed even in that, although the unfair and hostile publicity came in a very curious way through the office of the Woman's Peace Party, which one would suppose to be more open to attack than the Fellowship. Throughout the war the national office of the Woman's Peace Party was kept open in a downtown office building in Chicago. We did not remove any of our records, being conscious that we had nothing to hide, and our list of members with their addresses was to be found in a conspicuous card catalogue case. . . .

The secret service men finally entered the office in search of material not directly against us, but against the Fellowship of Reconciliation, which they considered as designed to lessen the morale of war. I have just read over some of the newspaper clippings; it is easy now to smile at their absurd efforts to give a sinister meaning to two such innocuous words as Fellowship and Reconciliation, but at the moment we all knew that it meant one more group put upon the index, as it were, and one more successful attempt to discredit pacifists. . . .

The Fellowship of course continued and fortunately was never disturbed in New York where its national office was located. As a member of the executive board I attended its meetings as often as possible and always found a certain healing of the spirit. . . .

[1915]   The press everywhere tended to make an entire nation responsible for the crimes of individuals, a tendency which is certainly fraught with awful consequences, even though the crimes for which the nation is held responsible may have originated in the gross exaggeration of some trivial incident. The very size and extent of the contention acts like a madness.

This perhaps accounts for the impression left upon our minds that in the various countries the enthusiasm for continuing the war is fed largely on a fund of animosity growing out of the conduct of the war. Germany is indignant because England's blockade was an attempt to starve her women and children; England is on fire over the German atrocities in Belgium. A young man in France said, "We hope to be able very soon to squirt petroleum into the German trenches so that everything will easily catch fire." I replied, "That seems very terrible." "Yes," he said, "but think of the poisonous gas and the horrible death of our men who were asphyxiated." . . .

Nevertheless the fanatical patriotism which has risen so high in these countries, and which is essentially so fine and imposing, cannot last. The wave will come down, the crest cannot be held indefinitely. Then men must see the horrible things which are taking place not as causes for continuing the war, but as that which must never be allowed to occur again. At the present moment, however, the man whose burning heart can find no slightest justification for the loss of the finest youth of Europe unless it results in the establishment of such international courts as will make war forever impossible, finds it difficult to discover a vehicle through which he may express this view. International ideals for the moment are treated not only with derision and contempt but as dangerous to patriotism.

In every country we found evidence of a group of men and women —how large, we were, of course, unable to determine—who although they were not opposed to the war and regarded their own countries as sinned against and not as sinning, still felt that their respective countries ought to be content with a limited programme of victory. Yet even in England a man who says that peace ought to be made with Germany on any other terms than dictation by the allies is attacked by the newspapers as pro-German, without any reference as to whether those terms are favorable or not to his country.

A good patriot of differing opinion finds it almost impossible to reach his fellow countrymen with that opinion, because he would not for the world print anything which might confuse the popular mind, for war belongs to that state of society in which right and wrong must be absolute.

The huge agglomerations of human beings of which modern society is composed communicate with each other largely through the printed word and, poor method as it is, apparently public opinion cannot be quickly discovered through any other agency. Certainly the most touching interview we had on the continent was with a man who had been in a responsible position in England when war was declared and who was overburdened equally with the sense that he had failed to convince his countrymen that the war was unnecessary and with the futility of making any further effort.

This lack of mobilization of public opinion in so many of the countries of Europe is at present a serious aspect of the war. Even in the most autocratic countries, Governments respond to public opinion and governmental policies are modified as men of similar opinion gather into small groups, as they make a clear statement of that opinion, and as they promote larger groups. At the present moment this entire process in the modification of governmental policies is brought to a standstill among the warring nations, even in England where the very method of governmental change depends upon the registry of public opinion.

But as like-minded people within the borders of a warring nation cannot find each other, much less easily can the search be conducted beyond the lines of battle. As we went from one country to another, people would say, "Did you find any one taking our line, thinking as we do?" The people, as a whole, do not know even the contemplated terms of settlement and could only learn them through a free and courageous press, while the governmental officials themselves could only thus obtain a full knowledge of public opinion concerning the continuance of the war. Every public man in Europe knows that before the rulers will think of peace, they must know that behind them, if they advocate peace, there would be a grateful and passionate opinion ready to support them against the militarists. Even pacifically inclined ministers in the Government itself dare not talk of treating with the enemy while the only vocal opinion in newspapers and speeches is in favor of fighting till the enemy surrenders unconditionally. Preëminently in Great Britain and Germany any peace negotiation can be stopped by the militarist elements, which predominate during war in Government circles. But how can peace processes be begun if none of the leading journals dare call upon "the various Governments to declare what to each nation is the essential and indispensable condition for ceasing the conflict," which would of course be but a preliminary to negotiations and the final terms of peace. If in the end adjustment must be reached through the coming together of like-minded people in the contending nations, it is a thousand pities that it should fail through lack of a mechanism whereby they might find each other. In the meantime, the very foundations of a noble national life are being everywhere undermined by the constant disparagement of other nations, and as each fears nothing more than an appearance of the weariness of the war, the desire for peace filling many hearts is denied all journalistic expression while the war spirit is continually fed by the outrages of the war, as flames are fed by fuel.

At moments I found myself filled with a conviction that the next revolution against tyranny would have to be a revolution against the unscrupulous power of the press. A distinguished European, accustomed to addressing the civilized world through the printed page, finding himself unable to reach even his own countrymen, suggested to us the plight of a caged lion as he vehemently walked up and down a little alcove in our hotel, expressing his exasperation and despair. To my mind the message he was not permitted to give was the one which Europe needed above all others and the self-exiled pacifists, French, German, Austrian, English, and Belgian, whom we met in Switzerland, were a curious comment on the freedom of the press.

Two conclusions were inevitably forced upon us. First: that the people of the different countries could not secure the material upon which they might form a sound judgment of the situation, because the press with the opportunity of determining opinion by selecting data, had assumed the power once exercised by the church when it gave to the people only such knowledge as it deemed fit for them to have. Second: that in each country the leading minds were not bent upon a solution nor to the great task that would bring international order out of the present anarchy, because they were absorbed in preconceived judgments, and had become confused through the limitations imposed upon their sources of information.

REACTIONS OF A PACIFIST IN WARTIME

[1922]   My temperament and habit had always kept me rather in the middle of the road; in politics as well as in social reform I had been for "the best possible." But now I was pushed far toward the left on the subject of the war and I became gradually convinced that in order to make the position of the pacifist clear it was perhaps necessary that at least a small number of us should be forced into an unequivocal position. If I sometimes regretted having gone to the Women's Congress at The Hague in 1915, or having written a book on Newer Ideals of Peace in 1911 which had made my position so conspicuously clear, certainly far oftener I was devoutly grateful that I had used such unmistakable means of expression before the time came when any spoken or written word in the interests of Peace was forbidden.

It was on my return from The Hague Congress in July, 1915, that I had my first experience of the determination on the part of the press to make pacifist activity or propaganda so absurd that it would be absolutely without influence and its authors so discredited that nothing they might say or do would be regarded as worthy of attention. I had been accustomed to newspaper men for many years and had come to regard them as a good natured fraternity, sometimes ignorant of the subject on which they asked an interview, but usually quite ready to report faithfully albeit somewhat sensationally. Hull-House had several times been the subject of sustained and inspired newspaper attacks, one, the indirect result of an exposure of the inefficient sanitary service in the Chicago Health Department, had lasted for many months; I had of course known what it was to serve unpopular causes and throughout a period of campaigning for the Progressive Party I had naturally encountered the "opposition press" in various parts of the country, but this concerted and deliberate attempt at misrepresentation on the part of newspapers of all shades of opinion was quite new in my experience. After the United States entered the war, the press throughout the country systematically undertook to misrepresent and malign pacifists as a recognized part of propaganda and as a patriotic duty. We came to regard this misrepresentation as part of the war technique and in fact an inevitable consequence of war itself, but we were slow in the very beginning to recognize the situation, and I found my first experience which came long before the United States entered the war rather overwhelming.

Upon our return from the Women's International Congress at The Hague in 1915, our local organization in New York City with others, notably a group of enthusiastic college men, had arranged a large public meeting in Carnegie Hall. Dr. Anna Howard Shaw presided and the United States delegates made a public report of our impressions in "war stricken Europe" and of the moral resources in the various countries we visited that might possibly be brought to bear against a continuation of the war. We had been much impressed with the fact that . . . many of the soldiers themselves were far from enthusiastic in regard to actual fighting as a method of settling international difficulties. War was to many of them much more anachronistic than to the elderly statesmen who were primarily responsible for the soldiers' presence in the trenches.

It was the latter statement which was my undoing, for in illustration of it I said that in practically every country we had visited, we had heard a certain type of young soldier say that it had been difficult for him to make the bayonet charge (enter into actual hand to hand fighting) unless he had been stimulated; that the English soldiers had been given rum before such a charge, the Germans ether and that the French were said to use absinthe. To those who heard the address it was quite clear that it was not because the young men flinched at the risk of death but because they had to be inflamed to do the brutal work of the bayonet, such as disembowelling, and were obliged to overcome all the inhibitions of civilization.

Dr. Hamilton and I had notes for each of these statements with the dates and names of the men who had made them, and it did not occur to me that the information was new or startling. I was, however, reported to have said that no soldier could go into a bayonet charge until he was made half drunk, and this in turn was immediately commented upon, notably in a scathing letter written to the *New York Times* by Richard Harding Davis, as a most choice specimen of a woman's sentimental nonsense. Mr. Davis himself had recently returned from Europe and at once became the defender of the heroic soldiers who were being traduced and belittled. He lent the weight of his name and his very able pen to the cause, but it really needed neither, for the misstatement was repeated, usually with scathing comment, from one end of the country to the other. . . .

Only once did I try a public explanation. After an address in Chautauqua, New York, in which I had not mentioned bayonets, I tried to remake my original statement to a young man of the Associated Press only to find it once more so garbled that I gave up in despair, quite unmoved by the young man's letter of apology which followed hard upon the published report of his interview.

I will confess that the mass psychology of the situation interested me even then and continued to do so until I fell ill with a serious attack of pleuro-pneumonia, which was the beginning of three years of semi-invalidism. During weeks of feverish discomfort I experienced a bald sense of social opprobrium and wide-spread misunderstanding which brought me very near to self pity, perhaps the lowest pit into which human nature can sink. Indeed the pacifist in war time, with his precious cause in the keeping of those who control the sources of publicity and consider it a patriotic duty to make all types of peace propaganda obnoxious, constantly faces two dangers. Strangely enough he finds it possible to travel from the mire of self pity straight to the barren hills of self-righteousness and to hate himself equally in both places.

From the very beginning of the great war, as the members of our group gradually became defined from the rest of the community, each one felt increasingly the sense of isolation which rapidly developed after the United States entered the war into that destroying effect of "aloneness," if I may so describe the opposite of mass consciousness. We never ceased to miss the unquestioning comradeship experienced by our fellow citizens during the war, nor to feel curiously outside the enchantment given to any human emotion when it is shared by millions of others. The force of the majority was so overwhelming that it seemed not only impossible to hold one's own against it, but at moments absolutely unnatural, and one secretly yearned to participate in "the folly of all mankind." Our modern democratic teaching has brought us to regard popular impulses as possessing in their general tendency a valuable capacity for evolutionary development. In the hours of doubt and self-distrust the question again and again arises, has the individual or a very small group, the right to stand out against millions of his fellow countrymen? Is there not a great value in mass judgment and in instinctive mass enthusiasm, and even if one were right a thousand times over in conviction, was he not absolutely wrong in abstaining from this communion with his fellows? The misunderstanding on the part of old friends and associates and the charge of lack of patriotism was far easier to bear than those dark periods of faint-heartedness. We gradually ceased to state our position as we became convinced that it served no practical purpose and, worse than that, often found that the immediate result was provocative.

We could not, however, lose the conviction that as all other forms of growth begin with a variation from the mass, so the moral changes in human affairs may also begin with a differing group or individual, sometimes with the one who at best is designated as a crank and a freak and in sterner moments is imprisoned as an atheist or a traitor. Just when the differing individual becomes the centro-egotist, the insane man, who must be thrown out by society for its own protection, it is impossible to state. The pacifist was constantly brought sharply up against a genuine human trait with its biological basis, a trait founded upon the instinct to dislike, to distrust and finally to destroy the individual who differs from the mass in time of danger. Regarding this trait as the basis of self-preservation it becomes perfectly natural for the mass to call such an individual a traitor and to insist that if he is not for the nation he is against it. To this an estimated nine million people can bear witness who have been burned as witches and heretics, not by mobs, for of the people who have been "lynched" no record has been kept, but by order of ecclesiastical and civil courts.

There were moments when the pacifist yielded to the suggestion that keeping himself out of war, refusing to take part in its enthusiasms, was but pure quietism, an acute failure to adjust himself to the moral world. Certainly nothing was clearer than that the individual will was helpless and irrelevant. We were constantly told by our friends that to stand aside from the war mood of the country was to surrender all possibility of future influence, that we were committing intellectual suicide, and would never again be trusted as responsible people or judicious advisers. Who were we to differ with able statesmen, with men of sensitive conscience who also absolutely abhorred war, but were convinced that this war for the preservation of democracy would make all future wars impossible, that the priceless values of civilization which were at stake could at this moment be saved only by war? But these very dogmatic statements spurred one to alarm. Was not war in the interest of democracy for the salvation of civilization a contradiction of terms, whoever said it or however often it was repeated?

Then, too, we were always afraid of fanaticism, of preferring a consistency of theory to the conscientious recognition of the social situation, of a failure to meet life in the temper of a practical person. Every student of our time had become more or less a disciple of pragmatism and its great teachers in the United States had come out for the war and defended their positions with skill and philosophic acumen. There were moments when one longed desperately for reconciliation with one's friends and fellow citizens; in the words of Amiel, "Not to remain at variance with existence but to reach that understanding of life which enables us at least to obtain forgiveness." Solitude has always had its demons, harder to withstand than the snares of the world, and the unnatural desert into which the pacifist was summarily cast out seemed to be peopled with them. We sorely missed the contagion of mental activity, for we are all much more dependent upon our social environment and daily newspaper than perhaps any of us realize. We also doubtless encountered, although subconsciously, the temptations described by John Stuart Mill: "In respect to the persons and affairs of their own day, men insensibly adopt the modes of feeling and judgment in which they can hope for sympathy from the company they keep."

The consciousness of spiritual alienation was lost only in moments of comradeship with the like minded, which may explain the tendency of the pacifist in war time to seek his intellectual kin, his spiritual friends, wherever they might be found in his own country or abroad. . . .

On the other hand there were many times when we stubbornly asked ourselves, what after all, has maintained the human race on this old globe despite all the calamities of nature and all the tragic failings of mankind, if not faith in new possibilities, and courage to advocate them. Doubtless many times these new possibilities were declared by a man who, quite unconscious of courage, bore the "sense of being an exile, a condemned criminal, a fugitive from mankind." Did every one so feel who, in order to travel on his own proper path had been obliged to leave the traditional highway? The pacifist, during the period of the war could answer none of these questions but he was sick at heart from causes which to him were hidden and impossible to analyze. He was at times devoured by a veritable dissatisfaction with life. Was he thus bearing his share of blood-guiltiness, the morbid sense of contradiction and inexplicable suicide which modern war implies? We certainly had none of the internal contentment of the doctrinaire, the ineffable solace of the self-righteous which was imputed to us. No one knew better than we how feeble and futile we were against the impregnable weight of public opinion, the appalling imperviousness, the coagulation of motives, the universal confusion of a world at war. There was scant solace to be found in this type of statement: "The worth of every conviction consists precisely in the steadfastness with which it is held," perhaps because we suffered from the fact that we were no longer living in a period of dogma and were therefore in no position to announce our sense of security! We were well aware that the modern liberal having come to conceive truth of a kind which must vindicate itself in practice, finds it hard to hold even a sincere and mature opinion which from the very nature of things can have no justification in works. The pacifist in war time is literally starved of any gratification of that natural desire to have his own decisions justified by his fellows.

That, perhaps, was the crux of the situation. We slowly became aware that our affirmation was regarded as pure dogma. We were thrust into the position of the doctrinaire, and although, had we been permitted, we might have cited both historic and scientific tests of our so-called doctrine of Peace, for the moment any sanction even by way of illustration was impossible.

It therefore came about that ability to hold out against mass suggestion, to honestly differ from the convictions and enthusiasms of one's best friends did in moments of crisis come to depend upon the categorical belief that a man's primary allegiance is to his vision of the truth and that he is under obligation to affirm it.

THE AMERICAN PANIC

[1922]   It was at the end of the winter of 1916-17 that the astounding news came of the Russian Revolution. Perhaps it was because this peasant revolution reminded me of Bondereff's "Bread Labour," a sincere statement of the aspirations of the Russian peasants, that the events during the first weeks of the revolution seemed to afford a sharp contrast between the simple realities of life and the unreal slogans with which the war was being stimulated. . . .

In the Russian peasant's dread of war there has always been a passive resistance to the reduction of the food supply, because he well knows that when a man is fighting he ceases to produce food and that the world will at length be in danger of starvation. Next to the masses of India and China, the Russian peasants feel the pinch of hunger more frequently than any other people on earth. Russia is the land of modern famines; the present one was preceded by those of 1891, 1906, and 1911. The last, still vivid in the memory of men at the front, affected thirty million people, and reduced eight million people to actual starvation. The Russian peasant saw three and a half years of the Great War, during which time, according to his own accounting, seven million of his people perished and the Russian soldiers, never adequately equipped with ammunition, food and clothing, were reduced to the last extremity. To go back to his village, to claim his share of food, to till the ground as quickly as possible, was to follow an imperative and unerring instinct. . . .

During the early days of the Russian revolution it seemed to me that events bore out the assumption that the Russian peasants, with every aspect of failure, were applying the touchstone of reality to certain slogans evolved during the war, to unreal phrases which had apparently gripped the leading minds of the world. It was in fact the very desire on the part of the first revolutionists in the spring of 1917 to stand aside from political as well as from military organizations and to cling only to what they considered the tangible realities of existence, which was most difficult for the outside world to understand. . . .

At that time the Allied nations were all learning to say that the end of this war would doubtless see profound political changes and democratic reconstruction, when the animalistic forces which are inevitably encouraged as a valuable asset in warfare, should once more be relegated to a subordinate place. And yet when one of the greatest possible reconstructions was actually happening before their very eyes, the war-weary world insisted that the Russian soldier should not be permitted to return to the land but should continue to fight. This refusal on the part of the Allied Governments suggests that they were so obsessed by the dogmatic morality of war, in which all humanly tangible distinctions between normal and abnormal disappear, that they were literally blind to the moral implications of the Russian attempt.

The Russian soldiers, suddenly turned into propagandists, inevitably exhibited a youthful self-consciousness which made their own emotional experience the center of the universe. Assuming that others could not be indifferent to their high aims, they placidly insisted upon expounding their new-found hopes. But all this made the warring world, threatened with defeat if the German army on the eastern front were released, still more impatient.

Possibly, as a foolish pacifist, wishing to see what was not there, I gave myself over to idle speculation. It may be true that the spiritual realism as well as the *real politik* was with the Allied statesmen who forced Kerensky to keep his men at war even at the price of throwing Russia into dire confusion.

These statesmen considered the outcome of the Russian Revolution of little moment compared to the future of civilization which was then imperilled by the possibility of a German victory if the men on the eastern front were allowed to reinforce the west. But such an assumption based on the very doctrines of war, was responsible for Brest Litovsk; for "peace after a smashing victory"; for the remarkable terms in the Versailles treaty; for Trotsky's huge army; for much of the present confusion in the world. Did the Russians, for one golden moment, offer a way out? or was the present outcome inevitable?

Three times in crucial moments in the world's history and with a simple dramatic gesture have representatives of Russia attempted to initiate the machinery which should secure permanent peace for all nations.

First: the proposals of the Russian Czar, Alexander I, in 1815, at the Peace Conference following the Napoleonic Wars, for "An All-Embracing Reform of the political system of Europe which should guarantee universal peace" and the resulting Holy Alliance which, according to historians, did not succeed "owing to the extremely religious character in which it was conceived."

Second: the calling of the first Hague Conference by Nicholas II, in 1899. His broad outline of the work which such a conference ought to do was considered "too idealistic" by the other powers, who tried to limit the function of the Hague Conferences to the reduction of armaments and to the control of the methods of warfare.

Third: the spontaneous effort of the first Russian revolutionists to break through the belief that any spiritual good can be established through the agency of large masses of men fighting other large masses and their naive attempt to convert individual soldiers. The string of Russian soldiers talking to their recent enemies stretched from the Baltic sea to the Carpathian Mountains. These simple men assumed that men wished to labor in the soil and did not wish to fight, while all the rest of the world remained sceptical and almost rejoiced over the failure of the experiment, before it had really been tried. Certainly the world was in no mood just then to listen to "mere talk." It was resounding with a call to arms.

With our Anglo-Saxon crispness of expression we are prone to be amused at the Russian's inveterate habit of discussion and to quote with tolerant contempt the old saying: "Two Russians—three opinions," without stopping to reflect that the method has in practice worked out excellently for the self-governing administration of village affairs throughout an enormous territory. . . .

We forget that to obtain the "inner consent" of a man who differs from us is always a slow process, that quite as it is quicker to punish an unruly child than to bring him to a reasonable state of mind; to imprison a criminal than to reform him; to coerce an ignorant man than to teach him the meaning of the law, so it is quicker to fight armies of men than to convince them one by one. . . .

I got a certain historic perspective, if not comfort at least enlargement of view, by being able to compare our widespread panic in the United States about Russia to that which prevailed in England during and after the French Revolution. A flood of reactionary pamphlets, similar to those issued by our Security Leagues, had then filled England, teaching contempt of France and her "Liberty," urging confidence in English society as it existed and above all warning of the dangers of any change. Hatred of France, a passionate contentment with things as they were, and a dread of the lower classes, became characteristic of English society. The French Revolution was continually used as a warning, for in it could be seen the inevitable and terrible end of the first steps toward democracy. Even when the panic subsided the temper of society remained unchanged for years, so that in the English horror of any kind of revolution, the struggle of the hand-loom weaver in an agony of adjustment to the changes of machine industry, appeared as a menace against an innocent community. . . .

Was the challenge which Russia threw down to the present economic system after all the factor most responsible for the unreasoning panic which seemed to hold the nation in its grip, or was it that the war spirit, having been painstakingly evolved by the united press of the civilized world, could not easily be exorcised? The war had made obvious the sheer inability of the world to prevent terror and misery. It had been a great revelation of feebleness, as if weakness, ignorance and overweening nationalism had combined to produce something much more cruel than any calculated cruelty could have been. Was the universal unhappiness which seemed to envelop the United States as well as Europe an inevitable aftermath of war?

So far as we had anticipated any contribution from the non-resistant Russian peasant to the cause of Universal Peace, the events in militarized Russia during the years after the war threw us into black despair. Not only had the Bolshevist leaders produced one of the largest armies in Europe, but disquieting rumors came out of Russia that in order to increase production in their time of need the government had been conscripting men both for industry and transportation. It was quite possible that the Russian revolutionists were making the same mistake in thus forging a new tool for their own use which earlier revolutionists had made when they invented universal military conscription. An example of the failure of trying to cast out the devil by Beelzebub, it had been used as a temporary expedient when the first French revolutionists were fighting "the world," but had gradually become an established thing, and in the end was the chief implement of reaction. It alone has thrown Europe back tremendously, entailing an ever-increasing cost of military establishment and consequent increased withdrawal of man-power from the processes of normal living. The proportion of soldiers in Europe has enormously increased since the middle ages; then out of every thousand men four were soldiers, now out of every thousand men a hundred and twenty to a hundred and fifty are soldiers. These were the figures before the great war. . . .

In some respects it was more difficult at that time to be known as a pacifist than it had been during the war, and if any of us had ever imagined that our troubles would be over when the war ended, we were doomed to disappointment. There were many illustrations of our continued unpopularity. In the early days of the armistice, for instance, a group of German women, distressed over such terms as the demand for the immediate restoration of 3000 milch cows to Belgium, cabled to Mrs. Wilson at the White House and also to me. My cable was never delivered and I knew nothing but what the newspapers reported concerning it, although the incident started an interminable chain of comment and speculation as to why I should have been selected, none of which stumbled upon the simple truth that I had presided over a Congress at The Hague attended by two of the signatories of the cable.

The incident, however, was but a foretaste of the suspicions and misinterpretations resulting from the efforts of Miss Hamilton and myself to report conditions in Germany and so far as possible to secure contributions to the fund the Friends Service Committee in Philadelphia was collecting for German and Austrian children. There was no special odium attached to the final report which we made to the Friends upon our return nor upon its wide distribution in printed form; it was also comparatively easy to speak to the International Committee for the Promotion of Friendship between the Churches and to similar bodies, but when it came to addressing audiences of German descent, so-called "German-Americans," the trouble began. The first Chicago meeting of this kind was carefully arranged, "opened with prayer" by a popular clergyman and closed by a Catholic priest, and it went through without difficulty although, of course, no word of it appeared in any Chicago newspaper printed in English. Milwaukee, St. Louis and Cleveland, however, were more difficult, although my theme was purely humanitarian with no word of politics. I told no audience that our passports had been viséed in Frankfurt in the city hall flying a red flag, that housing space was carefully proportioned with reference to the need of the inhabitants and other such matters, which would have shocked the audience of prosperous German-Americans quite as much as any one else. We always told these audiences as we told many others who invited us, about the work of the Friends' Service Committee in Northern France and over widespread portions of Central and Eastern Europe irrespective of national boundaries. Some money was always sent to Philadelphia for Germany but quite often it was carefully marked for one of the Allied countries in which the Friends' Service Committee was also at work. I was equally grateful for those contributions but I often longed to hear some one suggest that "to feed thine enemy if he hunger" might lead us back to normal relations with him, or to hear one of the many clergymen pray that we might forgive our enemies. No such sentiment was uttered in my hearing during that winter, although in the early Spring I was much cheered at a meeting in Denver when a club woman quoted apropos of feeding German children, from Bojer's "The Great Hunger": "I sow corn in the field of mine enemy in order to prove the existence of God."

It was a period of pronounced reaction, characterized by all sorts of espionage, of wholesale raids, arrests and deportations. Liberals everywhere soon realized that a contest was on all over the world for the preservation of that hard won liberty which since the days of Edmund Burke had come to mean to the civilized world not only security in life and property but in opinion as well. Many people had long supposed liberalism to be freedom to know and to say, not what was popular or convenient or even what was patriotic, but what they held to be true. But those very liberals came to realize that a distinct aftermath of the war was the dominance of the mass over the individual to such an extent that it constituted a veritable revolution in our social relationships. . . .

In the midst of the world-wide social confusion and distress, there inevitably developed a profound scepticism as to the value of established institutions. The situation in itself afforded a challenge, for men longed to turn from the animosities of war and from the futility of the peace terms to unifying principles, and yet at that very moment any attempt at bold and penetrating discussion was quickly and ruthlessly suppressed as if men had no right to consider together the social conditions surrounding them. . . .

A CHALLENGE TO THE LEAGUE OF NATIONS

[1922]   The later winter and spring of 1919 afforded a wonderful opportunity to talk about the League of Nations. It was all in the making and we, its advocates, had the world before us with which to illustrate "the hopes of mankind." . . .

We all believed that the ardor and self sacrifice so characteristic of youth could be enlisted for the vitally energetic role required to inaugurate a new type of international life in the world. We realized that it is only the ardent spirits, the lovers of mankind, who can break down the suspicion and lack of understanding which have so long prevented the changes upon which international good order depend. These men of good will we believed, would at last create a political organization enabling nations to secure without war those high ends which they had vainly although so gallantly sought to obtain upon the battlefield. . . .

During the first year of the League the popular enthusiasm seemed turned into suspicion, the common man distrusted the League because it was so indifferent to the widespread misery and starvation of the world; because in point of fact it did not end war and was so slow to repair its ravages and to return its remote prisoners; because it so cautiously refused to become the tentative instrument of the longed for new age. Certainly its constitution and early pronouncements were disappointing. During the first months of its existence the League of Nations, apparently ignoring the social conditions of Europe and lacking the incentives which arise from developing economic resources had fallen back upon the political concepts of the 18th century, more abstractly noble than our own perhaps, but frankly borrowed and therefore failing both in fidelity and endurance. . . .

. . . In the various armies and later among the civilian populations, two of men's earliest instincts which had existed in age-long companionship became widely operative; the first might be called security from attack, the second security from starvation. Both of them originated in tribal habits and the two motives are still present in some form in all governments.

Throughout the war the first instinct was utilized to its fullest possibility by every device of propaganda when one nation after another was mobilizing for a "purely defensive war."

The second, which might be called security from starvation, became the foundation of the great organizations for feeding the armies and for conserving and distributing food supplies among civilian populations.

The suggestion was inevitable that if the first could so dominate the world that ten million young men were ready to spend their lives in its assertion, surely something might be done with the second, also on an international scale, to remake destroyed civilization. . . .

. . . If from the very first the League of Nations could have performed an act of faith which marked it at once as the instrument of a new era, if it had evinced the daring to meet new demands which could have been met in no other way, then, and then only would it have become the necessary instrumentality to carry on the enlarged life of the world and would have been recognized as indispensable.

Certain it is that for two years after the war the League of Nations was in dire need of an overmastering motive forcing it to function and to justify itself to an expectant world, even to endear itself to its own adherents. As the war had demonstrated how much stronger is the instinct of self-defense than any motives for a purely private good, so one dreamed that the period of commercial depression following the war might make clear the necessity for an appeal to the much wider and profounder instinct responsible for conserving human life.

In the first years after the cessation of the great war there was all over the world a sense of loss in motive power, the consciousness that there was no driving force equal to that furnished by the heroism and self-sacrifice so lately demanded. The great principles embodied in the League of Nations, rational and even appealing though they were, grew vague in men's minds because it was difficult to make them objective. There seemed no motive for their immediate utilization. But what could have afforded a more primitive, genuine and abiding motive than feeding the peoples of the earth on an international scale, utilizing all the courage and self-sacrifice evolved by the war. All that international administration which performed such miracles of production in the prosecution of the war was defined by the British Labor Party at its annual conference in 1919 as "a world-government actually in being which should be made the beginnings of a constructive international society."

The British Labor Party, therefore, recommended three concrete measures apart from the revision of the Peace Treaty, as follows:

1. A complete raising of the blockade EVERYWHERE, in PRACTICE as well as IN NAME.

2. Granting CREDITS to enemy and to liberated countries alike, to enable them to obtain food and raw materials sufficient to put them in a position where they can begin to help themselves.

3. Measures for the special relief of children EVERYWHERE, without regard to the political allegiance of their parents.

How simple and adequate these three recommendations were and yet how far-reaching in their consequences! They would first of all have compelled the promoters of the League to drop the 18th century phrases in which diplomatic intercourse is conducted, and to substitute plain economic terms fitted to the matter in hand. Such a course would have forced them to an immediate discussion of credit for reconstruction purposes, the need of an internationally guaranteed loan, the function of a recognized international Economic Council for the control of food stuffs and raw material, the worldwide fuel shortage, the effect of mal-nutrition on powers of production, the irreparable results of "hunger œdema."

The situation presented material for that genuine and straightforward statesmanship which was absolutely essential to the feeding of Europe's hungry children. An atmosphere of discussion and fiery knowledge of current conditions as revealed by war once established, the promoters of the League would experience "the zeal, the tingle, the excitement of reality" which the League so sadly lacked. The promoters of the League had unhappily assumed that the rights of the League are anterior to and independent of its functioning, forgetting that men are instinctively wary in accepting at their face value high-sounding claims which cannot justify themselves by achievement, and that in the long run "authority must go with function." They also ignored the fact that the stimuli they were utilizing failed to evoke an adequate response for this advanced form of human effort.

The adherents of the League often spoke as if they were defending a too radical document whereas it probably failed to command widespread confidence because it was not radical enough, because it clung in practice at least to the old self-convicted diplomacy. But the comman man in a score of nations could not forget that this diplomacy had failed to avert a war responsible for the death of ten million soldiers, as many more civilians, with the loss of an unestimated amount of civilization goods, and that all the revolutionary governments since the world began could not be charged with a more ghastly toll of human life and with a heavier destruction of property.

During those months of uncertainty and anxiety the governments responsible for the devastations of a world war were unaccountably timid in undertaking restoration on the same scale, and persistently hesitated to discharge their obvious obligations.

It was self-evident that if the League refused to become the instrument of a new order, all the difficult problems resulting, at least in their present acute form, from a world war, would be turned over to those who must advocate revolution in order to obtain the satisfaction of acknowledged human needs. It was deplorable that this great human experiment should be entrusted solely to those who must appeal to the desperate need of the hungry to feed themselves, whereas this demand in its various aspects seemed to afford a great controlling motive in the world at the present moment, as political democracy, as religious freedom, had moved the world at other times. . . .

While the first year of the League held much that was discouraging for its advocates, the first meeting of the Assembly convened in Geneva in November, 1920, resolved certain doubts and removed certain inhibitions from the minds of many of us. The Assembly demonstrated that after all it was possible for representatives from the nations of the earth to get together in order to discuss openly, freely, kindly for the most part, and even unselfishly, the genuine needs of the world. In spite of the special position of the Great Powers, this meeting of the Assembly had so increased the moral prestige of the League of Nations that it was reasonable to believe that an articulate world-opinion would eventually remove the treaty entanglements which threatened to frustrate the very objects of the League. The small nations, represented by such men as Nansen and Branting, not by insistence on the doctrine of the sovereignty and equality of states, but through sheer devotion to world interests, were making the League effective and certainly more democratic. Perhaps these representatives were acting, not only from their own preferences or even convictions, but also from the social impact upon them, from the momentum of life itself.

In many ways the first meeting of the Assembly had been like the beginning of a new era, and it seemed possible that the public discussion, the good-will, and the international concern, must eventually affect the European situation. . . .

The International Labor Organization, from the first such a hopeful part of the League of Nations, had just concluded as we reached Geneva in August 1921, a conference upon immigration and possible protective measures which the present situation demanded. For many years I had been a Vice President of the American Branch of the International Association for Labour Legislation and had learned only too well how difficult it was to secure equality of conditions for the labor of immigrants. The most touching interviews I have ever had upon the League of Nations had been with simple immigrants in the neighborhood of Hull-House, who had many times expressed the hope that the League might afford some adequate protection to migratory workmen, to the Italian for instance, who begins harvesting the crops south of the equator and, following the ripening grain through one country after another, finally arrives in Manitoba or the Dakotas. He often finds himself far from consular offices, encounters untold difficulties, sometimes falling into absolute peonage.

It was interesting to have the International Labour Organization declare in its report that the two great "peoples" who had first recognized the large part the Office might play in conciliation and protection were (1) the Shipowners and Seamen, as had been shown by the conference at Genoa, and (2) "the immense people of immigrants, the masses who, uprooted from their homelands, ask for some measure of security and protection applicable to all countries and supervised by an international authority."

There was something very reassuring in this plain dealing with homely problems with which I had been so long familiar. I had always been ready to admit that "the solemn declaration of principles which serve to express the unanimity of the aspirations of humanity have immense value," but this was something more concrete, as were other efforts on the part of the Office to defend labor throughout the world and to push forward adequate legislation on their behalf. . . .

The food challenge was put up fairly and squarely to the second meeting of the Assembly of the League of Nations by the Russian famine due to the prolonged drought of 1921. A meeting to consider the emergency had been called in Geneva in August, under the joint auspices of the International Red Cross and the League of Red Cross Societies. We were able to send a representative to it from our Women's International League almost directly from our Third International Congress in Vienna. There was every possibility for using the dire situation in Russia for political ends, both by the Soviet Government and by those offering relief. On the other hand, there was a chance that these millions of starving people, simply because their need was so colossal that any other agency would be pitifully inadequate, would receive help directly from many governments, united in a mission of good-will. It was a situation which might turn men's minds from war and a disastrous peace to great and simple human issues; in such an enterprise the governments would "realize the failure of national coercive power for indispensable ends like food for the people," they would come to a coöperation born of the failure of force.

Dr. Fridjof Nansen, appointed high commissioner at the Red

Cross meeting in August, after a survey of the Russian Famine regions returned to Geneva for the opening of the Assembly on September 5th, in which he represented Norway, with a preliminary report of Russian conditions. He made a noble plea, which I was privileged to hear, that the delegates in the Assembly should urge upon their governments national loans which should be adequate to furnish the gigantic sums necessary to relieve twenty-five million starving people.

As I listened to this touching appeal on behalf of the helpless I was stirred to a new hope for the League. I believed that, although it may take years to popularize the principles of international co-operation, it is fair to remember that citizens of all the nations have already received much instruction in world-religions. To feed the hungry on an international scale might result not only in saving the League but in that world-wide religious revival which, in spite of many predictions during and since the war, had as yet failed to come. It was evident in the meeting of the Assembly that Dr. Nansen had the powerful backing of the British delegates as well as others, and it was therefore a matter for unexpected as well as for bitter disappointment when his plea was finally denied. This denial was made at the very moment when the Russian peasants, in the center of the famine district, although starving, piously abstained from eating the seed grain and said to each other as they scattered it over the ground for their crop of winter wheat: "We must sow the grain although we shall not live to see it sprout." . . .

THE WOMEN'S INTERNATIONAL LEAGUE FOR PEACE AND FREEDOM, 1919-1935

[1930]   When the Women's International League held its second international congress in Switzerland in May, 1919, groups of women came from twenty different nations, most of them having incurred great difficulty in travel. The ordinary means of transportation between countries had not yet been restored and in some instances there were such passport difficulties that the Australian delegation was able to arrive in Zurich the day before the French one did.

Because our congress met while the Paris peace deliberations were still going on we were enabled to be the first international group to point out the dangers to permanent peace contained in some of the provisions of the Treaty of Versailles, and as our delegates represented nineteen countries, we were the first group from both sides of the conflict, to consider the covenant of the League of Nations. The delegates changed the name of our organization to the Women's International League for Peace and Freedom, unwittingly approaching the name of a society founded by Victor Hugo in Switzerland, many years earlier, called Peace and Liberty.

It was after this congress that we established our International Headquarters in Geneva, when it had been decided to locate the League of Nations there. We hoped to avail ourselves of the ever-increasing data on international affairs, constantly accumulated by the Secretariat, and to share the companionship of like-minded people organized to promote every form of effort for better international service, who had also established themselves in Geneva. . . .

After the Zurich Congress and five days after peace had been officially declared, Doctor Alice Hamilton and myself went into Germany with a committee of Quakers from England and the United States, in order to make a survey for the work of rehabilitation undertaken by the Society of Friends in Germany as in all the other war-stricken countries. Happily, we did not go in absolutely empty-handed. The English Quakers had brought with them thirty thousand dollars, raised under the slogan of "Gifts of Love," with which had been bought through the Hoover Commission thirty-five tons of condensed milk, ten tons of cocoa, seventeen tons of sugar, and so forth, which we actually distributed among hospitals for children and crèches, principally in Chemnitz, Halle, Leipzig, and the smaller towns of the industrial district of South Saxony, where the starvation had been especially acute. Doctor Hamilton and I wrote our impressions and recommendations in a report which was published by the Friends Service Committee of Philadelphia, and it is of course unnecessary to describe once more the thousands of school children filing past us, with their sunken chests and shoulder blades standing out like sharp wings; or the piteous old people who had barely survived because they felt they had no right to a share of the scanty food. It was a great relief to be able to renew relations with social workers in various German cities—Sigmund-Schultze was not only the head of a settlement in Berlin but a lecturer on social ethics in the university. He had withstood the war madness, and although under the surveillance of the government had retained both positions. The gifted Alice Solomon, as head of the National School of Philanthropy, had made a valuable contribution in the study of the industrial status of women, as exemplified by their war work.

Upon our return from Europe, we traveled far and wide in the United States in an effort to procure food and money for the relief of the starving German children, working of course always with the Friends Service Committee. At first it was difficult and we met everywhere the charge of pro-Germanism, but gradually as time passed it became possible to secure impressive committees with the advantages of newspaper backing. Long before this, however, public approval or disapproval came to seem of little consequence compared to the tragic suffering we had seen face to face. The United States was in a curious state of mind during those first years after the war. Perhaps, because nothing save love stirs the imagination like hatred, there was a necessity for some object upon which the hatred stirred up during the war could vent itself. What so near at hand as the pacifists whom the newspapers had systematically identified with the enemy? Our unpopularity, however, was not all the aftermath of hatred. Some of it was due to the noblest emotions many of our contemporaries had ever known; Galsworthy has written:

The war was a great forcing house, every living plant was made to grow too fast; each quality, each passion; hate and love, intolerance, courage and energy, yes, and self-sacrifice itself, were all being forced beyond their strength, beyond the natural flow of the sap, forced until there came a wild luxuriant crop.

Perhaps it was our preoccupation with actual starvation that constantly drew us back to an examination of ultimate aims—to an interpretation of life itself. It led us to discuss that world-wide "tradition of a long and profound battle over what does in truth, constitute the spiritual life of mankind." Perhaps it was mere self-justification or only a rationalization of the position which we had irrevocably taken, that led us to make the reply accepted by at least a minimum of philosophers in every age: "If history has an ethical direction, its symbol is not the clansman or the warrior, but he who passively defends an idea."

[1922]   Our Third International Congress was held at Vienna in July, 1921, almost exactly two years after the Peace of Versailles had been signed. . . .

. . . The third Congress was convened in Vienna, which, as we realized, had suffered bitterly both from the war and the terms of Peace. The women from the thirty countries represented there had been sorely disillusioned by their experiences during the two years of peace, and each group inevitably reflected something of the hopelessness and confusion which had characterized Europe since the war. Nevertheless these groups of women were united in one thing. They all alike had come to realize that every crusade, every beginning of social change, must start from small numbers of people convinced of the righteousness of a cause; that the coming together of convinced groups is a natural process of growth. Our groups had come together in Vienna hoping to receive the momentum and sense of validity which results from encountering like-minded people from other countries and to tell each other how far we had been able to translate conviction into action. The desire to perform the office of reconciliation, to bring something of healing to the confused situation, and to give an impulse towards more normal relations between differing nations, races and classes, was evident from the first meeting of the Congress. This latter was registered in the various proposals, such as that founded upon experiences of the last year, that peace missions composed of women of different nations should visit the borders still in a disturbed condition and also the countries in which war had never really ceased.

There was constant evidence that the food blockade maintained in some instances long after the war, had outraged a primitive instinct of women almost more than the military operations themselves had done. Women had felt an actual repulsion against the slow starvation, the general lowering in the health and resistance of entire populations, the anguish of the millions of mothers who could not fulfill the primitive obligation of keeping their children alive. There was a certain sternness of attitude concerning political conditions which so wretchedly affected woman's age-long business of nurturing children, as if women had realized as never before what war means. . . .

The conditions in Southeastern Europe as we met them that hot summer of 1921 might well challenge the highest statesmanship. We saw much of starvation and we continually heard of the appalling misery in all of the broad belt lying between the Baltic and the Black Seas, to say nothing of Russia to the east and Armenia to the south. Even those food resources which were produced in Europe itself and should have been available for instant use, were prevented from satisfying the desperate human needs by "jealous and cruel tariff regulations surrounding each nation like the barbed wire entanglements around a concentration camp." A covert war was being carried on by the use of import duties and protective tariffs to such an extent that we felt as if economic hostility, having been legitimatized by the food blockades of the war, was of necessity being sanctioned by the very commissions which were the outgrowth of the Peace Conference itself. We saw that the smaller states, desperately protecting themselves against each other, but imitated the great Allies with their protectionist policies, with their colonial monopolies and preferences.

This economic war may have been inevitable, especially between succession States of the former Austrian Empire with their inherited oppressions and grievances. Yet we longed for a Customs Union, a Pax Economica for these new nations, who failed to see that "the price of nationality is a workable internationalism, otherwise it is doomed so far as the smaller states are concerned." . . .

And so we came back to what our own organization was trying to do, to substitute consent for coercion, a will to peace for a belief in war. Like all educational efforts, from the preaching in churches to the teaching in schools, at moments it must seem ineffectual and vague, but after all the activities of life can be changed in no other way than by changing the current ideas upon which it is conducted.

The members of the Women's International League for Peace and Freedom had certainly learned from their experience during the war that widely accepted ideas can be both dominating and all powerful. But we still believed it possible to modify, to direct and ultimately to change current ideas, not only through discussion and careful presentation of facts, but also through the propaganda of the deed. . . .

And although we were so near to the great war with its millions of dead and its starved survivors, we had ventured at the very opening of the Congress to assert that war is not a natural activity for mankind, that large masses of men should fight against other large masses is abnormal, both from the biological and ethical point of view. We stated that it is a natural tendency of men to come into friendly relationships with ever larger and larger groups, and to live constantly a more extended life. It required no courage to predict that the endless desire of men would at last assert itself, that desire which torments them almost like an unappeased thirst, not to be kept apart but to come to terms with one another. It is the very spring of life which underlies all social organizations and political associations.

[1930]   After the Hague meeting [1922] I met my friend, Mary Rozet Smith, in Paris, and in January, 1923, we started together upon a journey around the world, during which I saw many of the W.I.L. members as well as those of the Fellowship of Reconciliation and similar organizations. . . .

There were most cheering reports [W.I.L. Congress, 1924] showing that war inhibitions were lifting. Austria told of the bonfires made of old nationalistic textbooks, which cleared the schools for the use of classics culled from all countries and for a series of two hundred stories from twenty different nations. This report seemed almost as significant as the fact that "Austria has freely renounced a piece of Hungarian territory assigned her by the peace treaty." Czecho-Slovakia urged the establishment of chairs for peace in universities and told of the new museum of peace established by President Masaryk next door to the museum of war in Czecho-Slovakia; Holland reported the establishment of an international law school at The Hague; Switzerland was working out plans for civilian service to provide for the patriotism of the great number of conscientious objectors who now spend several months each year in prison rather than submit to military training; a Swiss group under the leadership of Cérésole cleared stones from flooded pastures and did other such works of restoration that they might thus demonstrate the possibility of substituting civil service for the military. Denmark, which had long been our largest national section, reported a W.I.L. representative in each electoral district and a woman member as the Minister of Education; Danish and German women had exchanged visits and organized public conferences in the territory ceded to Denmark after the war. These peace missions had been a constant feature of the International W.I.L. from the very beginning, when a committtee of our women with the Friends and the Fellowship of Reconciliation had lived in the Ruhr during the days of the greatest difficulty there, and later, when the Polish and German members of the W.I.L. had done what they could to mitigate the situation in Silesia. The Committee on Peace Missions told of a remarkable piece of work carried on in Finland and there was a moving report of the collection of money and jewelry made by the women of our German section in order to plant trees in the devastated areas of France. . . .

The proposition to outlaw war by international agreement was first made by a well-known attorney in Chicago and after a campaign exhibiting great devotion on the part of the originator and of its first adherents, Outlawry of War became a popular cause throughout the United States and finally resulted [1928] in the Pact of Paris more popularly known as the Kellogg Pact. This Pact eclipsed all former treaties by outlawing war itself as an institution, by making war as such, illegal; the signatories to the treaty pledged themselves never to use war as an instrument in international affairs. This comprehensive treaty illustrates, as nothing in all history has done, the genuine movement for peace taking place all over the world. It has been endorsed and ratified by government officials and voted upon favorably by hard-headed, even by hard-boiled politicians. The difficulties ahead lie in the enforcement of this high resolve and unless it is to prove an example, like the Prohibition Amendment, of government action outrunning public opinion every effort for popular backing must be made along both educational and empirical lines. Ramsay MacDonald has said in connection with these treaties that the mentality of the people must be transformed from a dependence upon military security to a dependence upon political security, the latter "rooted in public opinion and enforced by a sense of justice in a civilized world." . . .

If we continue to unite our unremitting efforts to organize for a more reasonable life upon the earth's surface, we will gradually make possible the utilization of a new dynamic. We will almost inevitably begin to grope our way toward what our generation calls human brotherhood but which the post-war generation would, I am sure, rather designate as a wider participation in life.

DISARM AND HAVE PEACE

[1932]   The chief skepticism pacifism meets comes from a widely accepted conviction that war is a necessary and inevitable factor in human affairs. Let us consider that in the light of one example.

In 1812 America and England were at war. Six years later representatives of the two governments agreed by treaty that the Canadian frontier should be unfortified. Neighbors along a frontier of almost four thousand miles, two peoples have lived during one hundred and fourteen years enjoying a sense of security neither treaties nor armaments can give.

By 1913, in each thousand men in Europe, one hundred and twenty were soldiers! Then came the crisis in 1914. We have wished to "forget the war." But I should like to recall it briefly.

At the end of it Europe was confronted by a crisis unequaled since the Great Plague, or the famine accompanying the Thirty Years' War, when a third of the population of Europe perished.

And yet, in spite of this lesson, a decade after the treaty was signed six million men were under arms in fifty-two nations; ten million were receiving military training; twenty-seven million were enrolled in military reserves!

During the period immediately after the Great War closed, political leaders had turned to a more arrant and arrogant "nationalism" than that which had gone before.

We have reached a stage in the advancement of civilization when we are quite willing to concede that finance, industry, transportation, science, medicine, culture, and trade are not bounded by national frontiers, but must be international. Must our political thought alone remain insular and blindly "national"?

Surely, now that we begin to comprehend the moral, social, and economic consequences of the late war, we must examine openly the question of how to avoid another.

It seems necessary that two things be done:

First, that peaceful methods substituted for war in the settlement of international disputes should be increased and strengthened.

Second, that these peaceful methods should be given a fair chance invariably to succeed, even in grave crises, by the final *abolition* of armaments.

Ten or a dozen of these peaceful methods have been developed in an unprecedented degree during the past generation. The chief of these were the Hague Court of Arbitration, the League of Nations, the World Court, and the Kellogg Pact. Each of these has been used repeatedly—the first one many times; and whenever they have been resorted to they invariably have succeeded.

But in a half dozen crises of the past generation, including the Chinese-Japanese crisis of today, they have been brushed aside and a resort has been made to armed force.

At the Geneva arms conference, which at this writing is about to open, a *principle* should be agreed upon and rigidly applied. The nations should pledge themselves—in another Kellogg Pact—never again to resort to armaments in their dealings with one another. The next step would be to agree upon methods of securing total disarmament. Experts now conceive of the warfare of the future as *bound to involve whole populations.*

At the last Women's International League Congress a report on disarmament was read which stated: "Defensive warfare will have no meaning, as nothing can any longer be defended; for modern war will inevitably be an attack on the civil population."

The history of one nation after another shows that it was the mothers who first protested that their children should no longer be slain as living sacrifices upon the altars of tribal gods. Women rebelled against the waste of the life they had nurtured.

I should like to see the women of civilization rebel against the senseless wholesale human sacrifice of warfare. I am convinced that many thousands of women throughout the world would gladly rise to this challenge.

The Women's International League for Peace and Freedom was organized at The Hague in 1915. I acted as chairman then and have served as president ever since. It is therefore a tribute to the peace efforts of women that I was chosen to share with Dr. Nicholas Murray Butler in the Nobel peace award.

FINAL ADDRESSES

Notes from Response by Jane Addams
at a Banquet of the Women's International League,
20th Anniversary Celebration, Washington, D.C.

[May 2, 1935]   I do not know any such person as is described here this evening. I think I have never met her. We all know much worse things about ourselves than anyone has ever said or printed about us. I have never been sure I was right. I have often been doubtful about the next step. We can only feel our way as we go on from day to day. But I thank you all.

We may not be able to "change human nature" but we do hope to modify human behavior. . . . Today we cannot get internationalism across. We are too near the last war to get it over and to act together. But when the time does come when men will accept internationalism in the place of separate nationalism, we must be ready with the League of Nations, with the World Court, with an instructed public opinion. . . .

The source of our difficulties lies in the lack of moral enterprise. . . .

At least we can seek to remove the difficulties which arise from each nation seeking to get the most for itself. It would be a splendid thing if the United States could lead the world in a new type of international relationship. . . . We move slowly, and yet much has occurred in twenty years. If we had said twenty years ago at The Hague that it would be possible to hold a disarmament conference, we would have been called idealistic visionaries. . . . Public opinion must come to realize how futile war is. It is so disastrous, not only in poison gas used to destroy lives, but in the poison injected into the public mind. We are suffering still from the war psychology. We can find many things which are the result of war, and one war is really the result of past war. . . . If it became fixed in the human mind that killing was not justified, it would be done away with along definite lines. It is a prerequisite to the lives of its citizens for a nation to build up a community relationship which destroys the feelings of distrust and inoculates good-will and international accord.

We may be a long way from permanent peace. We need education of ourselves; of others; development of public opinion; moral enterprise. . . . Woodrow Wilson said: "No issue is dead in the world so long as men have courage." It would be a great glory if the United States could lead in this new type of statesmanship.

Closing Paragraph, Jane Addams' Speech
Around the World International Broadcast, Washington, D.C.

[May 3, 1935]   The Women's International League joins a long procession of those who have endeavored for hundreds of years to substitute law for war, political processes for brute force, and we are grateful to our friends from various parts of the world who recognize at least our sincerity in this long effort.

References

List of Abbreviations

Democ. and Soc. Eth.	*Democracy and Social Ethics*
Excel. Bec. Perm.	*The Excellent Becomes the Permanent*
H. H. Maps	*Hull House Maps and Papers*
Long Rd.	*The Long Road of Woman's Memory*
New Conscience	*A New Conscience and an Ancient Evil*
Newer Ideals	*Newer Ideals of Peace*
Peace and Bread	*Peace and Bread in Time of War*
Philan. and Soc. Prog.	*Philanthropy and Social Progress*
Relig. in Soc. Ac.	*Religion in Social Action*
Sec. Twenty Yrs.	*The Second Twenty Years at Hull-House*
Spirit of Youth	*The Spirit of Youth and the City Streets*
Twenty Yrs.	*Twenty Years at Hull-House*
Women at Hague	*Women at The Hague*

I. Social Work

"First Days at Hull-House," **pages 5–9**: *Twenty Yrs.*, pp. 85, 87–89, 92–97, 101, 109, 90–91, 167, 111–112.

"Social Settlements"

"The Subjective Necessity for Social Settlements," **pages 9–10**: *Twenty Yrs.*, pp. 113–115; **pages 10–14**: *Philan. and Soc. Prog.*, pp. 1–6, 12–13, 15–17, 19–23.

"The Objective Necessity for Social Settlements," **pages 14–21**: *Philan. and Soc. Prog.*, pp. 28–37, 39–41, 44–45, 49, 52–56.

"Charitable Relationships," **pages 21–24**: *Democ. and Soc. Eth.*, pp. 13–14, 16–20, 34–36.

"A Function of the Social Settlement," **pages 24–25**: *Annals of the Academy of Political and Social Science* (May, 1899), XIII, 323–345.

II. Position of Women

III. Child Welfare

"Family Affection," **pages 141–142:** *Spirit of Youth,* pp. 31–34, 42–43; **pages 142–144:** *Excel. Bec. Perm.,* pp. 17–22; **pages 144–145:** *Democ. and Soc. Eth.,* pp. 77–82.

"Education," **pages 145–150:** *Democ. and Soc. Eth.,* pp. 178–181, 186–195, 198–200, 206–207, 211–215, 218–220.

"Adolescence," **pages 150–155:** *Spirit of Youth,* pp. 3–10, 15–17, 19–21, 26–27, 29–30, 45–47, 51–53, 58–60, 62–63, 69–71.

"Labor," **pages 156–159:** *Newer Ideals,* pp. 153–157, 166–173, 178–179.

"Justice," **pages 159–164:** *Sec. Twenty Yrs.,* pp. 304–319.

"Art and Recreation," **pages 164–167:** *Spirit of Youth,* pp. 82–84, 88–91, 94–95, 97–103; **pages 167–168:** *Sec. Twenty Yrs.,* pp. 344–347, 354–356, 358.

"Social Action," **pages 168–170:** *Spirit of Youth,* pp. 139–142, 160–162.

IV. The Arts

"The Arts at Hull-House," **pages 174–180:** *Twenty Yrs.,* pp. 371–381, 387–389, 393, 395.

"The Labor Museum," **pages 180–184:** *Twenty Yrs.,* pp. 235–237, 240–246, 256–258.

"The Play Instinct and the Arts," **pages 184–188:** *Sec. Twenty Yrs.,* pp. 367–371, 373–379.

V. Trade Unions and Labor

"Pioneer Labor Legislation in Illinois," **pages 192–200:** *Twenty Yrs.,* pp. 198–202, 205–214, 218–222, 224–230.

"The Settlement as a Factor in the Labor Movement," **pages 200–204:** *H. H. Maps,* pp. 184–191.

"Trade Unions and Public Duty," **pages 204–211:** *American Journal of Sociology* (Univ. of Chicago Press), Jan., 1899, pp. 448–462.

"Militarism and Industrial Legislation," **pages 211–215:** *Newer Ideals,* pp. 93–99, 115–116, 118–119.

"Group Morality in the Labor Movement," **pages 215–217:** *Newer Ideals,* pp. 145–150.

VI. Civil Liberties

"A Decade of Economic Discussion," **pages 223–225:** *Twenty Yrs.,* pp. 177–178, 184–185.

"Echoes of the Russian Revolution," **pages 225–235:** *Twenty Yrs.,* pp. 400–409, 411–418, 421–423.

"During and After the World War," **pages 235–247:** *Sec. Twenty Yrs.,* pp. 140–141, 153–165, 173–176, 180–187.

VII. International Peace

"Maturing Concepts of Peace," **pages 252–253:** *Report of the Thirteenth Universal Peace Congress* (Boston, 1904), pp. 261, 121; **pages 253–254:**

Newer Ideals, pp. 214, 217; **pages 254–255:** *Sec. Twenty Yrs.,* pp. 34–35, 37–38; **pages 255–257:** *Long Rd.,* pp. 136–140.

"First Reactions to War, 1914," **pages 257–259:** *Sec. Twenty Yrs.,* pp. 115, 116–117, 119–121; **pages 259–261:** *Peace and Bread,* pp. 1–3, 5–7, 9, 12–13.

"The Women's Congress at The Hague," **page 261:** *Sec. Twenty Yrs.,* pp. 124–125; **pages 261–265:** *Women at Hague,* pp. 124–126, 129–133, 139–141; **page 265:** *Sec. Twenty Yrs.,* pp. 125–126; **pages 265–275:** *Women at Hague,* pp. 56–66, 69–73, 75–81.

"The Ford Ship and the Conference of Neutrals," **pages 275–281:** *Peace and Bread,* pp. 26, 27–29, 33, 35–37, 40–46, 48.

"President Wilson's Early Policies," **pages 281–284:** *Peace and Bread,* pp. 50–53, 58–60, 66–70.

"Activities in 1915–1917," **pages 284–288:** *Sec. Twenty Yrs.,* pp. 127, 130, 131–133, 136, 137–140, 142, 144–145.

"After War Was Declared," **pages 288–294:** *Peace and Bread,* pp. 107–112, 117–118, 120–122, 126–128; **pages 294–297:** *Women at Hague,* pp. 84–85, 87–92.

"Reactions of a Pacifist in Wartime," **pages 298–303:** *Peace and Bread,* pp. 133–137, 139–144, 149–151.

"The American Panic," **pages 304–310:** *Peace and Bread,* pp. 91, 93–94, 97–98, 101–105, 191–194, 179–182, 187–188.

"A Challenge to the League of Nations," **pages 310–316:** *Peace and Bread,* pp. 196, 198, 201–203, 208–212, 215–221.

"The Women's International League for Peace and Freedom," **pages 316–319:** *Sec. Twenty Yrs.,* pp. 146–147, 149–152; **pages 319–321:** *Peace and Bread,* pp. 223, 224–225, 240–241, 243–244, 246; **pages 321–323:** *Sec. Twenty Yrs.,* pp. 169, 176–178, 218–219, 220.

"Disarm and Have Peace," **pages 323–325:** *Liberty,* March 12, 1932.

"Final Addresses"

   "Notes from Response by Jane Addams at Banquet of Women's International League, 20th Anniversary Celebration, Washington, D.C., May 2, 1935," **pages 325–326:** Jane Addams papers, Swarthmore College Peace Collection.

   "Closing Paragraph, Jane Addams' Speech, Around the World International Broadcast, Washington, D.C., May 3, 1935," **page 326:** Jane Addams papers, Swarthmore College Peace Collection.